RELIGION
AND
TECHNOLOGY

RELIGION AND TECHNOLOGY

*A Study in
the Philosophy
of Culture*

Jay Newman

Westport, Connecticut
London

Library of Congress Cataloging-in-Publication Data

Newman, Jay, 1948–
    Religion and technology : a study in the philosophy of culture /
Jay Newman.
        p.   cm.
    Includes bibliographical references and index.
    ISBN 0–275–95865–5 (alk. paper)
    1. Religion and science. 2. Faith and reason. 3. Technology—
Religious aspects. I. Title.
    BL240.N46   1997
    291.1'75—dc21   96–50321

British Library Cataloguing in Publication Data is available.

Library of Congress Catalog Card Number: 96–50321
ISBN: 0–275–95865–5

First published in 1997

Praeger Publishers, 88 Post Road West, Westport, CT 06881
An imprint of Greenwood Publishing Group, Inc.

Printed in the United States of America

The paper used in this book complies with the
Permanent Paper Standard issued by the National
Information Standards Organization (Z39.48–1984).

10 9 8 7 6 5 4 3 2 1

To the memory of my mother, Kitty—
  ever warm and kind, vibrant, bright and witty

Contents

Acknowledgments

I am grateful to the following institutions for facilitating my research and writing during the time in which this study was conceived and completed: the University of Guelph, which granted me sabbatical leave of absence for the academic year 1995–1996; Polytechnic University (New York), which accorded me a courtesy appointment as Visiting Professor in its Department of Humanities and Social Sciences in the Fall term of 1995 and provided me with liberal access to the resources of its faculty, Dibner Library, and Philosophy and Technology Studies Center; and the Centre for Studies in Religion and Society at the University of Victoria (British Columbia), which provided me with access to its research facilities in the Spring term of 1996. I particularly acknowledge the help that I have received from Harold Sjursen, director of the Philosophy and Technology Studies Center, and Harold Coward, director of the Centre for Studies in Religion and Society. Both have been true friends and exemplary academic colleagues. I am again indebted to Nina Pearlstein of Greenwood Publishing Group for her generous attention to the manuscript and her kindness to the author. My mother, Kate Rothbaum Newman, passed away on August 17, 1996. Anything good that I will have accomplished in this life can justly be attributed in large measure to her inspiration and guidance.

Religion and Antitechnology

AIMS OF THE INQUIRY

Sustained reflection on culture—on its historical (and prehistorical) foundations, existing patterns, and prospective conditions—almost inevitably
leads to consideration of both religion and technology, and it often leads
as well to consideration of some of the complex relations that obtain
between religion and technology. Religion is universally acknowledged as
one of the primary forms of human experience and culture; and whether
cultural theorists be pious defenders of some ancient faith, materialist
polemicists, or detached academic observers, they attest, with an imposing
consistency, to the historical and continuing cultural importance of religion. To be sure, not all of them can agree with the theologian Paul Tillich
that religion is the "substance" of culture,[1] or even with the severe critic
of religious "illusion," Sigmund Freud, that religion "has ruled human
society for many thousands of years."[2] They can, however, dutifully follow
a long line of renowned cultural theorists, from Plato, through Desiderius
Erasmus and Friedrich Nietzsche, down to Ernst Cassirer, Bronislaw Mali-
nowski, and humanistic and social scientific scholars of our own day, who
have reminded us in a series of impressive studies that whoever would arrive
at a clear understanding of culture had better do plenty of thinking about
religion.

　　While one's fascination with the latest high technology of our own age
may regularly result in a certain forgetfulness with respect to the historical
and prehistorical relations of technology and culture, technology too has

received its fair share of recognition from many of the most discerning cultural theorists, some of whom have actually seen it as having an even more seminal cultural importance than religion. Thus Thorstein Veblen, for example, has written that "in the growth of culture, as in its current maintenance, the facts of technological use and wont are fundamental and definitive,"[3] and Ortega y Gasset goes even further in maintaining that "man begins where technology begins. The magic circle of leisure which technology opens up for him in nature is the cell where he can house his extra-natural being."[4] Such assertions might well seem extravagant to those who insist upon associating technology primarily with the latest gadget that they purchased at the local electronics store. As such people are not ordinarily given to considering how, in D.S.L. Cardwell's words, "even a very simple human community can hardly function without a modicum of technics. Such a community must, if it is to rise above the level of the wandering food-gatherers, command the rudiments of agriculture; it must have acquired the basic skills needed to build houses, to weave cloth, to make weapons and to manufacture simple domestic utensils such as cooking pots, ovens, cutlery, querns and basic furniture."[5] It is, in fact, not difficult to understand why the term *technology* usually at first spontaneously brings to mind certain newfangled inventions, and we shall be turning our attention to this matter at various stages of our investigation. But to appreciate the close relations of technology and culture requires respect for technology's importance throughout history. Alois Huning writes that "the aim and function of technology is to transform nature into a human world, according to goals laid down by human beings on the basis of their needs and wants. Only rarely, if at all, can human beings survive independent of this transforming activity. Without technology human beings could not cope with their natural environment. Technology is thus a necessary part of human existence throughout history."[6] Technology was indeed a necessary part of human existence in the prehistorical phases of human cultural development, and without it the transition from prehistorical culture to historical culture would not have been possible.

Given that religion and technology are comparably situated at the very heart of any civilization, or of civilization as such, we can reasonably assume that their evolving relations—or at least the changing relations between particular religious phenomena (beliefs, attitudes, values, practices, institutions, and so forth) and particular technologies—have always had and will continue to have a powerful influence on social and personal development. We can assume further that at any given time, including our own, deeper insight into the prevailing state of those relations, and into the processes and circumstances by which the prevailing state of those relations has come about, can be of substantial value. Such insight would be of particular import to those religionists, technologists, and cultural observers who seek to improve their society, or perhaps even humanity, by promoting intelligent, creative, farsighted adjustments to the relations currently obtaining between particular religious phenomena and particular technologies, or between religion and technology generally. However, we must also be aware that while societies require for their survival some modus vivendi between the demands of religion and the demands of technology, the developing relations between religious phenomena and technologies (and between promoters and defenders of religion and promoters and defenders of technology) always involve a certain measure—and sometimes a very great measure—of tension, competition, and conflict as well as the requisite measure of balance, cooperation, and conciliation. Promoters of religion have often seen technology or particular technologies as representing a barbarous threat to religious tradition and the culture-nurturing values that it embodies. Conversely, promoters of technology have often seen religion or particular religions as arbitrarily restricting the technological advancement required for social and global progress or even human survival. The anxieties and resentments involved in such situations have not always been mere manifestations of self-righteousness, paranoia, or narrowness of vision.

In 1970 the ordinarily astute and sensible cultural observer, Herbert J. Muller, was moved to remark that

the subject of religion has been ignored in almost all the studies of a technological society that I am acquainted with. . . . The main reason for this neglect is doubtless simply that religion is no longer a vital concern of most contemporary thinkers, any more than it was a vital inspiration of the Industrial Revolution; never before has there been so little feeling of the "sacred" as a real power, since the powers of science and technology are so much plainer. Another reason is that technology has had a less direct impact on religion than on most other major interests, and so has itself been largely ignored by most religious thinkers.[7]

Even if we make appropriate allowance for how much has transpired since 1970, we should still react with astonishment to Muller's analysis. Almost every major philosophical or semi-philosophical writer on technology, and many another humanistic writer on the subject, has reflected aloud on the relations of religion and technology. Long before Muller wrote these lines, there was already an extensive body of literature on technology by theological and other religious authors. Indeed, Muller was himself familiar[8] at this time with the most influential work of Jacques Ellul,[9] a writer whose religious orientation is sometimes transparent. There has never been a time when religion has not been in one way or other a "vital concern" of most genuine "thinkers," and the sense of the "sacred" continues to manifest itself in rather conspicuous as well as more subtle ways, as I am sure that it always will. What is perhaps strangest in Muller's analysis is his failure to appreciate the historical and continuing importance of technology's impact upon religion and religious phenomena.

The range of relations between religion and technology that may be worthy of consideration is actually quite vast, and William B. Jones and A. Warren Matthews require page after page of fine print just to outline a "taxonomic scheme" that indicates the wide variety of these relations.[10] And although the literature on religion and technology was already extensive by 1970, it has increased considerably since then. Despite the rapid development in recent years of the academic field of philosophy of technology, and the broadening of the scope of philosophy of religion, there has not been very much so far in the way of systematic philosophical examination of the cultural context and cultural implications of the most basic and most abstract relations between religion and technology. This study is a contribution to such an examination. Friedrich Rapp, an analytical philosopher of technology, has suggested that the humanistic or historical orientation of the major philosophers of culture in the past resulted in a disinclination on their part to regard technology as a subject worthy of detailed discussion.[11] Although Rapp has overstated this point, it is fair to say that students of the philosophy of culture generally have not been as knowledgeable, as open-minded, or as comfortable in their approach to technology as in their approach to language, religion, philosophy, science, literature, the fine arts, historical study, politics, and certain specific technologies. And while, as Rapp observes,[12] there has recently been more interest among philosophers of culture in technology as a topic of research, it seems to me that this increasing interest has unfortunately been accompanied by a decline in the broad humanistic vision and commitment to historical understanding that have characterized not only the work of such great philosophers of culture as Plato, Erasmus, and Nietzsche, but also the work done in the first half of this century by the likes of Wilhelm Dilthey, George Santayana, José Ortega y Gasset, Benedetto Croce, R. G. Collingwood, and Ernst Cassirer.

The main focus of this opening chapter will be on religious antitechnology, a distinctively religious form of criticism that has been directed against technology itself (and not just particular technologies) because of technology's alleged role in undermining the religious world views, religious practices, and overall tone of spirituality needed to sustain a civilized society. After some preliminary considerations, we shall look at various versions and several dimensions of this general criticism, and our main concern at this stage will be to present the criticism. However, even here we will need to step back from time to time, if only out of a sense of desperation, and briefly respond to a particular claim. Though we could enter into an inquiry on religion and technology at any of a number of points, we shall find that religious antitechnology puts the fundamental issues into bold relief and provides us with a radical position from which we can back away in stages as we peel off the layers of rhetorical overstatement and conceptual muddle.

In Chapter 2, we shall take a closer look at the idea of technology in order to get a better understanding of what religious antitechnologists might be missing in their efforts to form a clear conception of the nature or essence of technology. We shall consider the problem of defining *technology*; paradigms of technology; aspects of the history of the usage of *technology*; and the relation of technology to *techne*, which in addition to being one of the classical Greek terms from which our word *technology* and such related words as *technique* and *technical* are derived, represents something to which the most important of all philosophers, Plato and Aristotle, gave considerable attention. By doing so, they greatly influenced subsequent philosophical and theological reflection on the relations of technology and culture. In the latter part of Chapter 2, we shall turn our attention to the important question of how different "modern" technology is from the technology of earlier ages; and we shall conclude this phase of our investigation with some general reflections on the complexity of the idea of technology.

In Chapter 3 we shall consider a number of ways in which religious antitechnologists have undervalued technology, and we shall concentrate particularly on technology's contribution to social, cultural, and personal progress. At this stage of our investigation, we shall have to consider, among other things, how desirable an end progress itself is.

In Chapter 4 we shall back away yet another few steps from the religious antitechnologist's position by considering ways in which technology qualifies as a religious endeavor of sorts. We shall focus on its compatibility with certain basic conceptions, attitudes, values, and obligations of the Western monotheistic faiths. In addition, we shall give some attention to the role of those faiths in having promoted technology, including some of the destructive technologies that religious antitechnologists have condemned.

Having thus gradually arrived at a heightened awareness of certain affinities and connections between religion and technology that are too easily overlooked in overwrought rhetoric about contemporary cultural decline, we shall be ready in Chapter 5 for a more comprehensive and systematic consideration of the relations of religion, technology, and culture. We shall consider first the usefulness of regarding religion itself as a kind of technology. Having done that, we shall consider the extent to which it is useful to regard religion, technology, and culture as all representing—in marked contrast to such forms of experience and culture as philosophy, science, and art—aspects of the same fundamental human endeavor, a general endeavor that underlies all the more specific forms of experience and culture. Having provided what I hope the reader will find to be a useful illumination of the nature of religion, technology, and culture themselves, as well as of some of their relations, I shall conclude the inquiry with some remarks about practical matters.

PRELIMINARY CONSIDERATIONS

Before we turn to the views of religious antitechnologists, a few preliminary considerations are in order. The first concerns our understanding of the ideas of religion and technology. There are occasions when it is useful or even necessary to have before us a specific definition of religion, but I shall assume that for the purposes of this inquiry the reader has an adequate working conception of religion based on his or her experience and reflection. However, it needs to be noted from the outset that the particular religions that will be the focus of our attention are Judaism and Christianity. Although it will sometimes be helpful to consider briefly other religions or personal forms of religion, we shall focus on Judaism and Christianity for several reasons. These are the two world religions that will be most familiar to—and will be of greatest interest and concern to—the overwhelming majority of readers of this study, and they are the only two that the author can discuss at length with much confidence. Moreover, the philosophical and semi-philosophical literature on religion and technology is predominantly by Western authors concerned with the relations of Western religion, technology, and culture, and these authors are mainly interested in "modern" technological developments that have generally had their origin and most significant effects in Western societies. Thus, while I often refer to religion as such, and do so on the assumption that what I am saying has some relevance to religions other than Judaism and Christianity, the reader may want to watch for places where I may have underestimated significant differences between world religions or different forms of religion.

The definition of technology, as we shall see, poses more immediate problems in this inquiry, and we shall have to give it some attention in the next chapter. But at this point I again assume that the reader has a working conception of technology based on experience and reflection and that there is general agreement in our society that certain things qualify as paradigms of technology. We have already considered, in passing, electronic gadgets and also such items on D.S.L. Cardwell's list as weapons and cooking pots and the skills needed to make them. As valuable as such paradigms are, it is imperative that we not forget the enormous breadth of the range of technologies. For example, in our fascination with the latest computer technologies, we must not forget about increasingly important biotechnologies; and even when we think back to ancient technologies, we must not allow our appreciation of the obvious importance of, say, building, transportation, and writing to diminish our respect for the importance of such rather different technologies as lighting, the cultivation of plants, and irrigation.

A consideration of a different order concerns the question of the appropriateness of assessing technology as such. It is obvious that some technologies are "good" in one or another way while other technologies are "bad" in a comparable way. It is also obvious that certain technologies can be used for good or for evil purposes. Moreover, a particular technology can be a source of good in some ways and a source of evil in others. Does it not follow then that technology as such is something "neutral," and that any attempt to pass judgment on technology itself, without precise reference to particular technologies or perhaps even to certain aspects or consequences of particular technologies, is bound to be fruitless or, in extreme cases, culturally destructive?

Mario Bunge, understandably irritated by the considerable portion of recent literature on technology that "consists of romantic wailings about the alleged evils of technology as such,"[13] has complained that the leading antitechnologists *characteristically* "fail to distinguish technology from its applications, and endow it with an autonomous existence and, moreover, with power over man."[14] Some social and cultural theorists have also stressed the need to assess technology in a particular context, so that Kai Nielsen, for example, maintains that "most of the problems attendant on our use of technology are not problems which are inherent in technology. Technology will go in one way under a social order in which profit and capital accumulation are the dynamic elements; technology will go in another way in a social order geared primarily to production to satisfy human needs."[15] Of course, technology is in fact routinely discussed, even by the leading antitechnologists, in terms of its pros and cons. A fair evaluation of technology, or of any particular technology, will obviously weigh both the pros and cons, and even if the latter substantially outweigh the former, which needs to be demonstrated, the former still deserve due acknowledgment. To complicate matters, the pros and cons of technology, or any particular technology, may be much more closely related than would appear on the surface. Emmanuel G. Mesthene, a scholar highly critical of antitechnologists, has suggested in this vein that new technology not only has both positive and negative effects, but it usually has the two "*at the same time and in virtue of each other.*"[16]

No reasonable person can fail to recognize, at least upon reflection, that certain technologies, at least when promoted and employed in certain ways, are uniformly "good" in the most profound senses of goodness of which human beings are capable of conceiving. Antitechnologists, with their inclination to romantic wailings, are not always reasonable, but they are often reasonable enough to deserve a hearing. If we are to give them a fair hearing, we must pay careful attention to their argument so that we can understand why they believe that despite the goodness and practical necessity of much technology, cultural criticism of technology is not to be confined to piecemeal criticism of particular aspects of particular technologies that are promoted and employed in particular ways in particular contexts. No reasonable critic of technology can be opposed to all technology; but we can still understand an antitechnologist's position concerning general aspects and consequences of technology even if we are troubled by the antitechnologist's devaluation of important particularities. When we listen closely to antitechnologists, we find that their criticism of technology is in fact being qualified in any number of ways, and the qualifications may be as important as the particularities that they undervalue. Furthermore, we need to leave a place in thought and discourse for useful general judgments. For example, the medication that I take for a chronic health problem has some distressing side effects, but I can still say without hesitation that this medication is basically a good thing for me because without it my life would be very much worse than it is and maybe even unbearable. The medication has pros and cons, and the cons are not insignificant; but a general judgment is still warranted. A general judgment about technology may involve the aggregate weighing of pros and cons, the assessment of the importance attached to technology in relation to the importance attached to other things, an evaluation of the overall influence of technology in its determination of social values and attitudes, and so forth. A judgment based on such considerations should not be dismissed outright as foolish simply because all of us, including the antitechnologists, know that there are good technologies. It remains, of course, that people who are given to allocating blame, especially for something as important as cultural decline, have an obligation to be very careful about their general judgments. Similarly, we have the right and sometimes an obligation to scrutinize their judgments.

SPECIMENS OF RELIGIOUS ANTITECHNOLOGY

Mesthene, though highly critical of antitechnologists, recognizes that some hostility to technology at least "has its source in very practical fears of the potential for harm resident in particular technological developments."[17] Although often the criticisms based on such fears are "one-sided and too facile,"[18] the fears themselves, when kept in reasonable perspective, are entirely legitimate. Mesthene takes note of five such fears: technology or a particular technology can deprive people of work, rob people of their privacy, poison the environment, repress individuality and rob people of dignity, and undermine democracy.[19] One does not have to be religious or attach great importance to the cultural role of religion in order to have such fears. Many people whose criticism of technology or particular technologies is based on such fears are avowed atheists, materialists, or secularists; and some critics of destructive technologies, as we shall see in a later chapter, actually see religion or particular religions as being responsible in large part for destructive technologies.

Mesthene finds it useful to contrast hostility to technology based on worries about the potential harm of particular technologies with a second, more general kind of hostility to technology that is harder to analyze and may be largely a matter of temperament.[20] Again, not all antitechnology of this kind—to the extent that it can be satisfactorily distinguished from the first kind—is rooted in a religious world view or a concern for protecting communal respect for religious attitudes and values. People who see themselves as aligned with a noble religious tradition find it much easier than most secularists do to move to a more general form of antitechnology. Religion, after all, is a realm in which one can properly expect to encounter on a regular basis such things as righteousness and self-righteousness, preaching and proselytizing, mistrust of excessive reliance on empirical data and hard facts, the mystic's sense of the limits of reason, and a heightened sense of the absurd. Now, it is not always easy or perhaps appropriate to distinguish as Mesthene does between two fundamental kinds of hostility to technology; and in any case, most of the versions of religious antitechnology that we shall examine combine elements of both. Nevertheless, it may be useful to bear in mind these two forms of antitechnology.

For our first specimen of religious antitechnology, let us turn to a diatribe by the widely respected academic theologian Langdon Gilkey, who writes, technological society promised to free the individual from crushing work, from scarcity, disease and want, to free him to become himself by dispensing with these external fates. In many ways, on the contrary, it has emptied (or threatens to do so) rather than freed the self by placing each person in a homogeneous environment, setting him as a replaceable part within an organized system, and satisfying his external wants rather than energizing his creative powers.[21]

Gilkey recognizes that we need technology but insists that technology must be "tempered and shaped" by religion so that it does not become "demonic": "From religion alone has traditionally come the concern with the human that can prevent the manipulation of men and the dehumanization of society; and from religion alone can come the vision or conception of the human that can creatively guide social policy."[22]

These comments effectively encapsulate the spirit of much of the religious antitechnology movement. They begin with a reference to "technological society," and this reference echoes the title of the English translation of Ellul's *La technique*, the most influential antitechnological study written after World War II and the Holocaust; it functions as a code by which Gilkey can endorse the core of Ellul's argument as well as associate himself with the agenda of the antitechnological movement generally and religious antitechnologists in particular. More importantly, it indicates that Gilkey is not merely troubled by the deleterious effects of certain technologies but by something more general, the "technological society" itself, which differs from other societies that are spiritually sound; so while Gilkey is undoubtedly aware that all societies require and to some extent thrive on their technology, he wants us to realize that there is something deplorable about a society in which technology is such a dominant presence—as in fact it now is, in a way that it has never been before, in our own pitiful society—that it is appropriate to characterize that society as "technological." Gilkey does not directly criticize here particular technologists or other participants in technological processes. Instead he attacks this "technological society" itself, which allegedly made a promise to someone (unidentified) at some time (not indicated) to do all sorts of wonderful things (and, in particular, promote freedom) and then not only broke the promise but proceeded to do the opposite of what it indicated that it would do. Gilkey proceeds to appeal to certain catchwords of the religious antitechnology movement by telling us that "technological society" has put the "individual" into a "homogeneous environment" and made him a mere "replaceable part" in an "organized system" that diminishes that person by focusing on the mere "satisfying" of "external wants" rather than on the noble "energizing" of "creative powers."

There is yet another dimension to this criticism that accentuates its distinctively religious character, and that is when Gilkey lets us know what it is rather than technology that really ought to be the dominant presence in our culture if our culture is to become healthy again. Academic theologian Gilkey has a simple and straightforward answer at hand: religion, from which *alone* has come the "concern with the human" that can prevent the "manipulation" and "dehumanization" of individuals. It must be a religion that can "guide" technology so that it does not become increasingly "demonic," that can "guide" all "social policy" so that the society can become a spiritually healthy community in which genuinely free individuals might reduce crushing work, disease, and the like without losing their souls.

Gilkey has delivered here some powerful rhetoric, but even given the few rudimentary observations that we made earlier in our inquiry, we can see that some critical questions are in order. Is it appropriate to endow the "technological society" with an autonomous existence and to focus on such a thing, whatever it might be, as opposed to particular aspects of particular technologies in particular contexts? In what sense can such a thing be regarded as having made and broken a promise? Is technology really so very much more dominant a presence in our society than it was in earlier societies? Is it now so dominant a presence in our own society—entirely subordinating not only religion but all other forms of experience and culture—that our society can appropriately be characterized as *primarily* a technological one? Are we really different from people in earlier societies or low-technological societies in the Third World in being mere "parts" in a homogenous system that has rendered us less free than our ancestors and fellows? How are we to reconcile the religious antitechnologist's lament about the "dehumanization" fostered by "technological society" with the earnest belief of deep thinkers like Ortega y Gasset, who commented that "man begins where technology begins"?

Faced with the distinctively religious character of an antitechnology like Gilkey's, we need to consider an additional group of problems. Gilkey not only believes that technology is too dominant of a presence in our society but also thinks that technology is notably dominant *at the expense of religion*. Concern about this *competition* is central to almost every major religious antitechnologist's position. Gilkey has remarkable confidence in the power of "religion" not only to temper technology but to guide all social policy. Not as impressed as he might have been by the historical and continuing contribution of philosophy, the arts and sciences, the humanities, and, of course, technology, he tells us that from religion *alone* has traditionally come an effective "concern with the human." Yet ironically, "religious society"—or at least a group of "traditional" or historically influential forms of institutionalized religious life—has long been severely criticized by liberal and progressive thinkers for having done through the millennia just the sort of things for which Gilkey criticizes "technological society." First and foremost, religion in at least some of its most important historical forms has been regarded by many astute cultural historians and theorists as a significant obstacle to personal and social freedom.[23] It has been shown to have been, in many of its most influential forms, authoritarian and politically, intellectually, and emotionally confining. It has been shown to have been in those forms in need of tempering through philosophy, the arts and sciences, and other forms of experience and culture that have helped to free individuals from mindless superstition, bigotry and sectarian hatred, hypocrisy, mechanical ritual, and plenty of other unattractive features of religious life that have contributed to the dehumanization of individuals and the maintenance of sick societies. Now, Gilkey knows that only certain kinds of religion can be relied on to fulfill the promise that he has made to us: "[I]t is only a religion related to history, to social existence and to the human in its social and historical context that can complement, shape and temper technology."[24] It is hard to know precisely what sort of religion Gilkey has in mind, and I worry a bit about whether the criticism of technological society is used by religionists like Gilkey as a means to justify their own theological preferences. At least Gilkey is aware that his lofty words about the cultural value of religion are themselves in need of some tempering, even if he does not appreciate the irony of the virtual interchangeability of his criticism of "technological society" with stock criticisms of "traditional" religion.

Religious antitechnologists are also given to criticizing a technological "mentality" that, again, not associated with any particular technologies or their applications, is a rival to the culture-sustaining mentality provided by a certain kind of religious commitment. Thus, George A. Blair informs us that "Christianity is something utterly other than technique; it involves a way of looking at things that is foreign to the way in which the technical mentality views things."[25] Blair is not only disturbed by the extent to which this "technical mentality" has supplanted the Christian mentality but seems particularly troubled by the way in which Christians, by succumbing to the "technical mentality," have allowed Christianity itself to become corrupted.[26] In a similar fashion, Jean Ladrière criticizes the "technician mentality," which, among other things, "brings with it a desacralization of the world":

[T]here is no longer any mystery; there is no longer any reference to any transcendence whatsoever; the world is spread out before us like some kind of transparent material, and if it is not quite transparent yet, then it certainly will be so. At the same time as this disappearance of the sacred, there is also a sort of devaluation of certain types of language, which are not those of technology: symbolic language for example.[27]

Ladrière cannot deny that there is value in technology, but he warns that if technology as such is not given "meaning" through "Christian hope," the distinctive *logos* at work in the "world of reason and technology" will expose us to the risk of nihilism.[28] Blair and Ladrière must make a place for technology in culture, but their criticism is directed not at particular uses of particular technologies but at a "mentality" that has somehow emerged and now threatens to infect Christianity and lead to nihilism.

Brent Waters, a chaplain, offers thoughts on fate and destiny in a "technological age" that he believes is significantly different from all the other ages in which technology has played such a vital role. A "technological age," he sullenly predicts, "has no future, only an endless process of planning and arrangement. We have purged ourselves of utopian dreams, much less hope for a new Jerusalem, and replaced them with a vague presumption that our rational knowledge and skill will somehow always lead to longer, healthier, and happier lives because of our growing mastery over capricious natural forces."[29] Although Waters's grim talk about a "technological fate"[30] is at least illustrated by some examples (the "banalities" of cable television and the "prospects of toxic waste or persistent vegetative states"[31]), his analysis and the "hope for a new Jerusalem" whose loss he mourns are in their own way as much matters of "vague presumption" as whatever precisely it is that he is criticizing; and as the persistence of the theodicy problem reminds us, God, who so often works in mysterious ways, can well seem as "capricious" as natural forces.

The Roman Catholic philosopher, Rudolf Allers, not inclined to confine his criticism to particular technologies, tells us that "the products of technology are, indeed, subservient to human needs; but they also tyrannize man, not only because they create new needs, but because they alienate man from himself. He is possessed by his possessions. He is the slave of his creations."[32] Speaking in a somber, prophetic voice, Allers asks, "Man is about to conquer the whole world, including the interstellar spaces. But: What does it avail him that he conquer the world and lose his soul?"[33] Sometimes even materialists talk casually about the dangers of "losing one's soul," but Allers clearly takes this expression more literally. Indeed, when religious antitechnologists speak of the threat posed by technology to human spirituality, a long tradition of theological and metaphysical soul-theory stands behind them. When they suggest that the cultural dominance of technology is imperiling salvation, they are rarely speaking in metaphorical terms. Another Roman Catholic philosopher, the proudly conservative Dietrich von Hildebrand, joins the chorus of antitechnologists with the announcement that "the triumph of technology has mechanized the world, deprived it of all poetry."[34] "In one word, instead of letting ourselves be fascinated by technology, instead of adapting ourselves to the spirit of instrumentalization—in the ridiculous fear of appearing reactionary and not up to date—we must refuse to adapt ourselves; we must consciously counteract all the immanent dangers of the development of technology; we must absolutely resist the temptation of making of technology the pattern of human life."[35] Although von Hildebrand singles out particular technologies for special criticism, particularly those that "try to apply the spirit of technology to the realm of the spiritual life of the person and personality" (such as the use of drugs and psychoanalysis to treat diseases of the soul),[36] he sees technology itself as going wild and usurping religion's proper role as the basic inspiration for the pattern of human life.

J. Mark Thomas does not attack technology itself. Yet he has harsh words for the "technicism" that, developed in the womb of classical liberalism,[37] has turned into a demonic quasi-religion, "elevating an authentic element of existence to the whole."[38] In the view of David E. Schrader, technology is "our contemporary snake":

Given technology's immense capacity to increase human power, the most central challenge that modern technology poses to religion lies in humankind's tendency to think that technology has enabled us to achieve power equal to that of God. In this sense, technology tempts us like the snake of old, promising that if we partake sufficiently of its fruits we shall attain equality with God. We fall prey, all too easily, to the idea that humanity is the central ordering force in the universe, that we can save ourselves from whatever perils might beset us, that we are therefore worthy of our own worship.[39]

Schrader grants that technologies have had positive effects, as in making the lame walk and healing the sick,[40] but like Gilkey, he sees technology as such as having made a promise that it cannot keep. Schrader wants us to understand that we must resist technology's temptation to believe that we can *save* ourselves.

The Russian Orthodox philosopher Nicolas Berdyaev is not only one of the most important of all Christian writers on technology but one of the most important twentieth-century philosophers of culture. Berdyaev can sometimes be quite subtle in his approach to technology, but at other times he preaches unadulterated antitechnology, as in this heated passage:

[T]he chief cosmic force which is now at work to change the whole face of the earth and dehumanize and depersonalize man is not capitalism as an economic system, but technics, the wonder of our age. Man has become a slave to his own marvellous invention, the machine. We may well call our epoch the epoch of technics. Technics is man's latest and greatest love. At a time when he has ceased to believe in miracles, man still believes in the miracle of technics. Dehumanization is, first of all, the mechanization of human life, turning man into a machine. The power of the machine shatters the integrity of the human image. Economic life is seen to be completely separated from spiritual life, which is pushed further and further into the background and is no longer permitted to direct life in general.[41]

Among the noteworthy features of this analysis are its emphasis on "technics" as such, its association of technology with a dehumanization that involves the turning of the human being into a machine, and the allusion to the usurpation of the role of spiritual life in directing life in general. Berdyaev indeed sees idolatry involved here, and he wants a revolution: "The present state of the world calls for a moral and spiritual revolution, revolution in the name of personality, of man, of every single person. This revolution should restore the hierarchy of values, now quite shattered, and place the value of human personality above the idols of production, technics, the state, the race or nationality, the collective."[42]

Finally, it is important to note even at this early stage of our investigation that religious antitechnology is not restricted to Christian writers of the twentieth century. We shall be giving due attention later to the ambivalence of the ancient Israelites and ancient Greeks toward technology, but it is useful to take note here of a contemporary Jewish scholar like David Novak who follows his teacher, the eminent Jewish philosopher, Rabbi Abraham Joshua Heschel, in regarding the Sabbath as a day on which to stop worshipping the idols of technical civilization.[43] Moreover, the philosopher Alan R. Drengson, in developing his theme that only a spiritual discipline can reverse the tendency toward the mechanization of the self,[44] purposefully focuses on the insights of Oriental religions rather than Western ones.[45]

The specimens that we have examined thus far give us a fairly good idea of the general tone of much religious antitechnology and introduce us to most of the basic themes and catchwords of the religious antitechnology movement. Some influential religious antitechnologists who should at least be noted in passing are Social Gospel theologian Alva W. Taylor;[46]

carver and engraver Eric Gill, who sees technology as fundamentally opposed to Christianity because of the former's connections with money and leisure and the latter's emphasis on poverty and simplicity;[47] Protestant kerygmatic theologian Emil Brunner;[48] and Roman Catholic existentialist philosopher Gabriel Marcel.[49] Also, a religious element can sometimes be detected in such widely read works as Friedrich Jünger's *The Failure of Technology*,[50] a relentless attack on technology, and E. F. Schumacher's *Small Is Beautiful*, which in effect attacks the materialism allegedly associated with advanced technology and exhorts readers to seek first the kingdom of God.[51] Although they would object—for different reasons—to being characterized as religious antitechnologists, such widely discussed writers on technology as Martin Heidegger,[52] George Grant,[53] and Hans Jonas[54] sometimes make statements that have extraordinary affinities with the major themes of religious antitechnology. To appreciate fully the great influence of religious antitechnology in recent years, it is necessary to turn our attention to the writings of Jacques Ellul.

THE ANTITECHNOLOGY OF JACQUES ELLUL

No literature on technology has received more attention in the last thirty years than the major writings of Ellul, whom Samuel C. Florman has perhaps fittingly characterized as the "founding father of the contemporary antitechnological movement."[55] Ellul's critics have sometimes been baffled by the importance that serious scholars have attached to his views on technology. As Ellul himself is often a strident, uncompromising critic— and at times an impolite critic—of those views of which he disapproves, his "romantic wailings" invite some particularly harsh evaluations. Yet Ellul's critics often seem to be more puzzled than angered by his remarkable influence. In Mesthene's eyes, "Ellul's examples, and the general position they are used to illustrate, . . . tend to range along a spectrum from the unintelligible to the trite";[56] with his "fundamental bias,"[57] Ellul is to be seen as "a living embodiment of nineteenth-century Romantic Idealism" and "a voice still crying out against the Age of Reason and the wreckage that it wrought upon the existentially rooted value structure of the medieval synthesis."[58] Joseph Agassi counts Ellul among those writers on technology whose discussion of the aimlessness of technological society is itself aimless;[59] and Langdon Winner sees Ellul as one of those "nontechnical thinkers" whose "uneasiness with problem solving seems to undermine the very basis upon which [they] have credentials to talk about technical matters at all."[60] Yet no less respected and orthodox a representative of "standard American sociology"[61] than Robert K. Merton, enlisted to write a foreword to the English translation of Ellul's most important book, characterizes Ellul's "social philosophy of our technical civilization" as wider in scope than Thorstein Veblen's, more incisive than Oswald Spengler's, more analytical than Lewis Mumford's, and more systematic than Siegfried Giedion's.[62] To some observers, Jacques Ellul is nothing less than a "prophet"—and in a very weighty sense of that term.[63]

That there is a significant relationship between Ellul's religious commitment and his attack on technology is not always clear—at least partly because Ellul himself often obscures it—and many who speak approvingly of what they know of Ellul's major views on technology are not even aware of the depth and relevance of Ellul's religious commitment. Among those who *are* aware of the importance that Ellul attaches to religion, there are some who have been favorably impressed by Ellul's general approach to technology despite their own lack of interest in religiocultural issues. Thus, there are those who would strongly object to the characterization of Ellul as a "religious antitechnologist," even though they would be prepared to grant that Ellul is an antitechnologist to whom both his own religious faith and religiocultural concerns in general are very important. Ellul certainly saw much of his antitechnology as capable of being accepted even by the radical secularist. There are places in his writings where he goes to some effort to emphasize that appreciation of his sociological analysis of the technological society does not require the adoption of a religious perspective. Still, one may wonder how much comfort Ellul could have derived from seeing his views on technology regularly associated with those of such secularist antitechnologists as Herbert Marcuse and Jürgen Habermas.[64]

When one actually tries to fit together Ellul's various religiocultural views, one may well find that it is a daunting task. In a presentation given very late in his life at a conference in his honor, Ellul, describing the main influences on his life and work, emphasized the central importance to him of "the hope of faith in Christ."[65] Ivan Illich, trying to rise to the occasion, praised the renowned sage by observing that "among modern thinkers, Ellul has always been one of a select few who understand that the place of the sacred is now occupied not by this or that artifact, but by *la technique*, the black box we worship."[66] Some years earlier, in a series of radio programs based on interviews, Ellul offered these provocative observations on the functional importance of religion in society: "In a society, religion has extremely well-known, extremely precise functions. It serves to hold a society together. When one destroys a religion, one will see the social group come apart. Religion gives people a kind of overall explanation of the world, which is very important. One cannot be satisfied with a purely logical and rational science, a science that knows it is limited."[67] In short, "we need a transcendence."[68] In the same discussion, Ellul noted how technology "reduces" Christianity,[69] and complained specifically about technology's responsibility for "deplorable" methods of analyzing Scripture such as those employing structural linguistics.[70]

These various remarks not only give us some indication of the importance that Ellul attaches to religion but also reveal some important tensions. Ellul, it would appear, was a genuine "believer," a devout Protestant Christian who worked at keeping the faith in his personal and professional affairs. He was also, as we shall see, a theologian who devoted much time and effort to the respectful exposition and application of Scriptural insights. As a devout believer and dedicated disciple of New Testament teaching, he was well aware of Jesus' injunction to his followers to witness for the faith, as in Matthew 24:14 ("And this gospel of the kingdom shall be preached in all the world for a witness unto all nations") and Matthew 28:19 ("Go ye therefore, and teach all nations, baptizing them in the name of the Father, and of the Son, and of the Holy Ghost"). Although devoutly religious people are not ordinarily being hypocritical when they strive to keep their personal faith from disrupting their performance of an essentially secular role in a religiously pluralistic community, a believer who finds himself theorizing on the world stage about cultural decline and the "dehumanization" of humanity can hardly afford to ignore the seminal importance of the faith that procures salvation. However, such a person may realize that if he also has a more general message, then coming across as a Christian preacher will result in the alienation of much of the audience to which he is appealing. Even so, it always sounds somewhat strange when a genuine believer talks about the functional, practical social value of religion; not only is the emphasis then on religion as such rather than the true faith that saves, but religion and "transcendence," even if shown to be needed to "hold a society together," are reduced to the status of utilitarian instruments, tools—technologies—whose mystical and poetic dimensions are relegated to the background. Moreover, as Illich's comment indicates, Ellul often stresses the extent to which technology has already won out over spirituality, and the quasi-deterministic aspect of Ellul's analysis can be very disconcerting to those seeking guidance on what action to take to restore human freedom, dignity, and spirituality.

For Ellul, these tensions are exacerbated by his fine appreciation of the corruptive cultural influences of propaganda. Ellul's work on propaganda is almost as widely known as his work on technology,[71] and Dennis Rohatyn has suggested that "despite his Luddite tendencies and a profound hatred for secularity, no one has done more than Ellul to advance our understanding of what propaganda is, what it does and why it exists."[72] Rohatyn has usefully observed that there is an important connection between Ellul's contempt for corruptive propaganda and certain theological ideas that Ellul has about how not to witness for the faith: "Ellul is a devout Protestant who (because he is French) is sometimes mistaken for Catholic. He has written several volumes of Biblical criticism, but his importance lies in his fervent opposition to all missionary zeal. Conversion is an inner experience which cannot be forced or even awakened by outsiders without corrupting the very faith one seeks to instill. This out-Luthers Luther."[73] Indeed, Ellul is inclined to dismiss evangelists like Billy Graham as propagandists.[74] Then where does that leave Ellul in his own effort to persuade his readers that it is crucially important that we at least understand the comparative cultural value of religion and *la technique?*

Ellul's quasi-determinist inclinations are relevant. In *The Technological System*, he writes, "We must then ask the question: Who is the man to whom one attributes the power of choice, decision, initiative, orientation? No longer a Greek in the time of Pericles, or a Hebrew prophet, or a twelfth-century monk. He is a man who is entirely immersed in technology. He is not autonomous in regard to these objects";[75] indeed, "man can choose, but in a system of options established by the technological process. He can direct, but in terms of the technological given. He can never get out of it at any time, and the intellectual systems he constructs are ultimately expressions or justifications of technology."[76] So although Ellul is not a strict determinist, we can see why he regards the "humanist" problems of such existentialist critics of technology as Jean-Paul Sartre and Martin Heidegger[77] as false and unrealistic. One reason—not the only reason, but an important one—why Ellul's approach to technology strikes someone like Joseph Agassi as "aimless" and someone like Langdon Winner as indicating an "uneasiness with problem solving" is that such readers do not appreciate the extent to which the piously Protestant Ellul is trying to impress upon his readers our dependence on Divine grace. This sense of the paramount importance of Divine grace is a significant force that shaped Ellul's attitude toward facing both the dehumanization produced by technological society and the problem of witnessing without corrupting the faith that one seeks to instill.

The tensions are not resolved by Ellul; indeed they are beyond resolution. Ellul often is, despite certain deeply held convictions inclining him in another direction, a religious propagandist whose attack on *la technique* and its displacement of the sacred is substantially (though not entirely) rooted in a profound hatred of secularity and a hope of faith in Christ. Furthermore, despite his quasi-determinist inclinations, Ellul is as much an advocate of human freedom as the existentialist philosophers whose "humanist" problems he undervalues. His copious and passionate writings are not offered up in the spirit of detached academic scholarship but are polemics meant to contribute to the promotion and realization of some distinctively Christian ideal of freedom. By virtue of his influence, if not the quality of his often confused and inconsistent ideas, he is the contemporary *religious* antitechnologist par excellence; and that he is not consistently recognized as such is to varying degrees a function of his own confusions, his intentional obscuring of his agenda, and the failure of readers to consider some of his specific observations (or works) in a sufficiently comprehensive context.

Ellul's credentials as an antitechnologist are impeccable. He can, when necessary, focus on a particular technology, such as television, which, "because of its power of fascination and its capacity of visual and auditory penetration, is probably the technical instrument which is most destructive of personality and of human relations. What man seeks is evidently an absolute distraction, a total obliviousness of himself and his problems, and the simultaneous fusion of his consciousness with an omnipresent technical diversion."[78] The references here to "distraction" and "diversion" should remind students of the humanities of similar passages in the *Pensées* of Blaise Pascal, that ardent seventeenth-century religious critic of the Age of Reason and its fascination with science, technology, and human powers.[79] (The affinities between Ellul and Pascal are generally noteworthy and are particularly apparent in their shared theological and anthropological opinions.) However, Ellul is fittingly regarded mainly as a critic of technology as such, of *la technique*. He is renowned for such passages as that in *The Technological Society* where he writes, "In our cities there is no more day or night or heat or cold. But there is overpopulation, thraldom to press and television, total absence of purpose. All men are constrained by means external to them to ends equally external. The further the technical mechanism develops which allows us to escape natural necessity, the more we are subjected to artificial technical necessities."[80] It is in this section of his most influential book that Ellul derides the "idealism" of philosophers like Henri Bergson and Emmanuel Mounier who naively believe that control can be regained over technical means by "an additional quantity of soul."[81] In *The Technological Society*, as elsewhere in his writings, Ellul passes his most severe judgment on the "technician," a person who "uses technique perhaps because it is his profession, but . . . does so with adoration because for him technique is the locus of the sacred."[82]

One of the central themes of Ellul's antitechnology is that there is a crucial difference between modern technology and the technology of earlier ages. "According to Emmanuel Mounier (and this is one of the reasons I broke with him), there is only a difference of degree between a flint arrowhead and the atomic bomb. In this case, I would have to very firmly apply Marx's notion that, on a certain level, quantitative change is qualitative change. Hence, when the human race moved from the flint arrowhead to the atomic bomb, there was a *qualitative* change."[83] The issue being addressed here is in fact one of the major issues in the philosophy of technology, and it obviously invites a number of perspectives involving various contexts of technology. For the religious antitechnologist, it is useful to be able to contrast technology in the highly secularized or pluralistic societies of our own day with the ostensibly more innocuous technology of earlier societies, a technology that was apparently able to coexist more harmoniously with traditional religious attitudes. Ellul realizes that if all societies throughout history have been "technological" in a fundamental sense, then it is inappropriate to blame technology as such for the kinds of dehumanization and cultural decline that are singularly characteristic of the "advanced" societies of our time. Now, because being clear on this issue is so important to understanding the relations of religion and technology, we must consider how muddled and inconsistent Ellul himself is when dealing with the issue. In *The Technological Society*, he sees himself as able "to assert with confidence that there is no common denominator between the technique of today and that of yesterday. Today we are dealing with an utterly different phenomenon."[84] No common denominator? An utterly different phenomenon? That Ellul himself does not consistently believe such things is evident in his historical speculations about the origins of technical activity ("the most primitive activity of man"[85] having developed "principally in the Near East"[86]) and the religious inspiration of such welcome ancient technologies as the domestication of animals and the cultivation of plants.[87] When it suits his antitechnological argument, Ellul can shift to the position that technique began with the *machine*—without which the world of technique would not exist[88]—and the machine created our distinctively modern world.[89]

On the final page of *The Technological Society*, Ellul takes a sarcastic jab at "technical experts" with his remark that "none of our wise men ever pose the question of the end of all their marvels."[90] It is, of course, lines like this one that Agassi has in mind when he refers to those critics like Ellul who discuss the "aimlessness" of technological society. Is Ellul's discussion, as Agassi contends, just as aimless? When we consider Ellul's reference to "the question of the end," we perhaps should not regard the use of the key term *end* as restricted to indicating clearly conceptualized human aims, motives, and objectives. Given our awareness of Ellul's theological concerns, we may well want to regard this reference as having eschatological import. Ellul, as a *religious* antitechnologist, believes that if we are to understand the most important matters properly, we must ultimately understand them not in terms of the ephemeral aspirations of God's woefully disobedient creatures but in terms of the Divine plan as indicated to us, however obscurely, in God's Holy Word. If one really wants to understand Ellul's agenda, one must move on from his "sociological" studies of technology to his unambiguously theological understanding of technology, particularly in *The Meaning of the City*.

It would give many secularist and liberal religious admirers of Ellul quite a shock to read *The Meaning of the City*, which not only is an aggressively pietistic work of Christian theology but is written in a peculiarly personal style that almost certainly reflects its author's antipathy toward the intellectually sophisticated approaches to the Word taken by leading contemporary academic theologians of culture. (The contrast between the theologies of culture of Ellul and Paul Tillich is particularly striking.) We noted earlier that Robert K. Merton, a respectable "mainstream" academic sociologist, characterizes Ellul's contribution to the theory of technology as a "social philosophy," almost as if Merton cannot bear to take Ellul at his word when Ellul characterizes his most widely known work as sociological. Samuel C. Florman, who clearly is not quite sure what to make of Ellul's vocation, characterizes him as a "theological philosopher."[91] While Ellul is comfortable enough dealing with abstractions and making value judgments, it is somewhat misleading to characterize him as a philosopher, for he appears to have rather little familiarity with (or at least use for) the texts and tools of the philosophical tradition. Whether or not he ever qualifies as a genuine sociologist or philosopher, Ellul certainly qualifies as a theologian when he gets down to explaining to his readers the "meaning" of the city.

Ellul emphasizes a special connection between technology and the city, which as we have noted, is a place that he has associated with "total absence of purpose." *The Meaning of the City* begins by looking at that rather abhorrent Scriptural figure, the murderer Cain, whom Ellul describes as the first builder of a city, the founder of craftsmanship, and a man who by carving stones thereby made them impure and unfit for use in an altar for God.[92] "It is man's high-handed piracy of creation that makes creation incapable of giving glory to God."[93] Ellul later turns his attention to the Israelites, God's chosen people; they obeyed a worldly king, the Pharaoh of Egypt, who forced them into ways not meant for a chosen people and reduced them to slaves used only for the building of cities.[94] Although the Israelites were always, in Ellul's view, separate *in spirit* from the city (and from the related obsession with human creations), they nevertheless were corrupted through secularization and suffered grievously as a result. Even long after the exodus from Egypt, in what might appear to have been their period of greatest glory, they could not avoid a destructive fascination with human creations that is vividly represented in Scripture by King Solomon's obsession with building.[95] "Jerusalem is there as a warning: As soon as man acquires righteousness and holiness by his work, we must be ready to leave that work, to abandon it to wrath; and woe to those who love it more than themselves!"[96]

However, with the coming of Jesus Christ, "God's greatest work,"[97] new horizons have opened for us.[98] It is crucial that we understand "God's fundamental action which, in Jesus Christ, leads from Cain to the New Jerusalem. God dissociates man's work from its spiritual power."[99] This theological antitechnology might seem almost quaint to the liberal thinker were it not for the fanaticism and nastiness that creep into Ellul's analysis. "Man sacrifices man to build his cities, instead of accepting the only true sacrifice which would enable him both to found them in truth and purify them of Satan's presence. I am sadly aware that these words mean nothing to the world's ears. The means chosen by God has no meaning for man's projects. But it is the only means."[100] Ellul the Satan-fighter, having not given up hope for the new creation in which "all that Christ came to accomplish is finally realized,"[101] wants the few of us who will listen to his prophetic words not to lose sight of the fact "that the powers defeated by Christ are still at work, that they refuse to admit their defeat and are struggling more violently than ever."[102] For Ellul the battleground on which the war against Satanic technology (and the dehumanization that it generates) is ultimately to be fought is a spiritual one; and the war itself is, in the last analysis, a Christian crusade.

ROOTS OF RELIGIOUS ANTITECHNOLOGY

Religious antitechnology has deep roots in Western civilization, and when we turn to the formative cultures of the ancient Hebrews and the ancient Greeks, we notice in both a pronounced ambivalence toward technology. Ellul's understanding of ancient Israel is obscured by his Christian-theological lenses, but he properly acknowledges Israel's ambivalence in his own peculiar way when he says that however secularized and urbanized the Israelites became, they remained in some sense separate "in spirit" from the city. It is certainly misleading for Katharine Temple to say that "the Jewish people never developed a high technology (prior to the twentieth century),"[103] and it is ironic for someone with her surname to make so blunt a generalization. In any case, Hebrew Scripture itself abounds with examples of a spiritualized respect for technological crafts-manship and creativity,[104] and Jewish craftsmen from the beginnings of the Diaspora to our own time have left an important mark on the cultures of the peoples among whom they have been dispersed.[105] Lewis Mumford views the urbanization of the Jews very differently than Ellul does. Im-pressed by the fact that the mainly urban culture of the Jews is one of only three great cultures that have a continuous history throughout the historic period, Mumford remarks that this culture is distinguished particularly for "practical intelligence," "rational morals," "kindly manners," and "co-op-erative and life-conserving institutions" that stand in stark contrast to the ways of the predominantly military and self-destructive forms of civiliza-tion.[106] At the same time, the ancient Hebrews (and later Jewish commen-tators) generally recognized their obligation to tend and guard the world rather than merely "dominate" it;[107] and the Garden of Eden is one of the most powerful images in world literature of a more glorious past in which human beings dwelled in a paradise unspoiled by human invention.[108]

Among the ancient Greeks, the ambivalence is even more marked. The philosopher Hans Jonas notes that it is powerfully displayed in the great Chorus from Sophocles's *Antigone* that begins at line 335 with the obser-vation that "many the wonders but nothing walks stranger than man."[109] Jonas observes:

This awestruck homage to man's powers tells of his violent and violating irruption into the cosmic order, the self-assertive invasion of nature's various domains by his restless cleverness; but also of his building—through the self-taught powers of speech and thought and social sentiment—the home for his very humanity, the artifact of the city. The raping of nature and the civilizing of himself go hand in hand. Both are in defiance of the elements.[110]

The myth of Prometheus even more arrestingly manifests this ambiva-lence, for in it we even more clearly see how, in A. George Schillinger's words, "the ancient Greeks found hubris a useful and unmistakable concept [but] also understood that technology shapes the lives of men, and exercises a profound influence over social existence."[111] Along with the image of Prometheus we should consider such classical Greek images as those of Pandora and Icarus,[112] but also that of the artisan god, Hephaestus, who is often praised in keeping with Homer's noticeable admiration for the craftsmen of his time.[113]

Classical Greek antitechnology received its most refined expression in certain texts by Plato and Aristotle. While their antitechnological views are obviously in a sense more philosophical than religious, it would be a mistake to undervalue the religious dimensions of (and religious influences upon) classical Greek philosophy. Even in its most sophisticated philosophical form, classical Greek antitechnology has a religious foundation. Thus, as Carl Mitcham has helpfully observed,

the ancient critique of technology . . . rests on a tightly woven, fourfold argument: (1) the will to technology or the technological intention often involves a turning away from faith or trust in nature or Providence; (2) technical affluence and the concomitant processes of change tend to undermine individual striving for excellence and societal stability; (3) technological knowledge likewise draws human beings into intercourse with the world and obscures transcendence; (4) technical objects are less real than objects of nature.[114]

A considerable part of this classical critique of technology carried over to Christianity, although we should bear in mind the relevance of a crucial difference between the Greek philosophical ethic and the Christian theological ethic. As Edward Goodwin Ballard points out:

To the Greek, man's initial non-being is a quite definite potentiality, a potentiality, moreover, which a man, exercising the appropriate rational discipline, could actualize himself and thus achieve that harmony of soul which is the perfection of humanity. This is a doctrine of self-salvation. Quite otherwise with the Christian. The Christian is plagued by the paradox of man's finite power set in contrast to his infinite destiny. . . . This Christian doctrine, therefore, must be a faith in salvation by the other.[115]

In any case, Plato and Aristotle were not consistently critical of technology as such. Aristotle was too practical of a fellow to be a consistent antitechnologist. Plato, despite the metaphysical Idealism that led him to regard technical objects as less real than the objects that should ordinarily occupy the wise person's attention,[116] understood the importance of the practical arts and respected honest and talented craftsmen. Indeed, the author of the *Republic* holds that the wisdom of the ideal *polis* resides in the class of Guardians, learned individuals who not only know the highest things but have mastered the *techne* of statecraft.[117]

One important area in which classical Greek influence upon Christian antitechnology can be seen is in the emphasis placed by Greek philosopher and medieval Christian theologian alike on the primacy of contemplation. As Hannah Arendt has observed, "Christianity, with its belief in a hereafter whose joys announce themselves in the delights of contemplation, conferred a religious sanction upon the abasement of the *vita activa* to its derivative, secondary position."[118] Although Plato and Aristotle could speak approvingly of *techne* in many of its forms, they never deviated from their position that contemplation is the highest of all human activities; and the followers of such saintly intellectuals as Augustine and Thomas Aquinas who transmitted Greek philosophical wisdom to the simple be-lievers of the Middle Ages maintained the position in some form, albeit a Christianized one. The independent thinkers of the Renaissance, Age of Reason, and Enlightenment dealt a series of mighty blows to the long-enduring medieval synthesis of Jewish, Greek, and Christian ideas, atti-tudes, and values. While religious antitechnology is still to a great extent reacting against the spirit of the Age of Reason and the Enlightenment, cultural historians generally acknowledge that there is also a significant connection between the rise of Protestantism and the heightening of the cultural profile of technology. The precise nature of this connection has been the subject of much debate; but having had to expose ourselves to the antitechnological preaching of the Reformed theologian Ellul, we are entitled to savor for a moment a certain irony.

One problem with theories that try to distinguish "qualitatively" be-tween destructive "modern" technology and the more innocuous technol-ogy of earlier times is that there is a basic ambiguity in the concept of the modern. This ambiguity reveals itself in discussions of technology as well as in discussions of philosophy, religion, literature, politics, and so forth. Some people are inclined to associate modern technology with develop-ments that have occurred since 1900 or even just since World War II. For such people, computer technologies and telecommunications technologies are often the paradigms of modern technologies. Many scholars associate the rise of modern technology with the nineteenth century and the Industrial Revolution, and they would agree with Albert Borgmann that "modern technology begins with the introduction of the steam engine in mines, factories, and for transportation."[119] Some of the greatest techno-logical shocks to traditional religion occurred in the nineteenth century,[120] and the impact of Darwinism, Marxism, and the "higher criticism" of Scripture immediately come to mind. And, of course, some people prefer to associate the emergence of modern technology—and its challenge to traditional religion—with scientific developments of earlier centuries, and with such names as Copernicus, Galileo, and Francis Bacon, or perhaps René Descartes, Benedict de Spinoza, and John Locke. The views of sociologist Max Weber provide us with yet another perspective.

In one of the most influential books ever written about religion and technology (as well as about other subjects), *The Protestant Ethic and the Spirit of Capitalism*, Weber argues that "ascetic Protestantism," particularly (but not exclusively) a kind of English Puritanism derived from Calvinism,[121] was the decisive factor in transforming basic Western attitudes toward labor, wealth, and technology. According to Weber, this ascetic Protestantism undermined religious and cultural traditionalism and paved the way for the rise of capitalism and a new kind of respect for technology. Weber observes that ascetic Protestantism taught that "wealth is . . . bad ethically only in so far as it is a temptation to idleness and sinful enjoyment of life, and its acquisition is bad only when it is with the purpose of later living merrily and without care. But as a performance of duty in a calling it is not only morally permissible, but actually enjoined."[122] With its emphasis on the steady production of useful *works* for the welfare of humanity and the glory of God, ascetic Protestantism was thus an impetus to technological creativity.[123] Its new social ethic paradoxically promoted—and was later intensified by—an important form of cultural secularization. Ascetic Protestantism had itself been influenced by the earlier asceticism of the monasteries at which free manual labor had acquired religious significance and dignity.[124] Thus, in Weber's view, "modern" technology and related forms of capitalism and secularization arose largely as a result of the effort of Calvinists and others to apply the asceticism of the monasteries to the whole of society. We should note, however, that Weber is not thinking here in terms of a simple one-way deterministic relationship and recognizes that the values of ascetic Protestantism were themselves gradually transformed as a result of economic, technological, and other cultural developments.[125]

This is an important theory, and even if it is not entirely correct, it at least reminds us that religious developments themselves contributed to the decline of the medieval synthesis of Jewish, Greek, and Christian ideas, attitudes, and values that had provided much of the foundation for traditional Christian antitechnology. It also reminds us that in discussing the relations of religion and technology, we need to be as careful in talking about religion as such as in talking about technology as such. Moreover, it leads us to ponder to what extent the Christian antitechnologists of our own day are prepared to return to the medieval synthesis.

ALTERNATIVES TO RELIGIOUS ANTITECHNOLOGY

We have seen that religious antitechnologists are typically troubled by what they perceive as the menacing competition that technology as such poses to some traditional or established religious dimension of culture; some religious antitechnologists understand this religious dimension broadly, and others understand it more narrowly. Most of them will grant that competition itself is not necessarily negative and that in some ways religious experience and religious institutions can be strengthened through competition.[126] Why then, we may wonder, is whatever competition technology poses to religion necessarily negative for society, for the individual, or even for religion itself? What most religious antitechnologists seem to believe is that there is something unfair about this competition. Forces, Satanic or otherwise, are ostensibly misleading the unsuspecting masses about the long-term effects of technological growth; and at the same time they are obscuring the true nature of religion and leading people to underestimate religion's vital cultural and spiritual importance. There are, of course, many technologists—and many people other than technologists—who are antipathetic to religion as such or to the kinds of religion that religious antitechnologists seek to defend and promote. Technologists and others regularly complain that religious leaders and groups often interfere with the "progress" required for the realization of the highest ideals. There is even in a sense a technological antireligion movement comparable to the religious antitechnology movement, although most critics of institutionalized religion would balk at being classified as *essentially* technological in their orientation. In any event, it does not follow from the facts that when competition takes place and someone is winning that competition that the competition itself is necessarily unfair; and most religious antitechnologists probably need to take a closer look at why religion is competing as unsuccessfully with technology as they think it is.

One can, to be sure, acknowledge significant competition between religion and technology, or between particular religious phenomena and particular technologies, without passing judgment on who is winning or who deserves to be winning. Ian G. Barbour, for example, works hard at analyzing aspects of the competition without sliding into polemics. Barbour recognizes that in a certain sense "in applied science and technology it is man who controls nature; the effective power is human rather than divine. Through his own abilities man reached the moon. Secular man trusts science, not God, to fulfill his needs."[127] Not given to romantic wailing, Barbour focuses instead on the extent to which contemporary religion must "come to terms" with scientific components of secularity,[128] and he works hard at developing an understanding of religion that will facilitate this coming to terms. Another sort of neutrality is evident in Frederick Sontag's recognition of the importance of both perspective and circumstances: "When we thought the rise of science and technology was all-good and the route to the salvation of man, we could find God in history and the hope for a new culture to emerge. When science and technology become liabilities and not total assets, God disappears because we are not prepared for this negative side."[129]

We must also be careful not to assume too close a connection between religion and antitechnology. There are many antitechnologists, including some of the most influential ones, who are not criticizing technology as such from a distinctively religious perspective. Some of these would undoubtedly characterize themselves as religious in some sense, but others would say that they have no special interest in defending religion, and some would point out that they have been openly critical of religion. Surveying a list of leading antitechnologists, including, among others, Jacques Ellul, Lewis Mumford, and Theodore Roszak[130]—and to which we could add, for example, Friedrich Jünger, Jean-Paul Sartre, Ivan Illich, Hans Jonas, and Herbert Marcuse[131]—Florman observes that they are an "unlikely combination."[132] Indeed they are, both generally and specifically with regard to their attitudes toward religion.

Correspondingly, many religious thinkers who have written about technology have not been antitechnologists; and as P. Hans Sun has observed, after surveying a wide range of religionists' opinions about technology, "[B]elievers as much as social philosophers fail to share any common judgment about technology."[133] There are certainly important theologians and religious philosophers who qualify in some sense as protechnologists, such as Emmanuel Mounier,[134] Teilhard de Chardin,[135] Harvey Cox,[136] and Walter J. Ong.[137] Much of the remainder of this study will be an attempt to shed light on the major aspects of the relationship between religion and technology that religious antitechnologists and others have failed to understand.

It is not hard to fathom why so many people who are unhappy with the society in which they live—or with the disappointing circumstances of their own lives, which they can conveniently attribute in part to the sorry state of their society—have a nostalgia for some of the old ways, including the religious attitudes of their parents, grandparents, or distant ancestors; and technology, symbolizing modernity and often demanding changes in our outlook and style of living, is undeniably responsible in large part for the passing of some of the old ways. But reason dictates that we avoid excessive and self-deceptive nostalgia and that we resist the temptation to make a scapegoat of something that has done so much to sustain and enrich human existence. Moreover, deeply reflective human beings (and many less reflective ones, too) cannot abide too much in the way of tradition, orthodoxy, and stability, and they often long for progress, variety, and novelty. A. George Schillinger has concisely described for us an underlying psychological and cultural dilemma:

One horn of the dilemma . . . is man's yearning to retain the simple, the familiar, the intelligible pattern of life he may enjoy at a given moment in as much harmony with his surroundings as possible. In the face of imminent change, his reaction is often to feel a sense of grief, bewilderment and fear.

The other horn of the dilemma is his enduring propensity to bring about change in the order of things, change in his natural and material environment, and change in human affairs. He optimistically regards reshaping the natural and material environment, his own niche in it, his social order, and his systems of production as human progress and as the primary means of improving the human condition, the quality of existence for the many. The principal instruments with which he has brought about change have been new knowledge and technology, from their pristine forms to their present state of great complexity, variety and scale.

These two human propensities have been at cross purposes throughout the ages, and man has been ambivalent about his preferences, letting one or the other tendency hold sway over his destiny.[138]

Although intellectuals have provided useful insights into the positive and negative aspects of religion, technology, tradition, progress, and so forth, much that has been said about such subjects has been deeply rooted in feelings and temperamental inclinations. This is evident, for example, in certain writings of George Grant. As a rational person, Grant clearly understands that even though justice requires the rejection of particular technologies, "meeting 'technology' face to face means for the thinker neither acceptance nor rejection but trying to know it for what it is."[139] While Grant rejected his earlier characterizations of the technological society and the secularist religion of progress,[140] he could not help railing against the "liberalism" that in promoting a certain form of freedom had made the contemplative life less and less accessible.

There are some observers who, not wishing to become (or be regarded as) full-fledged religious antitechnologists, are content to offer the somewhat bland albeit earnest advice that we draw on the religious resources of our civilization to help us to keep technological growth from going awry. When, for example, Larry Rasmussen puts forward "the modest proposal that an ancient tradition be reconsidered; more precisely, that some selected themes from Jewish and Christian traditions be reassessed for the frame of mind they might help promote in our circumstances,"[141] we would probably be churlish and obstinate if we did not respond, "Why not?" And when Rasmussen, focusing on the Hebrew tradition, reminds us of the profundity of Scriptural notions of creation, neighbor, justice, and peace, we are almost surely left in a better position to recognize bad technologies and destructive misapplications of the basically good technologies.[142] Even someone antagonistic to religion as such might be prepared to grant that a certain kind of religious world view can help particular individuals to be better producers and users of technology, just as it can help some people to be better philosophers, politicians, or—as so many of them have testified in the mass media—professional athletes. Meanwhile, those of us who are more open-minded with respect to the question of the value of religion can see from our own daily experience how religious commitment of a certain type can make individuals better human beings.

However, can we afford to forget that religion in some of its most important forms, including forms defended by prominent religious antitechnologists, has contributed mightily to making individuals and societies worse? Casting a skeptical eye on the wailings of religious antitechnologists, Herbert Muller points to the conspicuous failure of the major churches themselves to provide either moral or spiritual leadership in the emerging industrialized societies of the nineteenth century; indeed, "in spite of the shocking abuses of early industrialism, they mostly opposed movements toward social and political reform, and then the whole labor movement."[143] The very type of religion that can foster justice, spirituality, compassion, and hope, can also, when misappropriated—as it so commonly is—result in smug complacency, mindless superstition, bigotry, and hatred. I remember, as a child, seeing a picture that has left a great impression on me throughout the years, a picture of highly intricate torture devices used on victims of the Inquisition. Such elaborate machine technology, put to the service of the cruelest forms of dehumanization centuries before the invention of the steam engine, centuries before the Nazi death camps, is well worth remembering in an investigation of the relations of religion and technology. If the religious antitechnologist insists on seeing it as one more example of how technology has corrupted religion, the rest of us still have the prerogative of seeing it as also in part a powerful example of how religion has corrupted technology.

NOTES

1. Paul Tillich, *Theology of Culture*, ed. Robert C. Kimball (New York: Oxford University Press, 1959), 42.

2. Sigmund Freud, *The Future of an Illusion* (1927), trans. W. D. Robson-Scott (1953), revised and newly edited by James Strachey (1961), (Garden City, N.Y.: Doubleday, 1964), 60.

3. Thorstein Veblen, *The Instinct of Workmanship* (1914) (New York: W. W. Norton, 1964), v.

4. José Ortega y Gasset, "Man the Technician," in *Toward a Philosophy of History*, trans. not identified (New York: W. W. Norton, 1941), 117–18.

5. D.S.L. Cardwell, *Turning Points in Western Technology: A Study of Technology, Science and History* (New York: Science History Publications, a division of Neale Watson Academic Publications, 1972), 1.

6. Alois Huning, "*Homo Mensura*: Human Beings Are Their Technology—Technology Is Human," *Research in Philosophy and Technology* 8 (1985): 9.

7. Herbert J. Muller, *The Children of Frankenstein: A Primer on Modern Technology and Human Values* (Bloomington: Indiana University Press, 1970), 317.

8. Ibid.

9. Jacques Ellul, *The Technological Society* (1954), trans. John Wilkinson (New York: Knopf, 1964). The original French title of this work is worth noting: *La technique ou l'enjeu du siècle.*

10. William B. Jones and A. Warren Matthews, "Toward a Taxonomy of Technology and Religion," *Research in Philosophy and Technology* 10 (1990): 20–22.

11. Friedrich Rapp, *Analytical Philosophy of Technology*, trans. Stanley R. Carpenter and Theodor Langenbruch. *Boston Studies in the Philosophy of Science*, vol. 63 (Dordrecht, The Netherlands: D. Reidel, 1981), 8.

12. Ibid.

13. Mario Bunge, "The Five Buds of Technophilosophy," *Technology in Society* 1, no. 1 (1979): 67.

14. Ibid. Cf. Emmanuel G. Mesthene, "Technology as Evil: Fear or Lamentation?" *Research in Philosophy and Technology* 7 (1984): 65.

15. Kai Nielsen, "Technology as Ideology," *Research in Philosophy and Technology* 1 (1978): 132.

16. Emmanuel G. Mesthene, *Technological Change: Its Impact on Man and Society* (Cambridge: Harvard University Press, 1970), 26.

17. Mesthene, "Technology as Evil," 59.

18. Ibid., p. 65.

19. Ibid., pp. 59–65.

20. Ibid., p. 59.

21. Langdon Gilkey, "The Religious Dilemmas of a Scientific Culture: The Interface of Technology, History and Religion," in Donald M. Borchert and David Stewart, eds., *Being Human in a Technological Age* (Athens: Ohio University Press, 1979), 82.

22. Ibid., pp. 86–87.

23. For a critical survey of a broad range of arguments purporting to establish that religion is a hindrance to freedom, see Jay Newman, *On Religious Freedom* (Ottawa: University of Ottawa Press, 1991), ch. 2.

24. Gilkey, "The Religious Dilemmas of a Scientific Culture," 87.

25. George A. Blair, "Faith Outside Technique," in Carl Mitcham and Jim Grote, eds., *Theology and Technology: Essays in Christian Analysis and Exegesis* (Lanham, Md.: University Press of America, 1984), 45.

26. Ibid., pp. 47, 50.

27. Jean Ladrière, "Faith and the Technician Mentality," trans. Margaret House, in Hugh C. White, Jr., ed., *Christians in a Technological Era* (New York: Seabury Press, 1964), 67.

28. Ibid., p. 76.

29. Brent Waters, "A Meditation of Fate and Destiny in a Technological Age," *Bulletin of Science, Technology and Society* 12, nos. 4–5 (1992): 205.

30. Ibid.

31. Ibid.

32. Rudolf Allers, "Technology and the Human Person," in Robert Paul Mohan, ed., *Technology and Christian Culture* (Washington, D.C.: Catholic University of America Press, 1960), 38.

33. Ibid., p. 46.

34. Dietrich von Hildebrand, "Technology and Its Dangers," in Mohan, ed., *Technology and Christian Culture*, 81.

35. Ibid., p. 94.

36. Ibid., pp. 89–90.

37. J. Mark Thomas, "Are Science and Technology Quasi-Religions?" *Research in Philosophy and Technology* 10 (1990): 95, 98, 101.

38. Ibid., p. 101.

39. David E. Schrader, "Technology: Our Contemporary Snake," *Research in Philosophy and Technology* 10 (1990): 205–6.

40. Ibid., p. 208.

41. Nicolas Berdyaev, *The Fate of Man in the Modern World* (1935), trans. Donald A. Lowrie (Ann Arbor: University of Michigan Press, 1961), 80–81.

42. Ibid., p. 83.

43. David Novak, "Technology and Its Ultimate Threat: A Jewish Meditation," *Research in Philosophy and Technology* 10 (1990): 63–64. Cf. Abraham Joshua Heschel's *The Sabbath: Its Meaning for Modern Man* (New York: Farrar, Straus, and Young, 1951).

44. Alan R. Drengson, "The Sacred and the Limits of the Technological Fix," *Zygon* 19 (1984): 272.

45. Ibid., pp. 260–63.

46. Alva W. Taylor, *Christianity and Industry in America* (New York: Friendship Press, 1933).

47. See, for example, Eric Gill, *Christianity and the Machine Age* (London: Sheldon, 1940).

48. See, for example, Heinrich Emil Brunner, *Christianity and Civilisation* (London: Nisbet, 1948), vol. 2.

49. See, for example, Gabriel Marcel, *Being and Having: An Existentialist Diary* (1935), trans. Katherine Farrer (Boston: Beacon Press, 1951).

50. Friedrich Georg Juenger [Jünger], *The Failure of Technology*, trans. not identified (Chicago: Henry Regnery, n.d.).

51. E. F. Schumacher, *Small Is Beautiful* (New York: Harper and Row, 1973), 277.

52. See, for example, Martin Heidegger, *Discourse on Thinking* (1954), trans. John M. Anderson and E. Hans Freund (New York: Harper and Row, 1966).

53. See, for example, George Grant, *Technology and Justice* (Notre Dame, Ind.: University of Notre Dame Press, 1986).

54. See, for example, Hans Jonas, *The Imperative of Responsibility: In Search of an Ethics for the Technological Age* (Chicago: University of Chicago Press, 1984).

55. Samuel C. Florman, *The Existential Pleasures of Engineering* (New York: St. Martin's Press, 1976), 46.

56. Mesthene, "Technology as Evil," 67.

57. Ibid.

58. Ibid., p. 72.

59. Joseph K. Agassi, *Technology: Philosophical and Social Aspects, Episteme* series, vol. 11 (Dordrecht, The Netherlands: D. Reidel, 1985), 209.

60. Langdon Winner, *The Whale and the Reactor: A Search for Limits in an Age of High Technology* (Chicago: University of Chicago Press, 1986), 68.

61. Cf. Nicholas C. Mullins, *Theories and Theory Groups in Contemporary American Sociology* (New York: Harper and Row, 1973), esp. 40–70.

62. Robert K. Merton, "Foreword" to Jacques Ellul, *The Technological Society* (1954), trans. John Wilkinson (New York: Knopf, 1964), v-vii.

63. See, for example, David W. Gill, *The Word of God in the Ethics of Jacques Ellul,* American Theological Library Association monograph series, no. 20 (Metuchen, N.J.: American Theological Library Association and The Scarecrow Press, 1984), 179–85.

64. See, for example, Rosalia Berbekar, "Hephaestus—The God We Love to Hate: The Lingering Pro- and Anti-Technology Debate," *Bulletin of Science, Technology and Society* 8, no. 2 (1988): 172–82; Bunge, "The Five Buds of Technophilosophy," 67; Agassi, *Technology: Philosophical and Social Aspects,* 209.

65. Jacques Ellul, in "Statements by Jacques Ellul and Ivan Illich," *Technology in Society* 17, no. 2 (1995): 232.

66. Ivan Illich, in "Statements by Jacques Ellul and Ivan Illich," *Technology in Society* 17, no. 2 (1995): 237. Illich's statement is translated by Lee Hoinacki.

67. Jacques Ellul, *Perspectives on Our Age: Jacques Ellul Speaks on His Life and Work,* ed. William H. Vanderburg, trans. Joachim Neugroschel (Toronto: Canadian Broadcasting Corporation, 1981), 92–93.

68. Ibid., p. 101.

69. Ibid., p. 98.

70. Ibid., p. 99.

71. See in particular Jacques Ellul, *Propaganda: The Formation of Men's Attitudes,* trans. Konrad Kellen and Jean Lerner (New York: Knopf, 1968).

72. Dennis Rohatyn, "The (Mis)Information Society: An Analysis of the Role of Propaganda in Shaping Consciousness," *Bulletin of Science, Technology and Society* 10, no. 2 (1990): 79.

73. Ibid., p. 83.

74. Ellul, *Perspectives on Our Age,* 99.

75. Jacques Ellul, *The Technological System* (1977), trans. Joachim Neugro-schel (New York: Continuum, 1980), 311.

76. Ibid., 325.

77. Ibid.

78. Ellul, *The Technological Society*, 380.

79. See, for example, Blaise Pascal, *Pensées*, trans. A. J. Krailsheimer (Har-mondsworth, England: Penguin, 1966), 214, fragment 522 (fragment 140 in the Brunschvicg edition).

80. Ellul, *The Technological Society*, p. 429.

81. Ibid.

82. Ibid., p. 144.

83. Ellul, *Perspectives on Our Age*, pp. 35–36.

84. Ellul, *The Technological Society*, p. 146.

85. Ibid., p. 23.

86. Ibid., p. 27.

87. Ibid., p. 23.

88. Ibid., p. 3.

89. Ibid., p. 5.

90. Ibid., p. 436.

91. Florman, *The Existential Pleasures of Engineering*, 46.

92. Jacques Ellul, *The Meaning of the City*, trans. Dennis Pardee (Grand Rapids, Mich.: William B. Eerdmans, 1970), 1, 6. Ellul makes reference here to Exodus 20:25.

93. Ibid., pp. 6–7.

94. Ibid., p. 25.

95. Ibid., pp. 23–28.

96. Ibid., p. 146.

97. Ibid., p. 154.

98. Ibid., p. 147.

99. Ibid., pp. 163–64.

100. Ibid., p. 171.

101. Ibid., p. 177.

102. Ibid., p. 166.

103. Katharine Temple, "Doubts Concerning the Religious Origins of Technological Civilization," *Research in Philosophy and Technology* 6 (1983): 193.

104. See, for example, Florman, *The Existential Pleasures of Engineering*, 110–12.

105. See, for example, Henry Hodges, *Technology in the Ancient World* (London: Allen Lane, The Penguin Press, 1970), 171–72.

106. Lewis Mumford, *Technics and Civilization* (New York: Harcourt, Brace, 1934), 64.

107. Novak, "Technology and Its Ultimate Threat," 58. Cf. Temple, "Doubts Concerning the Religious Origins of Technological Civilization," 192; Mark

Swetlitz, "A Jewish Commentary on the Religious Origins of Technological Civilization," *Research in Philosophy and Technology*, 6 (1983): 197–204.

108. Cf., for example, Leo J. Moser, *The Technology Trap: Survival in a Man-Made Environment* (Chicago: Nelson-Hall, 1979), 4.

109. Hans Jonas, "Technology and Responsibility: Reflections on the New Tasks of Ethics" (1972), in *Philosophical Essays: From Ancient Creed to Technological Man* (Englewood Cliffs, N.J.: Prentice-Hall, 1974), 4. Cf. Sophocles, *Antigone*, trans. Elizabeth Wyckoff (1954), in David Grene and Richmond Lattimore, eds., *Greek Tragedies*, vol. 1 (Chicago: University of Chicago Press, 1960), 192–93.

110. Jonas, "Technology and Responsibility," 5.

111. A. George Schillinger, "Man's Enduring Technological Dilemma: Prometheus, Faust, and Other Macro-Engineers," *Technology in Society* 6, no. 1 (1984): 61.

112. Florman, *The Existential Pleasures of Engineering*, 75.

113. Ibid., p. 108.

114. Carl Mitcham, *Thinking Through Technology: The Path between Engineering and Philosophy* (Chicago: University of Chicago Press, 1994), 282.

115. Edward Goodwin Ballard, *Man and Technology: Toward the Measurement of a Culture* (Pittsburgh: Duquesne University Press, 1978), 37.

116. Cf. Friedrich Klemm, *A History of Western Technology* (1954), trans. Dorothea Waley Singer (New York: Charles Scribner's Sons, 1959), 18–19.

117. Cf. Winner, *The Whale and the Reactor*, 40.

118. Hannah Arendt, *The Human Condition* (Chicago: University of Chicago Press, 1958), 16.

119. Albert Borgmann, *Technology and the Character of Contemporary Life: A Philosophical Inquiry* (Chicago: University of Chicago Press, 1984), p. 57. Cf., for example, Arendt, *The Human Condition*, 148.

120. James K. Feibleman, *Technology and Reality* (The Hague: Martinus Nijhoff, 1982), 185.

121. Max Weber, *The Protestant Ethic and the Spirit of Capitalism* (1904), trans. Talcott Parsons (New York: Charles Scribner's Sons, 1958), ch. 4.

122. Ibid., p. 163.

123. Cf. Klemm, *A History of Western Technology*, 191.

124. Ibid., 64.

125. Cf. David Elliott and Ruth Elliott, *The Control of Technology* (London: Wykeham; New York: Springer-Verlag, 1976), 10–11.

126. For a detailed examination and appraisal of the main varieties of religious competition, see Jay Newman, *Competition in Religious Life*, Editions SR, no. 11 (Waterloo, Ont.: Wilfrid Laurier University Press, for the Canadian Corporation for Studies in Religion, 1989).

127. Ian G. Barbour, *Science and Secularity: The Ethics of Technology* (New York: Harper and Row, 1970), 3.

128. Ibid.

129. Frederick Sontag, "Theodicy and Technology: Is God Present in Technological Progress?" in Mitcham and Grote, eds., *Theology and Technology*, 301.

130. See, for example, Theodore Roszak, *The Making of a Counter Culture: Reflections on the Technocratic Society and Its Youthful Opposition* (Garden City, N.Y.: Doubleday, 1968).

131. See, for example, Herbert Marcuse, *One-Dimensional Man: Studies in the Ideology of Advanced Industrial Society* (Boston: Beacon, 1964).

132. Florman, *The Existential Pleasures of Engineering*, 48.

133. P. Hans Sun, "Notes on How to Begin to Think about Technology in a Theological Way," in Mitcham and Grote, eds., *Theology and Technology*, 172.

134. See, for example, Emmanuel Mounier, *Be Not Afraid*, trans. Cynthia Rowland (London: Rockliff, 1951).

135. See, for example, Pierre Teilhard de Chardin, *The Phenomenon of Man* (1955), trans. Bernard Wall (London: Collins; New York: Harper and Brothers, 1959).

136. See, for example, Harvey G. Cox, *The Secular City* (New York: Macmillan, 1965).

137. See, for example, Walter J. Ong, *In the Human Grain* (New York: Macmillan, 1967).

138. Schillinger, "Man's Enduring Technological Dilemma," 59.

139. George Grant, "Justice and Technology," in Mitcham and Grote, eds., *Theology and Technology*, 245.

140. George Grant, "Religion and the State," in *Technology and Empire* (Toronto: House of Anansi, 1969): 43–45, 58–59.

141. Larry Rasmussen, "Mindset and Moral Vision," *Research in Philosophy and Technology* 10 (1990): 123.

142. Ibid., pp. 123–24.

143. Muller, *The Children of Frankenstein*, 322.

Technology and Techne

DEFINITIONS AND PARADIGMS OF TECHNOLOGY

If technology were a person, she might be moved by now to propose that if only her critics knew her better, they would not be as hasty to blame her for so many contemporary cultural problems. Why should technology be difficult to know well? For one thing, grasping the concept of technology can be tricky. The term *technology* is used by "ordinary" users of our language in "ordinary" everyday situations, and most of us would object to being told by some self-proclaimed expert that we should avoid using it because it is basically a technical or semi-technical term best left to specialists of various kinds. Of course, as is often the case with words that we use in ordinary language, including some of the words that we use most frequently, it is not at all easy to provide, when requested, a straightforward definition of *technology* with which we can feel entirely comfortable. We generally are confident that we have a sound working conception of the nature of technology, and we understand on reflection that this conception is largely based on the consideration of particular technologies that we take to be paradigms. We assume that most people with whom we discuss technology have roughly the same group of paradigms in mind; and although sometimes we come to realize, in the course of a conversation, that the particular person with whom we are sharing use of the term *technology* has something significantly different in mind from what we do when she uses the term, that occasional surprise does not discourage us from keeping the word in our everyday vocabulary. Still, maybe we take for granted that such significant differences are uncommon; and maybe we are being naive or arbitrary in assuming that most people understand one another clearly when they use the term.

Consulting a few reliable dictionaries might enable us to use the term with more confidence, but dictionary definitions of abstract terms often cause more problems than they put to rest. When a *theorist* of some kind argues about the cultural impact of technology as such, we can be pretty sure that her own use of the term *technology* has a certain amount of theory built into it, and that such theory may well reflect her particular agenda for cultural reform as well as more obscure subjective factors. Indeed, in considering the assertions of such a theorist, it is prudent to watch out for uses of the term *technology* that are biased or manipulative.

Joseph Agassi has concluded that "technology in general is not definable in any narrow clear-cut definition."[1] The word *technology* "is used loosely in different contexts and it is not at all clear how it may be understood in general."[2] None of this, however, has discouraged Agassi from writing extensively on the subject. Samuel C. Florman recognizes that the term *technology* is "constantly being defined and redefined," but, inspired by its "wide use and common understanding," he tells us that he opts to "take it pretty much as I find it, without bothering about linguistic and grammatical subtleties."[3]

Robert E. McGinn rejects several definitions of *technology* that have been proposed;[4] and it is somewhat disconcerting that one of the definitions that he rejects—that technology is "what things are done or made" and "how things are done or made"—is offered at the beginning of the standard multivolume English language work on the history of technology.[5] Edward Ballard straightforwardly informs us, in answering the question, "What, then, is technology?" that "in a generic sense, technology refers us to any characteristically human use of instruments for any sort of production."[6] But before we have much time to ponder this concise definition, Ballard gives us the disappointing news that "so broadly understood, techniques would include primitive agriculture as well as modern applied science. But ordinarily the term is more narrowly used."[7]

Friedrich Rapp, who as a self-professed *analytical* philosopher might reasonably be expected to be exceedingly cautious with respect to matters of definition and usage, defines *technology* for us as "material technology which is based on action according to the engineering sciences and on scientific knowledge."[8] Even apart from the circularity of a definition that includes the definiendum in the definiens, there is plenty not to like about this definition, for despite Rapp's insistence that "this definition comes most closely to the usual understanding,"[9] I suspect that most users of the word *technology* will find it rather abstruse. Undaunted, Rapp goes on to suggest that his definition provides "the only practical approach, for if one were to actually include not only material technology for consideration, but *all* methodological procedures, then one would have to treat such topics as the construction of legal systems, the methods of political action, or the principles of warfare."[10] Rapp is entitled to treat whatever topics he wants, but it is not clear that he is entitled to beg the most important questions about the nature of technology.

Carl Mitcham has offered as a definition of *technology* "the making and using of artifacts,"[11] and when Mitcham talks, serious students of technology should listen carefully, for no scholar in recent years has done more than Mitcham to bring some order to the field of philosophy of technology. Moreover, Mitcham has an impressive familiarity with a wide range of historical sources and a commendable open-mindedness with respect to philosophical methodologies and approaches. To be sure, the term *artifact*, which looks ambiguous enough in its own right, raises its own problems. But if one is not inclined to give up completely on defining *technology*, or to take the term "pretty much as one finds it" while eschewing subtleties, or to dwell on the gap between the generic and ordinary uses of the term, or to beg the most important questions with respect to the term, then there is much to be said for a definition like Mitcham's. One will probably not find a general definition of *technology* that is simultaneously more compact, more transparent, and more innocuous. Having said that, however, I must add that there is enough wisdom in the observations of scholars like Agassi, Florman, Ballard, and Rapp to justify our maintaining considerable flexibility with respect to the matter of understanding the essence of technology. Maintaining the requisite flexibility involves making appropriate allowances for context and weighing the practical advantages of conceiving of technology in a particular way in a particular situation. It is also important to have a good idea of one's principal paradigms (and the paradigms of those whose views one is considering) and to strive for consistency and clear communication.

When one responds to an antitechnologist's argument, one may well be met with the response that one's conception of technology is too broad or abstract. The antitechnologist is then obliged to provide some account of what he takes to be the essence of technology—or of the technological society, technological attitude, technological mentality, technological ideology, or so forth. As soon as he provides it, we need to probe a bit to find out from him why he believes that we should join him in adopting so narrow a conception. The antitechnologist cannot adopt a very broad, generic conception of technology because then he is left in the awkward position of appearing to be critical of the cultural impact of, for example, "the things that are done or made" or "the making and using of artifacts." On the other hand, criticizing technology as such requires him to go beyond criticizing particular technologies. Hence, to distance oneself from the rhetoric of antitechnology, it is wise to move toward as broad a conception of technology as circumstances will permit. (If one counters the antitechnologist's narrow definition with an equally narrow definition, the result is an impasse; but appealing to the value of a more general definition is an authentic challenge to the antitechnologist with an arbitrarily narrow conception of technology.)

Few of us have the skills of a lexicographer or a linguistic philosopher like J. L. Austin, but ordinarily it is not all that hard to indicate what one takes to be some of the principal paradigms of technology (or of anything else). The more paradigms one specifies, the clearer one's communication is apt to be. One may be challenged with respect to one's choice of paradigms; and indeed, on reflection, one may regret that one did not initially specify a certain paradigm. But one's paradigms may also represent a challenge to the person with whom one is communicating; that person may see that some of his general statements cannot appropriately accommodate a particular paradigm that one has fairly indicated. When people are discussing philosophical or other abstract issues, this give-and-take is an important form of argumentation.

Let us return for a moment to the disagreement between Ellul and Mounier about the relationship between a flint arrowhead and the atomic bomb. For Mounier, these two technologies (or the two distinct technologies by which the products have been created) differ essentially in degree; but Ellul strongly disagrees, holding that the human race's move from one to the other must be regarded as essentially qualitative. Now, for our present purposes, we need not worry about the issue of quantity versus quality, but let us consider the two technological creations as paradigms. If a follower of Mounier asked an antitechnologist follower of Ellul to indicate what she regards as the most important paradigm of technology as such, and she were to answer, "the atomic bomb," then the follower of Mounier, though he might agree with her, might also be tempted to ask her why she did not regard a flint arrowhead as just as important. She could then observe that the atomic bomb is the technological creation that most obviously has the potential to destroy the entire human race, that it has killed and harmed more people at one time than any other weapon, that it is the most powerful symbol in literature and the fine arts of human destructiveness, that it is a technological creation that has caused unprecedented anxiety, and so forth. Although the follower of Mounier might well agree with her that these observations about the atomic bomb go a long way toward explaining its importance, he might still ask why a flint arrowhead is not in its own way as important a paradigm of technology. It is obviously, for one thing, of far greater *historical* importance than the atomic bomb, which has only been around for a few decades; and without the creation of the flint arrowhead, it is possible that nothing resembling advanced civilization could ever have come into being. Moreover, a flint arrowhead symbolizes dimensions of technology that the atomic bomb does not, as it has, for example, concrete connections with the hunting necessary for the survival of certain tribes.

There is no point in comparing apples to oranges, or even in arguing about what it means for a technological creation or process to be "important." A flint arrowhead and the atomic bomb are both paradigms of technology, and undoubtedly important ones, too; they have much in common insofar as they are technological creations and products of technological processes. They have yet more in common in virtue of being the particular *kinds* of technological creations that they are. If a person, when asked, were to name both as paradigms of technology, there would be little if anything to challenge in this answer, even if it too would be a revealing answer, as surely it would be. Still, a person who regards the atomic bomb as the most important paradigm of technology, or who even just specifies the atomic bomb when asked to name any paradigm of technology, has a specific understanding of the nature of technology and a specific attitude concerning the cultural importance of technology, and these are suggested by her response. The more paradigms that she named for us, whether as "important" paradigms or even just as paradigms that happened to come immediately to her mind, the better would be our understanding of her conception of technology and her appraisal of the cultural role of technology, not the least because of the countless types of technological creation that her list, however long, had *excluded*.

There is undeniably a major sense in which the most advanced technology of our own day is "important" to us in a way that the entire range of technologies that have long been obsolete is not. But outdated technologies are still important in their own way; and, in a vital sense, much more important are those ancient technologies that we still live by today and without which we could not survive or communicate or attain spiritual insight and fulfilment. Antitechnologists have an agenda that parallels their conceptions of the nature and cultural role of technology, and that agenda leads them to insist that the paradigms of technology on which they focus—technological creations and processes that they regard (perhaps appropriately) as destructive—are of *special* importance, of an importance so special that if we fail to recognize them as being so, we are necessarily naive fools, confused idealists, unwitting agents of the devil, or worse.

The specification of paradigms, particularly when it includes examination of both the paradigms that have been indicated and the paradigms that have been disregarded, is so useful in studying something like technology that it compensates in large measure for the limitations involved in efforts to arrive at a mutually satisfying definition of the abstract term in question. The nature of the antitechnologist's argument is such that it invites us to step back from it in part by moving toward a broader, more historically inclusive conception of technology. But if we did not find ourselves confronted with a position like the antitechnologist's, we might well be prepared to settle, in a rather different context, for a narrower conception, one involving a more restricted range of paradigms.

THE RANGE OF TECHNOLOGIES

There are terms and expressions in the definitions of *technology* that we have considered in passing that are useful to note, and these terms and expressions also happen to appear in many of the innumerable definitions of technology that we shall not be considering here. However unsatisfactory the definitions that we have considered may be, by one or another criterion, they all initially have at least the appearance of some degree of plausibility. None strikes us as thoroughly absurd because there is at least some significant connection between our working conception of technology and conceptions that we associate with the various terms and expressions included in these definitions. These terms and expressions are *instrument, production, applied science, engineering, methodological procedure, artifact*, and perhaps most notably, *things . . . done, things . . . made*, and *how* (specifically, how things are done or made). If one were a contestant on a game show on which one were asked to associate these various terms and expressions with one particular phenomenon, "technology" would be an excellent answer, although there might be other plausible answers that might not be too bad, such as "tool" or "machine" or "craft." In any case, thinking about the significance of these terms and expressions enhances one's understanding of technology, even if the definitions that we have seen built around them are not entirely satisfactory. Such thinking enables one to be more prudent in one's selection of paradigms of technology.

Let us consider now some paradigms of the *historically (and culturally) fundamental* types of technology; these are worth remembering here for various reasons but not the least because of the tendency of antitechnologists (religious and otherwise) to undervalue or utterly disregard them.

R. J. Forbes has remarked that "it is often little realized that the fundamental discoveries and inventions on which our modern civilization is based were made before the dawn of history."[12] That historically fundamental types of technology have had prehistorical origins is, I would think, yet another indication of their "importance." Rather than dwelling on this point, however, let us move ahead and note some of the fundamental types of technology that have been discussed at length in the first volume of the standard multivolume English language work on the history of technology. This first volume covers the period from "early times" to the "fall of ancient empires," an extremely long period of time that antedates "the modern world" by another extremely long period of time (although every culture, even an old-fashioned one, is to some extent "modern" in its own day). Entire chapters of this volume are devoted to, among other things, working stone, bone, and wood; rotary motion; fire making, fuel, and lighting; textiles, basketry, and mats; building in brick and stone; water supply, irrigation, and agriculture; mining and quarrying; extracting, smelting, and alloying; fine metal-work; land transport without wheels (including roads and bridges); wheeled vehicles; boats and ships; recording and writing; measures and weights; and ancient mathematics and astronomy.[13] This list, impressive as a whole, will be all the more impressive if one pauses at the reference to each category and reflects for a few moments on some of the practical cultural consequences of each specific class of technologies.

A few general observations are in order with respect to the paradigms that have just been presented. First, nearly every item on the list would be regarded by almost all ordinary speakers of our language, as well as advanced students of cultural theory, as referring to a type of technology (or a group of types of technology) that corresponds to an exceedingly large class of particular technologies. If someone were to remark to us, after looking at this list, that she could not understand the relevance of, say, textiles or quarrying or bridges or writing to the *subject of technology*, we would probably spontaneously assume that she either did not speak our language well or was suffering from some sort of mental disorientation. A case might be made for the position that some of the items on the list could better be regarded as something other than types of technology; but almost everyone would grant that all (or virtually all) the items on the list qualify as general paradigms of technology. Furthermore, they would almost certainly grant as well that all (or virtually all) the items on the list qualify as "important" types of technology, even if they are perhaps not important in all the ways that, say, the atomic bomb, television, and personal computer are important. I suggest that they would also justifiably endorse, maybe with varying degrees of conviction, all (or virtually all) of the following assertions about most of these important paradigms of technology:

- On the whole, it (that is, this particular paradigm of technology) has contributed greatly to the advancement of civilization and the amelioration of the human condition.

- Most of us usually take it for granted, but an advanced society like ours could hardly manage without it.

- Its initial and subsequent development strikingly exemplify some of the most admirable human qualities, including intelligence, creativity, dexterity, self-discipline, and cooperativeness.

- It has contributed greatly to freeing human beings from the need to perform certain onerous, time-consuming tasks and to providing people with increased opportunities for leisure and reflection.

- It does not in itself represent an obstacle to religious spirituality, and if anything, has contributed in certain ways to the development of religious spirituality.

We could easily add at least a dozen comparable assertions worthy of endorsement, but it is already clear by now that anyone who has taken some time to remember, understand, and appreciate the historical (and culturally) fundamental types of technology will have good reason to react with discomfort to the bald assertion that technology as such is "valued too highly" in relation to this or that or the next thing. We have barely scratched the surface of this discussion, however, and later there will be plenty more to consider.

Special attention may be given here to technologies related to recording and writing, without which our present endeavor would be inconceivable. S. H. Hooke may not be guilty of overenthusiasm when he suggests that "of all the discoveries and inventions by which man has created what we call civilization, the most decisive has been the instrument which enabled him to make a permanent record of his own achievements and history. Such an instrument is the art of writing."[14] Without writing, there would be nothing to read, but writing did not come "naturally" to our earliest ancestors. Our debt in this regard to ancient peoples of whom we rarely think—Sumerians, Hittites, Phoenicians, and so forth—is so immense that words can only barely do justice to it.[15] Yet the complex *religious* world views and institutions of these peoples are, perhaps with good reason, only of interest to a small number of specialist scholars.

We need not concern ourselves at this stage with the innumerable types of technology that arose in that extremely long period of time between the fall of ancient empires and the emergence of "the modern world." But it is

worth our while to consider briefly some of the recently developed technologies that are habitually undervalued or disregarded by antitechnologists preoccupied with the mechanization of human life. I am willing to
admit that I probably do not spend as much time thinking about the atomic
bomb as I should; but still, there are all sorts of recently developed
technologies that deserve to be regarded by me as important paradigms of
technology. The telephone, for example, enables me to communicate with
loved ones even though they live far away. Because of the airplane, I can
visit them without delay whenever special circumstances arise. New medi-
cations and therapies have prolonged their lives and relieved their pains.
Food remains fresh in my refrigerator. The dentist's drill is not nearly as
painful as it used to be. I can hear a live performance of *The Pirates of
Penzance* on the radio. And despite all of the problems it poses, environmental and otherwise—and they are undeniably considerable—can we not
find some generous words to say about modern plumbing?

THE CLASSICAL PHILOSOPHICAL
UNDERSTANDING OF *TECHNE*

In dealing with an abstract term whose usage poses serious philosophical
problems, it can be helpful to consider the history of some of the usages of
the term. R. G. Collingwood has rightly cautioned that the historical study
of a word must not be purely etymological, for "etymology inquires into one
aspect of a word's history and only one."[16] (In addition, we need to bear in
mind that what a word now means, in any of a number of possible
significations, is not necessarily what it originally meant, or even what it
meant just a relatively short time ago.) Still, Collingwood grants that
etymology is a good servant to the historical study of language "when it
helps to explain why words mean what in fact they do mean."[17] With
respect to the etymology of *technology* and related terms, one may want to
follow the path of Mario Bunge, who elects to "adopt the current lack of
respect for etymology and go over to more serious matters."[18] But as Bunge
himself has expressed dissatisfaction with the way in which leading antitechnologists conceive of technology, maybe a bit of etymology can be
more helpful than he allows.

The earliest known uses of the English term *technology* are to be found
in early seventeenth-century writings,[19] where, according to Carl
Mitcham, they have a connotation close to that of Peter Ramus's sixteenth-
century use of the term *technologia* in his Latin writings.[20] In the spirit of
Renaissance humanism, Ramus pointed to the need for a systematic
discourse on the relations of the various arts; and to designate such a

discourse, he put to new use the ancient Greek term *technologia*, which he believed could suitably be interpreted as referring to a *logos* ([theoretical or explanatory] discourse) on the relations of the various *technai* (arts).[21] The original Greek term *technologia*, which can be traced back to Aristotle,[22] was generally associated by the ancient Greeks with the study of grammar or rhetoric,[23] and its meaning has little if anything in common with modern connotations of *technology*. Yet the etymological consideration that is really important here concerns one of the two ancient Greek terms from which *technologia* and *technology* are derived. That is the term *techne*, which is also a root of such related terms as *technic, technical, technicality, technician, technicist, technique, technocracy,* and of course, *technological* and *technologist*.[24]

Porphyry, Sextus Empiricus, Cicero, and Ramus[25] might have been perturbed by what contemporary speakers of English have made of their word *technologia*, but they would have had little trouble discerning the conceptual connection between *technology* and *techne*. Contemporary understanding of the word *technology* (and of technology itself) still shows the influence of the ancient Greek understanding of the word *techne* (and of what *techne* represented to the ancient Greeks); of particular importance in this regard is the enormous influence of Plato and Aristotle, who have much of interest to say about *techne* in their writings, and whose writings have provided a large part of the foundation for humanistic, scientific, and spiritual reflection in the Western world.

According to the classical scholar F. E. Peters, Plato does not, generally speaking, have a "theory" of *techne* but rather employs the term in a "nontechnical and popular way" to refer to "any skill in doing and, more specifically, a kind of professional competence as opposed to instinctive ability (*physis*) or mere chance (*tyche*)."[26] However, *techne* does enter technical philosophical discourse in two of Plato's later dialogues, the *Sophist* and *Politicus*;[27] and Plato's student, Aristotle, characteristically opts to employ the term in a very precise way. At *Nicomachean Ethics* 1140a, Aristotle defines *techne* as a characteristic geared toward production rather than action. Putting together various other remarks that Aristotle makes in the *Ethics* and *Metaphysics*, we see that in Aristotle's view, this *techne* arises from individual experiences and develops through generalization into a knowledge of explanatory factors; it is a type of knowledge and can be taught; and unlike purely theoretical or scientific knowledge, it is concerned with the domain of becoming rather than the domain of being.[28] In both its "nontechnical and popular" usage and its narrower and more precise philosophical usage, the term *techne*, when found in the writings of Plato and Aristotle, is most appropriately translated as either "craft," "skill," "art," or "applied science."[29] It is meant to carry with it many of the associations that we make with these English words. However, translation at this level is a complicated matter, particularly because for Plato and Aristotle, and for those who have remained close to their intellectual vision, *techne* also carries with it the burden of designating a type of knowledge that is significantly inferior to the highest or purest knowledge.[30]

You may recall the ambivalence of Plato and Aristotle toward technology; though they recognize the importance of practical knowledge and admire the disciplined craftsman, there is also an antitechnological element in their world view. It is most noticeably represented by their positions on the inferiority of productive activity to contemplative activity and the inferiority of things produced to the highest realities that are deserving of our attention. These positions, as noted earlier, were to a great extent taken up by the intellectual and ecclesiastical leaders of medieval Christendom. Despite the influences of monastic labor, Baconian philosophy, ascetic Protestantism, the Enlightenment, Marxism, pragmatism, and so forth, these positions are still widely held in some form, even by people who would not ordinarily be regarded as antitechnologists in any sense. Bunge has suggested that the philosophy of technology may be seen as having started with Aristotle's elaboration of Plato's distinction between *techne*, practical knowledge, and *episteme*, theoretical knowledge; and this distinction, along with Aristotle's ontological distinction between the artificial and the natural, represented the core of philosophy of technology for more than two millenia.[31] In Joseph Pitt's view,

we must recognize that our current attitudes toward technology are the product of a long history from which we must liberate ourselves. Part of this history incorporates the continued use of an old and venerable distinction between the pure and the applied. This distinction, dating back to the Greeks and Plato's *Republic*, presupposes a value judgment in favor of whatever is viewed as pure. Thus, the world of contemplation is valued over that of the craftsman.[32]

When Pitt talks carelessly here about "our" current attitudes toward technology, he overlooks the fact that these current attitudes are quite varied and frequently rather complex. Furthermore, the Platonic-Aristotelian distinction between pure and applied, and the related glorification of the contemplative life, are still worth taking seriously, especially when one considers that most people in contemporary Western societies have found it all too easy to "liberate" themselves from their commitment to contemplation. Nevertheless, it would seem that in many and perhaps most contemporary uses, the term *technology*, unlike the terms *craft*, *skill*, and *art*, does carry over from its root term, *techne*, the burden of designating a type of knowledge, activity, or object that is in some important sense inferior or secondary, even if we find ourselves at a loss to explain precisely in what that inferiority or secondariness consists. This matter is, in a sense, an etymological one, and it has much to do with the classical philosophical attitude toward the cultural role and comparative value of *techne*.

If this idea sounds rather strange, it may help to take note of how other terms derived in part from the Greek root word *techne* have been similarly affected. Consider, for example, these somewhat disparaging uses of terms in the *techne* family:

- "This problem is simply a *technical* one that can be worked out later, but we agree on all of the important issues."

- "We found your presentation unnecessarily *technical* and could not understand why you weren't able to make your point more clearly."

- "The case was dismissed, but only on a mere *technicality*."

- "He is a genuine thinker; the other fellow is just a *technician*."

- "For him, acting is basically just a matter of *technique*, but she puts her soul into a role."

- "Our society, instead of becoming more aristocratic or even more democratic, is gradually turning into a *technocracy*."

There would appear to be a pattern here, so that while terms in the *techne* family are primarily descriptive, they lend themselves more easily than most other terms do to being employed in a slightly (or at times moderately) pejorative way to indicate a comparative lack of significance, scope, or vision. It must be granted that many ordinarily descriptive terms can be given pejorative force in special contexts, as, for example, when "mere *philosophy*" is contrasted with urgently required action or when "merely *religious* opinion" is contrasted with urgently required empirical evidence. But the applicability of terms in the *techne* family for purposes of devaluation is more general and more systematic.

We cannot know to what extent this phenomenon is the result of the classical philosophical attitude toward *techne*. In any case, we should not forget that in the Platonic-Aristotelian world view, there is also considerable respectability associated with *techne*. It is, in fact, conveyed in those terms usually employed in English as translations of *techne*, such as *craft*, *skill*, and *art*. *Craft*, for example, is now often used to indicate the excellence of the process by which something has been produced, and *skill* ordinarily

carries with it associations of competence, talent, and discipline. The term
art, of course, often has even loftier associations, as in, for example, such
expressions as "a true work of art" or "art for art's sake," and it is derived
from *ars*, the standard Latin translation of *techne*. Although Plato and
Aristotle undeniably regard the productive, the applied, the practical, and
the domain of becoming as significantly inferior to the contemplative, the
pure, the theoretical, and the domain of being—and, after all, these men
are *philosophers*—their appraisal of *techne* is not as condescending as analyses like Pitt's might suggest. Plato's attitude toward craftsmen generally is
indicated in a passage at *Apology* 22c–e, where he attributes to Socrates the
position that good craftsmen indeed have knowledge of many fine things
but tend to be misled by their success into believing that they are also wise
in more important fields that lie beyond a craftsman's specialized competence. For Aristotle, *techne* is one of the principal intellectual "virtues" or
"excellences." As such it is impressively included in a group with science,
practical wisdom, the capacity to grasp fundamental principles, and philosophical or theoretical wisdom.[33] The knowledge related to making or
producing things, while concerned with things that are not necessary and
eternal (but rather capable either of being or of not being), also involves
rationality, just as the knowledge of how to act well or live well does.[34]
Aristotle's example of *techne* at *Nicomachean Ethics* 1140a is building, and
it is a felicitous choice, not only in light of the etymology of the term *techne*
itself,[35] but because architecture involves such a wide range of constituent
arts, both "fine" and "industrial."

It is indeed crucial in appraising the precise influence of Plato and
Aristotle on the development of attitudes toward technology to remember
that the two philosophers group together the fine arts, industrial arts,
professions, and even statecraft as types of *techne*. Wolhee Choe, who
believes that "technology is primarily aesthetic in purpose, setting people
free from the destinies of biology or politics,"[36] suggests that it would
actually help us to understand technology better if we thought of it *more*
in the way that the classical philosophers do. She writes:

Technology, or *techne* as the Greeks understood it, referred not only to the
activities, skills, and artifacts of the craftsman but also to the arts of the mind and
the fine arts. An aspect of *poiesis*, it relates to making, fashioning, or constructing
an instrumental technique. Restoring this original context, [I argue] that the
primary human activity is shaping reality for oneself and contributing an aspect of
shape to reality, through both physical and mental acts of construction. Such a
notion cannot be understood in technological terms as used today, for technology
is too often construed as limited either to hardware/software or techno-social

systems of manufacture and use. All but traces of _poiesis_ have been eliminated from technology.[37]

The narrowing of the idea of technology that has resulted in part from distancing it from the classical philosophical conception of techne is, in Choe's view, related to the overvaluing of the abstract and quantitative at the expense of the concrete and qualitative;[38] but Choe's criticism is as applicable to the antitechnologists' understanding of technology as it is to the unreflective technologists'.

Whether or not one believes that we would have a richer understanding of technology if we thought of it more in the way that the classical philosophers do, it is clear that in ordinary usage, _technology_ rarely if ever has been understood as meaning precisely what the classical philosophers mean by _techne. Mitcham is right to caution against the "facile historical identification" of technology with techne._[39] For one thing, the _logos_ root of _technology_ requires some consideration; and Mitcham has provocatively suggested that modern technology differs from techne precisely in that it proposes to furnish a _logos_ of the production process.[40] Of course, the term _technology_ has constantly been redefined. In any case, historical study of the term can only take us so far, especially if one believes, as do many technologists and many antitechnologists alike, that modern technology is qualitatively as well as quantitatively different from anything in the ancient world.

HOW DISTINCTIVE IS "MODERN" TECHNOLOGY?

The distinctiveness of "modern" technology still poses conceptual and practical problems for us. While antitechnologists may be prepared to grant that the term _modern_ is exceedingly ambiguous, that there are significant continuities and affinities between modern technology and the technology of earlier ages, and maybe even that prehistorical and ancient technologies have been as important and influential in their own way as the technologies of our own century, they are compelled by their basic agenda to remain committed to a strong version of what we can call the "distinctiveness theory." The antitechnologist is a critic and would-be reformer of contemporary culture. When she focuses on technology, she does so in part because she believes that there is something about the technology of our time that renders it very much more dangerous and more destructive than the technology of the preceding millennia. In the case of the religious antitechnologist, there is a need to establish some connection between what she takes to be the escalating domination of our culture by technological attitudes and interests, the decline of authentic religious commitment and traditional religious institutions, and the increasing dehumanization of individuals and overall deterioration of civilization. Antitechnologists, religious and otherwise, are encouraged by the fact that the "distinctiveness theory" is widely accepted by observers who are not committed to the antitechnologist agenda, including many if not most technological optimists.

For those committed to the "distinctiveness theory," historical, linguistic, and etymological approaches to understanding technology are largely tangential, trivial, irrelevant, or evasive. (You may recall that while Ellul admired Mounier, an authentically religious man with a keen sense of the intellectual's obligation to address urgent social problems, Ellul could not abide Mounier's fascination with flint arrowheads and the like, and felt obliged to break with him.) The proponent of the "distinctiveness theory" needs, of course, to do enough in the way of historical, linguistic, and etymological analyses to justify his assertion that what he is talking about is really technology and that technology and its cultural role are now significantly (and perhaps qualitatively) different from what they used to be. Beyond that he will stress our obligation to open our eyes and concentrate on the present and future, the concrete, and the practical.

Whether we be inclined to technological pessimism, technological optimism, or technological "neutrality," those of us who remain skeptical about the "distinctiveness theory," at least in its stronger versions, will still worry about the ambiguity of the term *modern* and the tendency of so many observers to undervalue the importance, influence, and relevance of the technology and technological attitudes of earlier ages. We skeptics also have plenty to encourage us. For example, defenders of the "distinctiveness theory" are conspicuously at odds with one another, even with respect to some of the most fundamental issues. Their disagreement is noteworthy in itself; yet what is of greater interest to us is the extent to which they expose the arbitrariness of each other's speculations. Perhaps even more interesting is the extent to which their individual positions are internally inconsistent. Of course, we cannot afford to ignore the extent to which their individual positions are simply unclear.

Consider first some of Bertram Morris's efforts to explain the distinctiveness of modern technology. At one point, Morris tells us that "the contrast between technology in primitive society and modern society is seen in the kind of knowledge that developed in each. Basically, the distinction is between the knowledge of the artisan and that of the scientist. The former is a doer; the latter a thinker."[41] It is not clear what Morris has in mind here by "modern society," but the *suggestion* that a modern society is in essence one that is simply not primitive is difficult to swallow. When did the scientific knowledge that Morris has in mind develop? Morris himself is none too clear with respect to this matter. At one point he attaches great importance to the "science and technology" of classical Greece.[42] He later goes on to draw attention to "Renaissance science," which he tells us came into conflict with religion and initiated a form of secularism.[43] At another point, he advances the widely held position that "the unique aspects of today's technology are to be found in the supplanting of tools by machines," and his examples of machines perplexingly include the cart, pulley, lathe, and computer.[44] Still later he offers an entirely different perspective when he suggests that "the context of sophisticated technology is the political power that controls the distribution of economic benefits."[45] What he regards as crucial in this respect is that "the context of technology is no longer mythical but political."[46] Now, it might be said in Morris's defense that nowhere here does he refer specifically to the criteria by which modern technology is to be distinguished from earlier forms of technology. But that is not much of a defense, for Morris talks in turn about "technology in . . . modern [as opposed to primitive] society," "today's technology," and "sophisticated technology." In addition, he stresses the connection between modernity and the knowledge of the scientist (as opposed to the knowledge of the artisan) and then focuses on the importance of science in civilizations separated by many centuries. His association of "today's" technology with machines is undermined by his grouping together of machines that were invented many centuries apart, such as the cart and the computer. His point about the political having replaced the mythical as the context of technology is not only inconsistent with some of his other themes but could be seen as applying equally to any of the last five centuries, and perhaps some earlier centuries, too. (Consider in this regard the symbolic importance of such politically conscious under-miners of myth as Plato, Thomas Hobbes, Benedict de Spinoza, François Voltaire, Karl Marx, and Jean-Paul Sartre.)

Ballard introduces still another consideration when he contends that technology, productive activity controlled by consciousness and reason, "becomes modern when the reason involved is subjectivity disciplined to measurement and calculation with an eye for efficiency."[47] We may note right off that Ballard's categorical assertion leaves little if any room for the considerations that we encounter in Morris's account. Ballard, a thinker much influenced by the cultural criticism of postwar French and German philosophers, is clearly concerned about the apparent dehumanization that has been growing as a result of the burgeoning "technism" into which modern technology has been allowed to deteriorate.[48] Yet while Ballard's attention is mainly fixed on modernity, his talk about reason, measurement, calculation, and efficiency may apply as much to technology in the age of Galileo, the age of Archimedes, or the age of the pyramids as it does to technology in the age of Microsoft and Disney.

Many advocates of the "distinctiveness theory" hold forth at length about the fundamental relationship between modern technology and the machine. We have just noted Morris's view on the subject, and in the preceding chapter we took note of the widely held position that modern technology begins with the steam engine, or at least with certain applications of the steam engine. Ellul attaches immense importance to the machine,[49] as, of course, do all antitechnologists who bemoan the escalating "mechanization" of personality, life, and culture. Hannah Arendt offers a provocative theory about the singular technological importance of the machine when she writes that

there never was any doubt about man's being adjusted or needing special adjustment to the tools he used; one might as well have adjusted him to his hands. The case of the machines is entirely different. Unlike the tools of workmanship, which at every given moment in the work process remain the servants of the hand, the machines demand that the laborer serve them, that he adjust the natural rhythm of his body to their mechanical movement.[50]

However, before we accept the proffered conceptual connection of modern technology and the machine, we would do well to remember that machines have constituted a prominent feature of human culture since ancient times. Even if we opt for a rather narrow conception of what a machine is, we must still recognize that the steam engine had an imposing line of machinery leading up to it. Mumford complains that "popular historians usually date the great transformation in modern industry from Watt's supposed invention of the steam engine. . . . But the fact is that in Western Europe the machine had been developing steadily for at least seven centuries before the dramatic changes that accompanied the 'industrial revolution' took place."[51] Mumford's date is a particularly interesting one for those of us concerned with the relations of religion and technology, for seven centuries before the invention of the steam engine, the Christian church had not yet reached the pinnacle of its temporal power, and the Middle Ages were far from over.

In any case, if one insists on associating modern technology with the emergence of sophisticated machinery, one need not focus on the eighteenth and nineteenth centuries. One might focus instead on, say, the seventeenth century, which brought us, among many other things, the telescope, the barometer, the air pump, and the pendulum clock. Or one might focus on the fifteenth century, which, as Pamela McCorduck has impressively shown, can be usefully seen from the standpoint of the historian of technology as rather much like the twentieth century,[52] with Johannes Gutenberg's printing press being the "emblematic machine" of the fifteenth century in much the same way as the computer is the emblematic machine of the twentieth century.

A theorist might also elect to emphasize the special distinctiveness of only the most recent technology. That is to say, it may well be that the typical proponent of the "distinctiveness theory" is being exceedingly arbitrary in regarding late twentieth-century technology as a *continuation*, indeed a mere *extension*, of a "modern" technology that began a century or more earlier. It should not take much imagination to appreciate profound differences between this century and the previous two centuries, or for that matter, between the computer and the steam engine. It is no wonder then that Henryk Skolimowski, an analytical philosopher of technology, can complain that "mistaken ideas about the nature of technology reflect what technology was a century or two centuries ago and not what it is today. In the twentieth century, and particularly in our day, technology has emancipated itself into a semi-autonomous cognitive domain."[53] There are actually people who habitually talk as if what happened last month happened "a very long time ago" and is "virtually ancient history"; and at times we may be tempted to agree with them.

An appealing feature of Marshall McLuhan's approach to the study of technology is his appreciation of the advantage of our understanding both the continuities and discontinuities in the history of technology. In his chief work, *Understanding Media*, McLuhan takes the fashionable term *media* and tries to show that it can be suitably applied not only to mass communication technologies but to all technologies, insofar as any new technology is an "extension of ourselves";[54] and he goes on to attempt to show the consistent applicability of a general theory of technology[55] to both recently created technologies and long-established technologies, including some developed in prehistorical and ancient times. For McLuhan, appreciating the continuities is very important. By understanding the origins, operations, and influences of long-established technologies, we can better understand technology as such and can apply our general understanding of technology to fathoming emergent and future technologies. At the same time, McLuhan draws our attention to the importance of discontinuities, or at least radical changes in the direction of technology. So on one level, McLuhan helps us to understand the automobile, television, and automation by shedding light on such long-established technologies as roads, money, clocks, and print; on another, he alerts us to the need to recognize that the mechanical age is now receding and that we must be adroit and imaginative if we are to adjust successfully to the demands of the electric age.

In *Mechanization Takes Command*, Siegfried Giedion (who, by the way, influenced McLuhan to a degree that is rarely appreciated) emphasizes the historical importance of the emergence of full or high mechanization. Giedion recognizes that there is nothing particularly "modern" about a machine as such; but he attaches great historical consequence to the nineteenth-century transition, particularly in America, from complicated handicraft to mechanized production.[56] According to Giedion, in the age of the assembly line ("the symptom of full mechanization")[57] observers routinely identify the inventive impulse with the mechanization of production, and here we can see how different the technological attitude is now from what it was in the days of the ancient Greeks, who "placed their inventive gifts in the service of the miracle."[58] Although Giedion makes an impressively detailed case for a position that fits comfortably with the outlook of most antitechnologists, Giedion himself is no antitechnologist for while he grants that "future generations will perhaps designate this period as one of mechanized barbarism, the most repulsive barbarism of all,"[59] he explicitly refuses to take a stand "for or against mechanization" and is critical of those who believe that we can "simply approve or disapprove."[60] We must, to Giedion's mind, "discriminate between those spheres that are fit for mechanization and those that are not."[61]

It is questionable that Giedion has provided much support for the "distinctiveness theory" itself. While we can understand Giedion's fascination with the simultaneous decline of complicated handicraft and emergence of high mechanization in nineteenth-century America, we must remember that mechanization as such, at least according to Giedion's own conception of it, is just about as old as the machine. In fact, Giedion's explanation of the nature of mechanization goes some way toward taking the sting out of antitechnologist complaints that technology has led to the "mechanization" of human beings and human life. Here we have Giedion's simple, dispassionate account of the essential nature of mechanization: "The hand can be trained to a degree of automatic facility. But one power is denied it: to remain unvaryingly active. . . . It cannot continue a movement in endless rotation. That is precisely what mechanization entails: endless rotation."[62] Conceived of in this way, mechanization is rather less terrifying than antitechnologists would have us believe. Moreover, Giedion recognizes that the distinction between full or high mechanization and mechanization prior to the nineteenth century is essentially quantitative rather than qualitative; and in his view, the key practical question to be considered in the employment of machines is not even "How much?" but rather "Under what circumstances?"

We may note that even since the emergence of what qualifies in Giedion's mind as full or high mechanization, there has still been plenty of intricate handicraft; and in some spheres, such handicraft has actually been on the rise. (Giedion's principal paradigm of technology is the door lock, and while his history of this technology is a scholarly triumph, the limitations of such a paradigm should by now be evident.) Again, it is harder and harder to find people who actually *identify* the inventive impulse with the mechanization of production. And there is an abundance of technology in our society that is not in any sense mechanical, even if much of it has been machine produced (which is a separate matter); for example, a pharmaceutical, whether prepared by a pharmacist for an individual customer or mass-produced by means of complex machinery, is not in any sense a machine, was not initially conceived by a machine, does not serve a machine, and does not turn its user into a machine (although it may have dehumanizing effects of another order).

Putting the matter of machines behind us, let us turn to a quite different theme associated with the "distinctiveness theory." We can understand the temptation to associate "modern" technology with "modern" science; and for the proponent of the "distinctiveness theory," a chief advantage of this approach is that the idea of a distinctively "modern" science, fundamentally different from all the science that came before it, has been consecrated by many generations of historians of science and culture. This is not the place to consider the wisdom of this cherished opinion, but we may note some problems that have arisen with respect to the linkage of modern technology and modern science. Arendt, for example, is quite convinced that "it is a matter of historical record that modern technology has its origins not in the evolution of those tools man had always devised for the twofold purpose of easing his labors and erecting the human artifice, but exclusively in an altogether non-practical search for useless knowledge."[63] Setting aside the obvious hyperbole here, the characteristic overstatement that lends an eccentric charm to so much of this author's work, we may note the conviction that scientific-intellectual motives rather than the ostensibly traditional ones gave rise to a whole new order of technology that warrants being categorized as distinctively "modern." (Arendt's principal paradigm is the watch.) We took note earlier of problems that arise with respect to Morris's ambiguous thesis that technology in "modern" society is directly related to the knowledge of the scientist; and some of those problems also arise here. But we can focus at this point on the alternative perspective of Hans Jonas, Arendt's colleague at The New School for Social Research. Jonas writes that "it is a common misconception that the evolutions of modern science and modern technology went hand in hand. The truth is that the great, theoretical breakthrough to modern science occurred in the seventeenth century, while the breakthrough of mature science into technology, and thereby the rise of modern, science-infused technology itself, happened in the nineteenth century."[64] Jonas is not directly contradicting Arendt here; and Jonas is not only clearly defending the "distinctiveness theory" in these lines but has impressive credentials as an antitechnologist whose work has significant affinities with that of the leading religious antitechnologists. There is, however, something of a tension here. According to Arendt, modern technology has its origins in the search for pure scientific knowledge; according to Jonas, however, it took technologists two centuries to figure out that the extraordinary insights attained in the age when modern science emerged are profoundly relevant to matters of production. Thus, the historical record is not so clear here, and we have yet another reason to worry about the confidence with which advocates of the "distinctiveness theory" talk about a "modern" technology.

There is undoubtedly a certain truth to Ortega y Gasset's observation that "our technical methods are radically different from those of all earlier technologies."[65] We might even do well to endorse Jonas's observation that "our collective technical practice constitutes a new kind of human action, and this not just because of the novelty of its methods but more so because of the unprecedented nature of some of its objects, because of the sheer magnitude of most of its enterprises, and because of the indefinitely cumulative propagation of its effects."[66] But I do not think that we are simply being mischievous or obstinate when we maintain that these observations of Ortega y Gasset and Jonas could have been appropriately made, using the language of their own time and place, by observers in the age of Galileo and Descartes, the age of Gutenberg and Leonardo, the age of Archimedes and Eratosthenes, and the ages that witnessed the creation of flint arrowheads, alphabetic writing, and the "wonders of the world." If I have belabored this point, it is because it is centrally important to a proper understanding of the relations of religion and technology. Throughout the millennia, religion has survived wave after wave of radically new technology; it has to a great degree inspired many of them, and perhaps to an even greater degree it has been substantially transformed by them. Like so many things, from the city of Paris to Freudian psychoanalysis, "*Fluctuat nec mergitur*,"[67] and like technology itself, it is always what it is, nothing more and nothing less, and yet perpetually "modern" and vital. These are facts that it will be useful to bear in mind when we move on to more complicated matters.

THE COMPLEXITY OF THE IDEA OF TECHNOLOGY

One can easily become discouraged when one reflects on the ambiguity of a key term, especially when one has been striving to clarify its meaning; and the more that one dwells on linguistic and conceptual confusions related to the term, the more one is likely to feel that the subject matter of one's investigation is gradually slipping out of one's grasp. I suspect that this fear of losing control of one's subject matter and getting lost among all the competing perspectives has contributed greatly to turning many a subtle philosophical mind into a dogmatic ideologist. Besides, the "crowd" often prefers boldness to subtlety and rewards it accordingly. I suggest then that we keep our spirits up at this stage by accentuating the positive and reminding ourselves that we have been making great progress in our exploration of the *complexity* of the idea of technology. We have as yet some way to go in this exploration.

Although some people use the term *technology* to designate a quasi-mystical force, and others use it in a somewhat archaic sense to signify, say, a specialized terminology, language, or form of discourse,[68] people normally now use it to signify either some sort of productive activity, process, or procedure; or the tools, instruments, or artifacts employed in the performance of this activity, process, or procedure; or the actual product that has resulted from the activity, process, or procedure. People sometimes use the term generically to refer abstractly to all productive activity of this sort, or even to productive activity generally; or to the totality of tools, instruments, or artifacts that have been employed in all productive activity of this sort, or in productive activity generally; or to the totality of actual products that have resulted from all productive activity of this sort, or from productive activity generally. Sometimes people use the term specifically to refer to a particular productive activity; or to tools, instruments, or artifacts employed in that particular productive activity; or to products that have resulted from that particular productive activity. Thus, for example, *technology* is used to denote my radio or my pen or both; some feature of my radio or my pen or both; some class of objects to which my radio and pen both belong; the complex procedure by which either came into being; the general category of procedure by which both came into being and by which objects like them generally come into being; the instruments employed to produce them and objects like them; and so forth.

Furthermore, some people tend to restrict their use of the term to refer only to newly invented products and the instruments and processes by which they were created (and, by extension, to future products, instruments, and processes like these), whereas other people feel quite comfortable about talking about "ancient technology" and "sixteenth-century technologies." Some people tend to restrict their use of the term to refer only to material products and the instruments and processes by which they are created, whereas other people do not hesitate to use the term to refer to products that are not material, such as, for example, systems, modes of perception, states of mind, or patterns of social organization. In addition, we sometimes use the term *technology* to refer to a fairly specialized vocation or branch of learning, one that is closely related to engineering, as when we say, for example, "She has dropped out of journalism school and is now pursuing a career in technology." This bewilderingly expansive diversity of uses of the term certainly contributes considerably to the "complexity" of the idea of technology.

Another dimension of the complexity of the idea is related to the range of individuals who may be involved in a productive activity. George Kimball Plochmann invites us to consider in this regard who it is that "makes" a machine: "The designer? The capitalist? The manager? The factory worker? Certainly all of these take a hand and are makers in a loose, participatory sense, but only the designer can be considered the maker in any primary sense because making is not the material supplied or the fabricating operations conducted, but is the imposing of artificial form upon the material."[69] Plochmann's analysis raises several difficulties. For one thing, a visionary thinker who conceives of and describes in detail a product that he does not know how to bring into existence certainly qualifies as a designer, but he hardly qualifies as a maker, and he has little if any of the requisite practical knowledge of how to make or produce the kind of product that he has envisioned. (An obvious example here is the "inventor" Rube Goldberg.) On the other hand, a meticulous craftsman who painstakingly produces machines, furniture, wines, or religious articles in the "classical" or "traditional" manner, faithfully following to the most minute details the pattern laid down by his revered ancestors and predecessors, cannot fairly be regarded as merely a marginal figure in the making or productive process. Again, designs are not always immutable; a designer will sometimes alter his plans as he sees the other participants in the production process bringing those plans to fruition. And, of course, many a maker—often because she has no choice—combines the skills of designer, capitalist, manager, and laborer, and each of these sets of skills involves a distinctive form of practical knowledge. (We may note in this regard that many a distinguished playwright or film director has benefited greatly from his experiences as an actor or production designer; and in many fields there has long been widespread agreement about the advantages to be gained from serving a period of apprenticeship in some subordinate role.) These various problems related to forming a conception of who properly qualifies as a maker or "technologist" contribute further to the complexity of the idea of technology. All too often the antitechnologist or the "neutral" observer, upon hearing the term *technology*, spontaneously and uncritically forms in her mind the image of a middle-aged senior executive of a mammoth "high-tech" corporation or, perhaps just as arbitrarily, of a brilliant and internationally renowned inventor, or maybe even more arbitrarily, of some pathetic drudge slaving away on the assembly line of a dingy factory in China or the southeastern United States. But the world of technology includes all sorts of people; in this respect, it is not unlike the world of religion, which includes the Dalai Lama, the earnest undergraduate who is not quite sure whether she has lost her faith, the fanatical religious bigot, the frail cleric who has devoted his life to helping lepers, and the simple soul who keeps mailing off checks to televised evangelists in the hope that they will pray for her.

Every so often, a serious student of technology, disheartened by the impreciseness of ordinary language, boldly recommends linguistic and conceptual revisions. A notable example is Lewis Mumford's effort to popularize the term *technics*. "We ordinarily use the word technology to describe both the field of the practical arts and the systematic study of their operations and products. For the sake of clarity, I prefer to use technics alone to describe the field itself, that part of human activity wherein, by an energetic organization of the process of work, man controls and directs the forces of nature for his own purposes."[70] Talk about "technics" was fashionable for a while among students of technology, but most ordinary speakers of English and even many academic scholars would now be inclined to regard persistent use of the term *technics* as pretentious, maybe a bit arch, and generally not very helpful.

The term *technology* is sometimes directly associated with specialization and the specialist, although probably less frequently than the terms *technical* and *technician* are. This point is worth noting insofar as antitechnologists who disparage the technological "attitude" or technological "mentality" are sometimes troubled primarily (or at least substantially) by the excessive specialism that they see as having been cultivated and promoted at the expense of those things that they see as providing individuals with a "wide view," such as religion, philosophy, general education, the liberal arts, and the humanities. This tendency is evident in the antitechnology of

Friedrich Jünger, who asserts that "because technology pursues its own ends, it fails to produce a bigness of mind capable of visualizing as a whole the evolutionary trends which evolve from the mechanization and organization of human labor. This would require a freedom of spirit that cannot be expected of any specialist. For the specialist, whatever his field, is in the service of technical organizations."[71] There is an irony in Jünger's invocation of the name of Plato in support of this position. Accompanying Plato's intense commitments to philosophical thinking, metaphysical Idealism, and the contemplative life, and his acute sensitivity to the limits of the craftsman's practical knowledge, is a powerful conviction that specialization, or the division of labor, is the key to the just state, in which every individual does the special job for which he or she is naturally suited and properly trained and does not attempt to perform any other vocational role in society.[72]

We can, with a little imagination, envision a person who is proficient at a broad range of technologies. Leonardo, the "Renaissance man," may come to mind, or the proverbial jack of all trades, or the uncle who could fix almost anything around the house and in his spare time made pottery and wrote a little poetry. But proficiency of the highest order, especially in an advanced society, requires natural ability, specialized training, a professional attitude, and association with professional colleagues, all of which add up to specialization and the specialist mentality. With the growth of knowledge and things to be known in any specialized area, the specialist is virtually forced to become narrower and to reduce the time and energy available for those pursuits that enable one to be contemplative and to take a "wide view." This is a genuine existential and cultural problem, and it requires the constant attention of educators, statesmen, religious leaders, television programmers, and others. However, the most advanced societies have reached a stage where citizens will no longer allow certain very important tasks to be consigned to inspired amateurs or semiprofessionals, and there is good reason for that. Moreover, many of those things that traditionally could be relied upon to equip people with a wider view have themselves become more specialized. Natural scientists regularly complain about the typical humanist's ignorance of even the most rudimentary natural scientific truths. Humanists have more and more trouble communicating with one another. Scholarship in the liberal arts seems to be becoming increasingly arcane, at least to judge from the learned journals and conference presentations. Despite enormous efforts at ecumenism and reconciliation, religionists of countless creeds and practices remain divided with respect to matters of theology, ritual, and authority. Philosophy, once widely regarded as the most humanizing and integrative of all intellectual disciplines, has become so abstruse at times as to appear almost ridiculous.

The case of philosophy is illuminating. Along with theologians and other religious intellectuals, philosophers have been conspicuous among the ranks of prominent antitechnologists; and criticism of the technological mentality has been a regular feature of existentialist philosophy in particular. This century has also witnessed a notable decline in the cultural influence and public prestige of philosophy, despite the discipline's entrenchment in the university curriculum. It is not surprising then that certain philosophers, resentful of and worried by their discipline's declining status, and eager to promote the discipline as a revitalizing and rehumanizing force, have seen the technological mentality as a suitable target for criticism. Yet many critics of contemporary philosophy, including a good number of open-minded undergraduates who have been compelled to suffer through hours of unnecessarily abstruse philosophy lectures on apparently trivial topics, have with more than a little fairness complained that the main philosophical schools of our time have increasingly turned a noble discipline once known for promoting a "wide view" into an increasingly technical and overspecialized discipline. Now, one could regard the increasing specialization of philosophy as evidence that increasing specialization is to some extent an almost inescapable consequence of the growth of knowledge in any intellectual discipline, so that technology as such cannot properly be blamed for promoting the excessive specialism of our day. But the philosophical antitechnologist, like the religious antitechnologist, may find it fitting (and perhaps convenient) to blame technologists and the technological mentality rather than the growth of knowledge—or his own colleagues—for the excessively narrow and technical character of his own discipline. For example, the philosopher Michael Zimmerman, who is convinced that "the technological culture is absolutely certain that its way of understanding the world is the *only* rational (correct) way,"[73] concludes that "it was inevitable that philosophy itself become another 'sector' or 'field of specialization' within the technological society, that its practitioners succumb to the subtle pressure that radical reflection is worthless and irrational because technical thinking, not mere reflection, has answered in the best possible way who man is and what he must do."[74] This analysis, however, is sociologically one-dimensional. The excessive specialism that has characterized much recent philosophy is the result of several factors, the most important being probably the increasing professionalization of philosophy.[75]

Understanding the term *technology* is also complicated by users' implicit and peculiarly inconsistent attitudes with respect to the relations of tech-

nology and science, technology and art, and science and art. The common
expression (or category) "science and technology" testifies to the regularity
with which technology is now associated with science; so too, to some
extent, does the spontaneity with which we substitute the expression
"applied science" for the term *technology.* Much more is involved here than
a linguistic habit. For example, the *techne* of medicine is so habitually
regarded nowadays as being more closely related to such sciences as
biochemistry and physiology than to the *techne* of, say, carpentry or painting
that many people find it easier to regard medicine as a science than an art.
The principal national agency in Canada that awards grants in the natural
sciences also awards grants in engineering but not grants in the social
sciences. To be sure, the practitioner of the art of medicine needs to have
knowledge in such fields as biochemistry and physiology, and the engineer
needs to have knowledge in the natural sciences. But associating technology closely with the sciences can result in losing sight of the importance
of medicine and engineering as arts. For Plato and Aristotle, who attached
so much import to the fundamental distinction between *techne* and
episteme, or for the later thinkers who stressed the parallel distinction
between *ars* and *scientia,* the excessive linkage of technology and science
at the expense of the equally important associations of the various forms
of technology would have been confounding.

While the classical insight into the crucial difference between the "pure"
knowing of the scientist and the "practical" knowing of the technologist
is often worth calling to mind, we can also see that since the time of Galileo
and Descartes, and more and more as the years pass, the mathematical
precision and general quantitative conception required in both the physical sciences and "high" technology have brought prominent paradigms of
science and technology conceptually closer.[76] Science and technology are
closely linked not only in the minds of many scientists, technologists, and
general observers, but also in the minds of many critics of science and
technology. Thus, it is not surprising to find a religious antitechnologist
like J. Mark Thomas attacking the "philosophical apologists for a scientific
and technological culture"[77] or attacking the twin "quasi-religions" of
"scientism" and "technicism."[78]

Since it is the relations of religion and technology that constitute our
basic concern here, we can note in this regard that religious antitechnology
not only can be closely related to religionists' fear and resentment of
scientific inquiry but can often conveniently function as a blind for a
religionist's antiscientific agenda. Religionists have generally felt more
directly threatened by scientific discoveries than by technology as such;
the responses of panicky ecclesiastics to the work of Copernicus and

Darwin are notable examples. But the more sophisticated contemporary defender of religion may well be hesitant to attack science as such and any materialist agenda that it may be harboring, for many educated people and skeptical younger people take a dim view of ecclesiastical science bashing and see it as reflecting the superstitious irrationalism of old-fashioned "blind faith." The religious antitechnologist can high-mindedly attack the "dehumanization" and "mechanization" that she associates with spiritually bankrupt forms of positivism without putting herself in the awkward position of attacking scientific orthodoxy directly and suggesting that teachers and professors of the sciences are systematic liars and deceivers. One may have to dig very deeply to uncover the antiscientific core of a particular religious antitechnology; and a religious antitechnologist is not necessarily antiscientific. Even so, often the digging will turn out to have been worthwhile.

Competing attitudes toward the relations of technology and art are even more bewildering. That we still often associate technology with *techne*-as-art is perhaps best evidenced by our frequent use of the term *art* to refer to a technology, as, for example, when we speak of the "art" of medicine, flower arrangement, or motorcycle repair.[79] The term *art* often spontaneously leads us to think of one of the fine arts, and painting in particular; but upon reflection it is clear that *art* has a much wider use in everyday language. Nevertheless, technology has also been prominently attacked in the name of art by thinkers who have gone to great effort to contrast technology and art. Among these critics, one of the most influential has been Mumford, despite the characteristic elusiveness of this author's argument. Mumford is well aware of the historical association of "technics" with *techne*-as-art, but he considers it crucial that we recognize that there is a sense in which art can be separated from technics. That sense involves "the domain of the person; and the purpose of art, apart from various incidental technical functions that may be associated with it, is to widen the province of personality, so that feelings, emotions, attitudes, and values, in the special individualized form in which they happen in one particular person, in one particular culture, can be transmitted with all their force and meaning to other persons or to other cultures."[80] This is a nice bit of aesthetic theory, but once Mumford glorifies the profound artist as symbol-maker at the expense of the plebeian artist as toolmaker, there is a risk of antitechnological rot setting in: "[M]an is both a symbol-maker and a toolmaker from the very outset, because he has a need both to express his inner life and to control his outer life. But the tool, once so responsive to man's will, has turned into an automaton; and at the present moment, the development of automatic organizations threatens to turn man himself into a mere passive tool."[81] This sort of aesthetic antitechnology can easily be incorporated into religious antitechnology, for the aesthete and the religionist ostensibly share a concern with human spirituality.

It has also been argued that technology directly undermines art of this loftier kind. Especially well known is Walter Benjamin's argument that the aura of the work of art withers in the age of mechanical reproduction.[82] According to Benjamin, "To an ever greater degree the work of art reproduced becomes the work of art designed for reproducibility";[83] one of his most intriguing observations is that the film actor, unlike the stage actor, acts to a "mechanical contrivance," the camera, rather than to other human beings.[84] Benjamin almost inevitably moves toward antitechnology: "The destructiveness of war furnishes proof that society has not been mature enough to incorporate technology as its organ, that technology has not been sufficiently developed to cope with the elemental forces of society."[85]

Quite a different view is taken by Wolhee Choe, who, as we noted earlier, sees technology as primarily aesthetic in purpose. Choe is impressed by the affinities between creativity in the fine arts and creativity in technology generally. She is also struck by the role that technology plays in initiating aesthetic experience.[86] Aesthetic antitechnology, and the religious antitechnology that incorporates it, may well fail to appreciate the degree to which technological artifacts are "objects that communicate meaning."[87] The other side of the coin is that the symbol-maker's work can to some extent be helpfully analyzed by reference to general technological categories and concerns. In fact, despite the aesthetic antitechnologist's agreement with the religious antitechnologist that unrestrained technology leads to the "mechanizing" of humanity,[88] some knowledgeable observers have noted with interest the likenesses between works of fine art and machines. As Choe points out, "Edgar Allen Poe saw the machinery of all works of art and found the recognition pleasurable. William Carlos Williams defined the poem as a machine made of words. And structuralist critics have spent recent decades studying the poetic artifact as a structure of describable functional elements."[89]

If aesthetic creations rich in symbolic meaning can be helpfully analyzed by reference to general technological categories and concerns, then there is all the more hope that so too can religious creations rich in symbolic meaning. But we are getting ahead of ourselves, for what is specifically of interest to us at this point is the complexity of the idea of technology, which as we have seen, involves, among other things, competing attitudes toward the relations of technology and art. A price has to be paid for any effort, no matter how well-meaning, to simplify a complex idea, especially when the complexity of the idea is at the heart of some serious controversies. That price is essentially a matter of limiting vision and understanding, though it may also involve the impeding of authentic dialogue. Unfortunately, sensitivity to the complexity of a key idea can be so humbling as to discourage us from continuing our inquiry into concrete matters deserving of our consideration; and then the public discussion of those matters will be left to people who are not sensitive to the complexity of key ideas. So, again accentuating the positive, let us note that an important reason why the relations of religion and technology are rather more complex than the typical religious antitechnologist would have us believe is that technology itself, as the complexity of the idea of technology indicates, is a complex and multifaceted phenomenon that can be viewed from many different perspectives and can be seen as related to all sorts of culturally significant phenomena. Moreover, while we must avoid the facile historical identification of technology with what the ancients called *techne*, we can now see that the most serious oversimplifications of the idea of technology are those that reveal an observer's neglect or undervaluation of those aspects of technology that are in fact most directly related to its historical connection with what the ancients called *techne*.

NOTES

1. Joseph K. Agassi, *Technology: Philosophical and Social Aspects*, Episteme series, vol. 11 (Dordrecht, The Netherlands: D. Reidel, 1985), 23–24.

2. Ibid., p. 21.

3. Samuel C. Florman, *The Existential Pleasures of Engineering* (New York: St. Martin's Press, 1976), x.

4. Robert E. McGinn, "What Is Technology?" *Research in Philosophy and Technology* 1 (1978): 180.

5. Charles Singer, E. J. Holmyard, and A. R. Hall, eds., *A History of Technology*, vol. 1: *From Early Times to the Fall of Ancient Empires* (Oxford: Clarendon Press, 1954), vii.

6. Edward Goodwin Ballard, *Man and Technology: Toward the Measurement of a Culture* (Pittsburgh: Duquesne University Press, 1978), 195.

7. Ibid.

8. Friedrich Rapp, *Analytical Philosophy of Technology*, trans. Stanley R. Carpenter and Theodor Langenbruch, Boston Studies in the Philosophy of Science, vol. 63 (Dordrecht, The Netherlands: D. Reidel, 1981), 35.

9. Ibid. Cf. pp. 33–36.

10. Ibid.

11. Carl Mitcham, *Thinking Through Technology: The Path Between Engineering and Philosophy* (Chicago: University of Chicago Press, 1994), 1.

12. R. J. Forbes, *Man the Maker: A History of Technology and Engineering* (London: Abelard-Schuman, 1958), 14.

13. Singer, Holmyard, and Hall, eds., *A History of Technology*, vol. 1, ch. 6, 9–10, 16–17, 19–21, 23, 26–31.

14. S. H. Hooke, "Recording and Writing," in Singer, Holmyard, and Hall, eds., *A History of Technology*, vol. 1, 744.

15. Ibid., pp. 744–68.

16. R. G. Collingwood, *The New Leviathan* (Oxford: Clarendon Press, 1942), 281.

17. Ibid.

18. Mario Bunge, "Technology as Applied Science," *Technology and Culture* 7, no. 3 (1966): 329.

19. The *Oxford English Dictionary* (1933) indicates the date 1615.

20. Mitcham, *Thinking Through Technology*, 130.

21. Ibid.

22. Ibid., pp. 119–20.

23. Ibid., p. 129.

24. It may be worth noting that, according to the *Oxford English Dictionary* (1933), the only one of these terms that can be found used in English earlier than *technology* is *technic*, for which the O.E.D. gives the date 1612.

25. Cf. Mitcham, *Thinking Through Technology*, 129–30.

26. F. E. Peters, *Greek Philosophical Terms: A Historical Lexicon* (New York: New York University Press, 1967), 190.

27. Ibid.

28. Ibid., p. 191.

29. Ibid., p. 190.

30. See, for example, Wolfgang Schadewaldt, "The Concepts of *Nature* and *Technique* According to the Greeks," trans. William Carroll, *Research in Philosophy and Technology* 2 (1979): 164–66; Mitcham, *Thinking Through Technology*, 117–25.

31. Mario Bunge, "The Five Buds of Technophilosophy," *Technology in Society* 1, no. 1 (1979): 67.

32. Joseph Pitt, " 'Style' and Technology," *Technology in Society* 10, no. 4 (1988): 448.

33. Aristotle, *Nicomachean Ethics* 1139b–1141b.

34. Ibid., 1140a.

35. Cf. Mitcham, *Thinking Through Technology*, 117–18.

36. Wolhee Choe, *Toward an Aesthetic Criticism of Technology* (New York: Peter Lang, 1989), 184.

37. Ibid., p. 1.

38. Ibid., p. 178.

39. Mitcham, *Thinking Through Technology*, 133.

40. Ibid., p. 128.

41. Bertram Morris, "The Context of Technology," *Technology and Culture* 18, no. 3 (1977): 408.

42. Ibid., pp. 405–6.

43. Ibid., p. 407.

44. Ibid., pp. 410–11.

45. Ibid., p. 417.

46. Ibid., p. 418.

47. Edward Goodwin Ballard, *Man and Technology: Toward the Measurement of a Culture* (Pittsburgh: Duquesne University Press, 1978), 204.

48. Ibid., pp. 203–4.

49. See, for example, Jacques Ellul, *The Technological Society* (1954), trans. John Wilkinson (New York: Knopf, 1964), 3.

50. Hannah Arendt, *The Human Condition* (Chicago: University of Chicago Press, 1958), 147.

51. Lewis Mumford, *Technics and Civilization* (New York: Harcourt, Brace, 1934), 3.

52. Pamela McCorduck, *The Universal Machine: Confessions of a Technological Optimist* (New York: McGraw-Hill, 1985), 18–29.

53. Henryk Skolimowski, "The Structure of Thinking in Technology," *Technology and Culture* 7, no. 3 (1966): 382.

54. Marshall McLuhan, *Understanding Media: The Extensions of Man* (New York: New American Library, 1964), 23.

55. Ibid., ch. 1–7.

56. Siegfried Giedion, *Mechanization Takes Command: A Contribution to Anonymous History* (New York: Oxford University Press, 1948), 51–76.

57. Ibid., p. 5.

58. Ibid., p. 32.

59. Ibid., p. 715.

60. Ibid., p. 720.

61. Ibid.

62. Ibid., p. 47.

63. Arendt, *The Human Condition*, 289.

64. Hans Jonas, "Seventeenth Century and After: The Meaning of the Scientific and Technological Revolution," in *Philosophical Essays: From Ancient Creed to Technological Man* (Englewood Cliffs, N.J.: Prentice-Hall, 1974), 71.

65. José Ortega y Gasset, "Man the Technician," in *Toward a Philosophy of History*, trans. not identified (New York: W. W. Norton, 1941), 155.

66. Hans Jonas, *The Imperative of Responsibility: In Search of an Ethics for the Technological Age* (Chicago: University of Chicago Press, 1984), 23.

67. The creator of psychoanalysis took as the motto for the first section of "On the History of the Psychoanalytic Movement" (1914) the motto on the coat of arms of the city of Paris: "It is tossed by waves, but does not sink." See Sigmund Freud, *The History of the Psychoanalytic Movement and Other Papers*, ed. Philip Rieff (New York: Collier Books, 1963), 41.

68. Cf., for example, *Oxford English Dictionary* (1933); *Webster's Ninth New Collegiate Dictionary* (1991).

69. George Kimball Plochmann, "The God from the Machine May Soon Be Dead," *The Philosophy Forum* 9, nos. 3–4 (1971): 273–74.

70. Lewis Mumford, *Art and Technics* (New York: Columbia University Press, 1952), 15.

71. Friedrich Georg Juenger [Jünger], *The Failure of Technology*, trans. not identified (Chicago: Henry Regnery, n.d.), 74.

72. See, for example, Plato, *Republic* 369b–370b, 397d–e, 432b–434c.

73. Michael Zimmerman, "Technological Culture and the End of Philosophy," *Research in Philosophy and Technology* 2 (1979): 141.

74. Ibid., p. 144.

75. Cf. Bruce Kuklick, *The Rise of American Philosophy* (New Haven, Conn.: Yale University Press, 1977), 565–72.

76. Cf. Choe, *Toward an Aesthetic Criticism of Technology*, 178.

77. J. Mark Thomas, "Are Science and Technology Quasi-Religions?" *Research in Philosophy and Technology* 10 (1990): 95.

78. Ibid., p. 98.

79. Cf. Leo J. Moser, *The Technology Trap: Survival in a Man-Made Environment* (Chicago: Nelson-Hall, 1979), 168.

80. Mumford, *Art and Technics*, 16.

81. Ibid., p. 161. Cf. pp. 33–58.

82. Walter Benjamin, "The Work of Art in the Age of Mechanical Reproduction," in *Illuminations*, trans. Harry Zohn (New York: Schocken, 1969), 221. Cf. Jünger, *The Failure of Technology*, 149–52.

83. Ibid., p. 224.

84. Ibid., pp. 229–30.

85. Ibid., p. 242.

86. Choe, *Toward an Aesthetic Criticism of Technology*, 176.

87. Ibid., p. 7.

88. Mumford, *Art and Technics*, 5. Cf. p. 10.

89. Choe, *Toward an Aesthetic Criticism of Technology*, 3–4.

Technology and Progress

THE SECULAR DIMENSION OF RELIGIOUS ANTITECHNOLOGY

Understanding technology better helps us to understand better the cultural relations obtaining between religion and technology; this increased understanding has value as pure, theoretical, philosophical knowledge but can also be useful to the practical person who is interested in influencing attitudes toward religion and technology in hope of bringing about constructive cultural change (or curbing destructive cultural change). Technological optimists and others who are enthusiastic about the positive cultural potential of technology tend to be quite practical-minded by temperament, but there is some irony in the fact that religious antitechnologists and aesthetic antitechnologists who champion the primacy of contemplative activity rarely approach the matter of the cultural relations of spirituality and technology in a detached, disinterested way. Rather, they are inclined to adopt the stance of the polemical reformer, agitator, preacher, or prophet. The preacher and prophet have a pivotal role to perform in the religious life of a community, but if the antitechnologist were to mistake the preacher or prophet for a contemplative type, she would be revealing that her understanding of the complexity of religion is in important ways as limited as her understanding of the complexity of technology. Preacher and prophet normally exhort those who will listen to them to be better human beings and to contribute to the betterment of their society. Nothing could be more practical than endeavoring to get individuals and communities to mend their iniquitous and misguided ways; no impulse could be less inward in its direction than the impulse to "save" one's fellow human beings.

The antitechnologist is well aware that most people see familiar forms of technology as enriching personal and communal life. She also knows that most people routinely associate technology with "progress," which they generally take to be an intrinsic good. If she is to convince her audience that far too many people in our society have made technology into an idol, she needs to do at least one of two things; either she must show that the prevailing confidence in technology has held back rather than contributed to overall cultural progress, or she must show that progress itself has been overrated as a cultural ideal. It is not enough for her to establish that particular technologies have had, or are likely to have, devastating cultural consequences, for even the most irredeemable pro-technologist acknowledges that there are destructive technologies that the world would be better off without. She must show that technology as such, in the guise of the technological "attitude" or "mentality" or "fascination," is itself anticultural in some basic way and that restoring the cultural agenda of our society to a condition of soundness requires a form of "conversion" through which there can be a restorative calibration of concerns and a reaffirmation of the primacy of the spiritual by both individuals and the society as a whole.

The religious antitechnologist could concentrate exclusively and directly on ways in which technology makes people less religious, but in fact religious antitechnologists rarely adopt this strategy. That is in part because religious antitechnology more often than not has an apologetic dimension; the religious critic of technology is usually trying to *show* that the inadequacies of the technological idol indicate the need for a traditional form of faith in a transcendent object of veneration and the corresponding need for cultural institutions in which such a faith can be embedded and fostered. The religious antitechnologist may to some extent be preaching to the converted, but he is sensitive to the fact that even most of those who regard themselves as religious are not entirely steadfast in their conviction and may actually entertain skeptical doubts about the practical relevance of traditional religious conceptions to most of their everyday concerns. He may also be sensitive to the imprudence of appearing to be dogmatic or biased, especially if he is trying to reach listeners and readers who are earnestly troubled by the corruptions of religion that manifest themselves in various forms of fanaticism, hypocrisy, superstition, and intolerance.

Another factor that can be taken into account is that the religious antitechnologist is not always on the offensive; his strategy must enable him to deal effectively with the arguments of defenders of technology. The defender of technology is not required to defend some technological "mentality," "attitude," or "fascination"; she indeed would likely deny that any such thing exists, at least in the antitechnologist's sense. It is thus sufficient for her to offer up a list of universally respected technologies, to note that technology in these forms is now virtually indispensable, to observe that most people seem to believe that technology generally does less harm than good, and to suggest that the antitechnologist's assertions about technology as such are gratuitously speculative. She can also, if she so chooses, proceed to a more assertive type of argument and attempt to establish that technology in significant ways promotes the realization of such ideals as freedom and wisdom, or maybe even religious spirituality itself. Confronted with such a defense of technology, the religious antitechnologist ordinarily cannot afford to appear to undervalue the benefits of universally respected technologies or the need to realize such transcultural ideals as freedom and wisdom. If he even merely suggests that religion may be more important than such things, he runs the risk of leading even many of the religious people in his audience to wonder whether perhaps religion has outlived its usefulness as a form of culture. Thus the religious critic of technology is almost inevitably drawn into the discussion of certain technologies and the role that they play in *hindering* the realization of transcultural ideals.

This is not to say that the typical religious antitechnologist does not *believe* that technology as such tends to make people less religious; it is simply to explain why so much of the religious antitechnologist's argument is secular, at least on the surface, and especially so in its initial stages of development. We can, with a bit of imagination, conceive of a religious critic of technology who does not see technology as making people less religious, but we are not likely to encounter such a person. Now, the general impact of technology upon religious commitment is a matter to which we shall be giving considerable attention later. At this point it will be useful to consider certain ways in which technology in some of its specific forms has contributed to social, cultural, and personal progress. The religious antitechnologist might well insist that he has never denied the value of these specific technologies, but the basic thrust of his argument prevents him from doing full justice to them.

TECHNOLOGY AS AMELIORATIVE

For most speakers of our language, the term *progress* almost always has positive connotations. Indeed, in its most common uses, it is directly associated with goodness; in these uses, it is to be understood as denoting improvement—getting *better*—rather than, say, change per se. People do disagree a great deal about what specifically constitutes such progress and about whether particular changes genuinely represent such progress; and people commonly allow that such progress can bring concomitant difficulties that need to be addressed. But when, as is usually the case, *progress* denotes improvement—getting better—it is obviously a "pro" word. Therefore, when people use *progress* to denote something essentially negative, or even something to be given a neutral evaluation, they are using the term in a fairly special way. For example, when they talk about the "progress" of a disease, as in the grim observation that "the progress of the cancer has been so rapid that surgery is now absolutely necessary," *progress* is a negative term. For now, *progress* will be employed to denote some sort of improvement or getting better. Moreover, in accordance with what may well be its most popular uses, it will be employed here primarily to denote improvement in societies and cultures. It will secondarily denote improvement in the personalities and lives of individual human beings, although we know that it could also be correctly employed to indicate the improvement of, say, a hockey team or an industry.

The vast majority of people who associate technology with progress associate technology with the improvement of societies, cultures, and human beings; and not very many defenders of technology are capable of uttering more than a few sentences without making reference to "technological progress," "progress through technology," "technology's contribution to progress," or something else along these lines. For many people, the connection between technology and progress is so important that the word *progress* leads them to think of certain technologies, even though they will grant, if pressed, that such things as "moral" progress and "intellectual" progress are as important in their own way as the kind of progress that is directly associated with technology.

There are almost as many ways of getting better as there are ways of being good, for there are relatively few good things that are perfect and incapable of being better than they are. Societies, cultures, and individual human beings can all be better than they are, even if they are pretty much satisfied with the way they are; and although being imperfect has profound disadvantages, it enables people to have lofty aspirations, and conceiving and realizing these aspirations imparts to them a distinctive kind of nobility that a perfect being could not attain. Assessments of improvement are usually made with reference to particular times and particular conditions, so that, for example, when I say, indirectly praising a product of medical technology, that "I've made some progress," I mean that it is specifically such things as my health and state of mind that have improved and that they have improved from roughly the time that my new medication began to take effect. Whenever it is said that progress has taken place, or that something has improved or gotten better, we may appropriately ask, if the answers are not already obvious, what specifically it is that has improved, in what sense it has improved, and relative to what point in time it has improved. These observations may sound rather trite or pedantic, but we need to keep them in mind if we are to counter such arguments as "technology has not substantially contributed to progress, for there were people in ancient times who were both nobler and happier than most people in technologically advanced modern societies are." The premise of this argument is plausible enough, but the inference reveals the arbitrariness of the speaker's frame of reference.

Focusing on our own concrete personal situation—and that does not seem to me to be an inappropriate point at which to start, particularly in a humanistic (as opposed to scientific) investigation—we can all give examples of how technology has made us better off than we were a specific number of years ago. Speaking from personal experience, I can wholeheartedly express my unqualified gratitude for the technological progress represented by certain developments in medicine, dentistry, transportation, and communications. Undoubtedly, you could do the same, as could the honest antitechnologist. I can also express my *general* gratitude for other technological developments, such as word processing, even though I am aware that in some ways they have negatively influenced my life and the lives of those who matter most to me.

Then we can compare our situation with that of people who do not have access to technologies that we enjoy. I recall the poignancy with which a friend described to me some years ago how his mother and brothers in a small village in Assam, not having the plumbing and water purification systems that people in technologically advanced societies normally take for granted, constantly have to make inconvenient trips to a well to draw water that is often far from hygienic. It could be fairly observed that the diet and life-style of some Assamese villagers are in noteworthy ways more healthful than those of most middle-class North Americans; but there is not much to be said for having to spend a large part of one's life walking a long distance in inclement weather to draw polluted water from a well.

It can also be instructive to listen to stories told by people who remember the days when technologies that we now take for granted did not exist or were only available to the very privileged. I still listen attentively when elderly relatives tell me about what life was like before they had refrigerators, televisions, and antibiotic drugs, and before they could take a trip by airplane to visit their loved ones, to shake hands with an animatronic Minnie Mouse, or to play at the slot machines in Las Vegas. These elderly relatives retain their nostalgia for certain aspects of their life in the "good old days," and they can be heard from time to time to comment on how much worse "things" always seem to be getting. However, they do not like it at all when their refrigerator and television are not working properly, and they reflect with an almost unbearably intense sadness on how a rudimentary antibiotic or vaccination would have spared their beloved parents, baby nephews, and childhood friends from a cruel death at an early age.

Focusing on our own concrete personal situation, we can also give examples of how technology has made us "better" in ways that transcend being "better *off*." That is to say, we can show how new technologies not only have sustained us, made things less painful and less difficult for us, and enabled us to do things that previously we could not do, but they have actually made us finer human beings by criteria of moral, intellectual, or theological virtue. The inexpensive paperbound book represents a relatively new technology whose educational impact, though generally undervalued, mirrors to some degree that of Gutenberg's printing press. The numerous paperbound books on my bookshelves that deal with some serious subject matter have not only enlarged my moral and intellectual understanding but have provided me with ready access to many of history's most profound insights, and that access has helped to keep me from lapsing into parochialism and small-mindededness. Given our basic interest in the relations of religion and technology, we may note here the role that recent advances in educational and communications technology—from the paperbound book to the Internet—have played in the dissemination of religious teachings that, whatever their imperfections, have been uplifting to many a desperate soul.

The antitechnologist is typically aware of much of the good that has been accomplished by these technologies, but she is definitely not as impressed by it as I am. Unlikely to be satisfied by any perfunctory acknowledgment on my part that there are numerous bad technologies and abuses of technology, she will insist that a "wider" or "more balanced" view is necessary. She can then move to the debit side of the ledger and list all sorts of dreadful technologies, such as those employed in Nazi concentration camps and those that have resulted in the wholesale despoliation of some of the most beautiful natural environments. She can also show that many of the recent technologies for which I have expressed my admiration have done a great deal of harm. Thus, for example, medicines have frequently had terrible effects, especially when unwisely prescribed or used; transportation vehicles have polluted the atmosphere and deprived people of opportunities for healthful exercise; and television programs and paper-bound books have promoted ignorance and hatred as well as wisdom and compassion. She may well object to the autobiographical frame of reference with which my assessment of technology begins; she may regard it as egoistic and excessively subjective as well as shortsighted in its concerns and arbitrary in its weighing of factors. Given her anxieties about technology as such, she will regard my concentration on particular technologies, technology in some of its specific forms and manifestations, as evasive in its refusal to look at the big picture.

The critic of technology may well be right in believing that assessments of technology regularly fail to pay sufficient attention to the debit side of the ledger, and that in time most technological optimists and apathetic observers (or their unfortunate progeny) will be sorry that they allowed their uncritical association of technology with personal, cultural, and social improvement to blind them to the need to speak out against bad technologies and the abuse of good (and potentially good) technologies. She may be right in believing that in time, more and more people will realize how naive they have been in not recognizing the great harm that has been done to them and to their fellows by technologies that have seemed on the surface to be essentially ameliorative. She may be justified in her conviction that if one focuses a great deal on the role of technologies in one's own life, one risks being too selfish to be able to adopt a responsible view of technology.

Yet assessments of technology, and evaluative judgments generally, can never be objective in the way that most empirical and mathematical judgments can be. While I am not advocating a relativistic view of such assessments, I see it as critical that we appreciate the extent to which the determination of the relevance of concerns or the weighing of numerous complex factors normally involves such things as commitment to a particular world view, a preferred decision-making procedure, the selective acceptance of particular sources as authoritative, and unconscious inclinations. There is still plenty of room left here for roles to be played by practical reason and impersonal logic, public dialogue and consensus building, scientific research, the uncovering of suppressed information, and so on. The critic of technology must not take lightly here the role of subjective factors, however. (Ironically, religious, aesthetic, and philosophical critics of technology customarily complain about the devaluation of subjectivity to which science and technology have led; so they sound somewhat hypocritical as well as dogmatic when they aggressively dismiss positions on technology that differ from their own.)

In addition, to those who remain confused or troubled by the antitechnologist's talk about a technological "mentality," "attitude," or "fascination," the position that a person can be overly impressed by particular forms and manifestations of good technology will likely seem to be much like the position that a person can be overly impressed by instances of good music, good literature, good politics, good science, or good religion. As for such questions as "Is technology now generally doing more good than harm?", "Has technology throughout history generally done more good than harm?", and even "Is technology now generally doing more harm than it used to do?", a sensible person will realize at once that whoever works at answering such questions will arrive at answers largely determined by the parameters that she has laid down and the methods that she has adopted when initially determining how to approach the questions.

Still, I am prepared to grant that perhaps I have been a bit egoistic and even somewhat evasive. So it is appropriate now that we turn to the ideas of observers who can help to provide us with something in the way of a wider view. These observers all have a special interest in certain technologies, but they are also interested in the general phenomenon of technology. Furthermore, they are willing to talk about technology itself and the general cultural impact of technology, although not all of them would countenance critical reflection on a technological "mentality."

TECHNOLOGY AS A SOURCE OF HAPPINESS AND FREEDOM

When we consider the relation of technology to a "progress" that we understand to be a matter of improvement or getting *better*, it is fitting that we turn our attention to what would appear to be relevant conceptions of good or goodness; we need to have some idea of the principal types of good that might reasonably constitute the criteria by which the change that technology brings about could be assessed as being for the better. In the famous opening line of the *Nicomachean Ethics*, Aristotle announces that every *techne* (along with every inquiry, action, and choice) aims at some good, so that the good has been suitably defined as that at which all things aim.[1] In Aristotle's view, both ordinary people and highly cultured ones agree that happiness is the highest good,[2] but popular views of what happiness is (for example, that happiness is pleasure) are demonstrably unsatisfactory,[3] and careful reflection eventually leads us to the realization that happiness is the contemplative life.[4] We noted earlier some of the historical impact of the classical Greek philosophical emphasis on contemplation, especially insofar as it influenced religious attitudes toward the value of technology; but what is more germane to this phase of our inquiry is the unqualified endorsement that one of the greatest figures in the history of thought gives to a view that is as widely held in our own day as it was in his, the "common sense" position that happiness, whatever it may be, is the highest good. Many later philosophers, such as the English utilitarians,[5] had no compunction about identifying happiness with pleasure, but they remained respectful of the importance almost universally ascribed to happiness as a primary ideal. When a revolutionary thinker such as Nietzsche ridicules those who regard happiness as a suitable ideal for a superior man, the incisiveness of his argument cannot altogether compensate for the counterintuitive quality of his position.[6]

There is obviously something strange about such questions as "Does technology generally tend to make people happy?" and "Has technology in the last hundred years tended to contribute less to happiness than earlier technology did?" It is hard to get a handle on these questions, and any answer that one gives to a question of this kind will be largely determined by the specific and often arbitrary conceptions, assumptions, and methods with which one begins one's answering. Yet if one is going to take a "wide view" of technology and progress and make a broad assessment of technology itself, apart from its specific forms and manifestations in specific contexts, then maybe one needs to say something plausible about technology and happiness.

The subject has been provocatively addressed by Nicholas Rescher, an analytical philosopher who has no particular sympathy for the agenda of religious and aesthetic antitechnologists. Rescher singles out for praise such happiness-producing technologies as the prevention of childhood diseases through innoculation, anaesthetics, plastic and restorative surgery, waste disposal, and temperature control through heating and air conditioning;[7] but he also observes that historical research suggests that the "bloom of ameliorative hopefulness" with respect to technology was already fading fast by the time of Thomas Malthus and Charles Darwin.[8] Rescher recognizes that views on the relation of technology to happiness are apt to be "distorted" by a deep-rooted tendency to think well of certain aspects of the past;[9] and there is a provocative impartiality, one likely to be somewhat irritating to antitechnologist and technological optimist alike, in Rescher's observation that "contentment and satisfaction seem to depend on very basic elements of the human condition, factors which our technical progress leaves largely untouched and which actually do not admit of ready manipulation."[10] Rescher does not remain consistently impartial, however, for at a key moment in his analysis, he feels obliged to answer in the negative the question of whether technological progress promotes human happiness; and he does so, regretfully, "because of the hard facts we encounter when we go into the field and look at the reactions we get from people themselves."[11]

One might think that Rescher's conclusion would give some comfort to religious, aesthetic, and philosophical antitechnologists, especially since Rescher insists that he is not speaking here as a "humanistic curmudgeon."[12] But Rescher's conclusion actually raises more problems than it solves. For one thing, Rescher clearly believes that the "hard facts" obtained out in the "field" indicate that people generally do not make an idol out of technology or fall prey to some technological "mentality" but rather tend to react negatively toward technology. Furthermore, their negative attitudes toward technology would appear to be fundamentally irrational, not only because attitudes toward technology are "distorted" by nostalgia but because, if Rescher is correct, then happiness actually depends on basic elements of the human condition that technological progress leaves largely untouched. It is noteworthy in this regard that Rescher himself sees certain recently developed technologies as representing genuine *progress*. Rescher's analysis thus tends to confirm Aristotle's view that while ordinary, unreflective people are in some sense striving to attain happiness, they are quite confused about what happiness is and how it is to be attained. Moreover, despite what Rescher himself is prepared to count as the "hard facts" about attitudes toward technology, human beings generally would appear to be just as confused in their thinking about their chances of deriving happiness from technology as they are in their thinking about happiness itself.

The major teachings of Judaism and Christianity seem for the most part to assure the faithful that they will attain a happiness of a more elevated and more abstract kind than mere pleasure, a bliss or joy or rapture that is somehow tied to fulfilment or salvation. Although prophets and teachers of the major monotheistic faiths have at times described the reward of piety in concrete, temporal terms that a relatively unreflective individual could grasp,[13] they usually keep the matter of the nature of the reward for religious devotion as obscure as possible and prefer to approach it through allegorical or abstract language; and the medieval Jewish and Christian philosophers, writing to an intellectually sophisticated audience, usually characterize the good to be attained by the righteous in language that is in places intentionally close to that of Plato and Aristotle. We shall be considering technology as a religious endeavor in the next chapter, but it may be noted here that the role of technology in leading to happiness and unhappiness in any conventional secular sense has traditionally been a very minor consideration in mainstream Western religious teaching; and the major religious antitechnologists of our time, though they have sermonized at length about the earthly consequences of technology and even about the joylessness of the "technological society," have usually left their audience periodic reminders that as men and women of faith, they are not hedonists or utilitarians and are not ultimately concerned about how technology as such tends to make people "feel."

We should not be surprised then that broad discussions of technology and progress only rarely focus directly on technology as a source of and hindrance to happiness. Their main focus is usually on freedom. Freedom too may be a somewhat vague conception, but it is not nearly as vague a conception as happiness.[14] Freedom—what it is, how it is to be attained, and why it is important—must be regarded as one of the three or four central themes of both the Western monotheistic tradition[15] and the classical philosophical tradition. Not coincidentally it is invariably one of the two or three major concerns of critics of technology, whether they be religious or not. It also happens to be one of the major concerns of most defenders of technology, and when the issue of technology and progress arises, freedom is almost always the chief concern.

The critic who sees technologists as promoting, insidiously or naively, the dehumanizing mechanization of the human person, human life, and human institutions is obviously very much committed in principle to the defense of human freedom, autonomy, and self-determination. She may see freedom as important because it is a major condition of happiness, self-realization, dignity, or salvation; or she may take the existential philosophical view that freedom is of primary importance in its own right and is misunderstood when it is regarded as being of essentially instrumental or practical value. This distinction is a significant one for us. Those who defend freedom because they see it as a major condition of something even more important, such as happiness or salvation, may well find themselves in a predicament when confronted with arguments plausibly purporting to show that freedom can sometimes be an obstacle to attaining a higher end; on the other hand, existential thinkers may well strike us as being arbitrary, fanatical, confused, or insincere when they insist that freedom absolutely transcends all other ideals, collectively as well as individually, including happiness, salvation, justice, and peace. Either way, there is a serious problem for the self-professed defender of freedom. The disciple of Jacques Ellul and the disciple of Martin Heidegger are both greatly concerned by the threat to freedom posed by technology, but their attitudes toward freedom are very different, and each can see the danger of the other's position. Religious existentialists like Nicolas Berdyaev and Gabriel Marcel are simultaneously faced with both difficulties, which is just one of the costs of adopting a world view that is rooted in a fundamental tension.

The defender of technology is not obliged to assign great importance to freedom. Unlike the religious, aesthetic, and philosophical antitechnologists who habitually worry about such things as spirituality, salvation, dignity, freedom as a condition, and freedom in its own right, the defender of technology can be an outright hedonist, behaviorist, or materialist without being disloyal or inconsistent. But he does not *have* to be one, and he may legitimately resent an antitechnologist's unwarranted assumption that he *is* one. More to the point, he can make an impressive case for the position that technology, even when viewed "broadly" after the peculiar manner of the antitechnologists, has on balance promoted freedom. In doing so, it has contributed to progress, maybe even in a way that religion and other forms of culture cannot. If bold enough, he can carry his argument a step further and try to show that technology has brought about social, cultural, and personal progress partly by undermining certain cultural influences of religion, the fine arts, and philosophy. Though the defender of technology is not obliged to show how technology promotes freedom, it is usually prudent for him to make the effort because the people that he is trying to impress will probably regard freedom as a great good, even if they have not bothered to think much about what it is. In addition, the defender of technology will find that, curiously, antitechnologists themselves sometimes indirectly help him to make this case.

For the ancients, freedom was mainly to be contrasted with slavery.[16] Peter C. Hodgson has pointed out that the term *freedom* is in fact linguistically "a product of those who are masters and who define their mastery vis-à-vis slavery"[17] and that a corresponding pattern can be detected with respect to the development of terms used to designate freedom in all Indo-European languages.[18] The contrast between freedom and slavery is generally sharply defined in the writings of the classical Greeks. It is even more striking in the Torah, in which the exodus of the Hebrew slaves from Egypt is perhaps the central event, and in which God's Ten Commandments begin with the words, "I am the Lord thy God, which have brought thee out of the land of Egypt, out of the house of bondage."[19] Although *freedom* and such related terms as *liberty* and *autonomy* have gradually taken on a variety of connotations, the ancient contrast between freedom and slavery is notable here not only because of its historical importance in the development of Western religious conceptions of freedom, but because it is regularly applied by defenders of technology, who plausibly observe that expendable machines and other technologies effectively perform a role that human slaves were once forced to perform.[20] The decline of institutional slavery—which we should not forget still exists in certain forms—is perhaps the most vital evidence of how technology, broadly conceived, has promoted social, cultural, and personal progress. The "labor saving" devices introduced by technologists have taken the place of human slaves, and in doing so, they have contributed greatly not only to freeing human beings from onerous labor but to inhibiting one of the most fundamental forms of dehumanization.

Just as *freedom* has by extension taken on new connotations, so to some extent has *slavery*; a person is not simply speaking metaphorically when he says that thanks to his new microwave oven, or a newly invented agricultural implement, or a newly developed medical procedure, he is no longer a "slave" to this or that. A labor-saving device really "frees" us from a task that to some degree we have been performing "against our will." Even if previously we had not recognized that task as being particularly burdensome, it now appears so because time has been freed up for us to pursue activities that we regard as more meaningful or more fulfilling. What then could qualify more clearly as progress?

The critic of technology has several possible responses, all of which pose problems of their own. Illich warns that "we must come to admit that only within limits can machines take the place of slaves; beyond these limits they lead to a new kind of serfdom."[21] This admonition sounds moderate enough, but when Illich offers his "alternative to technocratic disaster," the "vision of a convivial society," he emphasizes the need for "social arrangements that guarantee for each member the most ample and free access to the tools of the community and limit this freedom only in favor of another member's equal freedom."[22] According to such a view, technology is an obstacle to freedom only when people are denied access to it. There is a conspicuous irony here, one that reminds me of Illich's inability many years ago to answer my question about how he could reconcile his enormous admiration for the "simple" lives of peasants with his desire to see them given access to sophisticated technologies that would make them more and more like their supposedly neurotic capitalist exploiters.

Antitechnological extremist Friedrich Jünger's alternative response is that "the notion that manual labor is monotonous and that this so-called tedious monotony is eliminated by technical progress—this notion is false. The opposite is true."[23] Traditional types of manual labor are not necessarily monotonous, and the work done by assembly-line workers in factories or oral surgeons in offices inundated by the latest technological devices of their profession may be very monotonous indeed. There is thus perhaps a sense in which the assembly-line worker and oral surgeon can be said to be "unfree." The fact that many people who earn their living by working with the latest technologies detest their work is of vital importance, and the critic of technology, religious or otherwise, is right to draw our attention to it. However, it should be considered together with other matters. Monotonous work may be on balance much less onerous—and rather more remunerative—than the available alternatives. In a socioeconomic system in which people are normally expected to earn a living rather than pass all their time in leisure activities, the demands of consumers, clients, employers, and fellow citizens in general are not to be dismissed as inherently oppressive. Many people have not adequately demonstrated that they possess the intelligence, skill, discipline, and patience that are necessary for the satisfactory performance of the kind of job that they would prefer. Most importantly, we must resist the temptation to view manual labor as such through rose-colored lenses, and we must work at remembering how much more difficult many socially necessary and ameliorative tasks would be without the familiar technologies that workers and consumers alike customarily take for granted.

There may well be some who believe that the average individual who works on an assembly line is no better off than the ancient slave. We must not ignore the exploitation of factory workers during the Industrial Revolution—and in many places in the world today—but neither should we assume that a factory assembly-line worker, simply because of the nature of her work, has been denied the benefits of technological progress. What else might she have had to do to earn her living? And does she not have accessibility in her home, the marketplace, and the domain of cultural and entertainment institutions to many fruits of technological progress? There is as much condescension as compassion in the typical antitechnologist's general attitude toward those who earn their living by "monotonously" working with the latest technologies; and in this regard he has succumbed to an old prejudice.[24] In any case, our own technologically advanced society is not predominantly populated by miserable assembly-line workers and oral surgeons and other supposed victims of the technological "mentality." It is a society in which, despite its serious shortcomings—and they are decidedly very serious—a remarkable number of citizens have opportunities to get a higher education, participate in the political process, vacation at tropical resorts and in faraway lands, obtain redress for violations of their civil rights, and witness epoch-making events.

Another response is offered by those who grant that technology has indeed promoted freedom but insist that the kind of freedom that it has tended to promote is culturally corruptive. This position is usually advanced by religious and cultural "conservatives" who are antipathetic toward those features of contemporary social life that they see as having been directly shaped by the application of the tenets of "liberalism." You will perhaps recall how J. Mark Thomas sees demonic technicism as having been nurtured in the womb of liberalism. Thomas suggests that "in the history of ideas, it is significant that the bearers of classical liberalism and the philosophical apologists for a scientific and technological culture were essentially the same thinkers."[25] He sees the cultural chaos to which scientism and technicism have led as revealing that "the original human-istic intentions of the liberal ethos" have fallen into ruin.[26] The connection between liberalism and a protechnological agenda is not as tight as Thomas's comments would lead us to believe, even in the case of the thinkers that Thomas has in mind, such as John Locke, Adam Smith, and Jeremy Bentham. In fact, conservatives, liberals, and radicals are amply distributed among the ranks of both protechnologists and antitechnolo-gists. Nevertheless, it is interesting to see a religious antitechnologist associating technological optimism with the one sociopolitical philosophy that has been based on the fundamental objective of optimizing personal freedom. There can be no doubt that particular technologies have served well the agenda of classical liberalism. That is why, for example, Ronald Reagan, an influential proponent of at least certain ideals of classical liberalism, could enthusiastically praise the *democratic impact* of the elec-tronic revolution in communications and information technology.[27] It is in fact in the dissemination of knowledge and theory that technology fosters some of the most important forms of freedom and perhaps does most to earn its reputation as a source of progress. We shall return to this matter shortly; at this point, however, I feel the need to pronounce that while attacks on classical liberalism are much in fashion these days in many intellectual and pseudointellectual circles, the constructive legacy of clas-sical liberalism should not be taken lightly by anyone who has the privilege of enjoying such fundamental freedoms as freedom of religion, speech, assembly, and the press. In particular, people who love ideas and believe that ideas are in great measure what make life worth living must never forget that these freedoms are as vulnerable as they are noble and that they have been attained and preserved only at the expense of immense effort, ingenuity, passion, and willingness to sacrifice.

To understand technology's foremost contribution to freedom, perhaps we should move to a more abstract level of reflection. We took note earlier of Wolhee Choe's contention that technology sets people free from the destinies of biology and politics. The intelligent productive act enables an agent to take control of some aspect of her condition, some aspect of the environment, and often also some aspect of the social order. When she works in cooperation with her fellow human beings, the range of possibili-ties can be expanded exponentially. Richard A. Peterson has incisively observed that "we are on the threshold of accurately manipulating sentiments with drugs, repairing or replacing body parts with ease, and even changing man's genetic structure. In all these advances, technology gives a new meaning, which we . . . now only dimly comprehend, to the age-old idea of the 'self-made man.' "[28] It is understandable that one may be frightened by such advances and that one may fear that they will result in freedom for few and slavery for many. But as existential philosophers have maintained from Søren Kierkegaard on, true awareness of one's freedom and responsibility for self-determination is terrifying in and of itself. Technology is frightening in part because it perpetually places new demands on the agent who is keenly conscious of his freedom and responsibility. "Technology," Emmanuel Mesthene tells us, "has a direct impact on values by virtue of bringing about . . . changes in our available options," and "by adding new options in this way, technology can lead to changes in values in the same way that the appearance of new dishes on the heretofore standard menu of one's favorite restaurant can lead to changes in one's taste and choices of food."[29] Behind Mesthene's quaint analogy is the powerful theme that one of the main freedoms that technology contributes to social, cultural, and personal progress involves an ever-expanding range of options that will periodically induce the reflective, self-assured, creative individual to reconsider traditional and conventional values as well as those that are more intimately—more "existentially"—his own. The religious, aesthetic, and philosophical antitechnologists who parade their uncompromising dedication to the promotion of immutable values and eternal truths are at the very least insightful in their recognition that such freedom is exceedingly *dangerous*.

TECHNOLOGY AS A SOURCE OF KNOWLEDGE

Defenders of technology understandably have much to say about the constructive role played by technology in the acquisition and dissemination of knowledge. We need only to consider in this regard how much of our own personal knowledge has been acquired by means of tools, instruments, and devices of various kinds, with books presumably being the most obvious and telephones, radios, televisions, and computers reminding us of the importance of more recent technologies. The connection between knowledge and progress is for most of us virtually intuitive. It is apparent to us from a very early age that the more one knows, then generally speaking, the better off one is. Soon after that realization, we come to associate the acquisition of knowledge with being better human beings; we see that knowledge is not only practically advantageous but something that makes us worthy of respect in the eyes of loved ones, friends, and rivals—

and even eventually in our own eyes. People appreciate the practical uses to which our knowledge can be put, but they also admire us simply for having certain knowledge that they themselves may or may not have, as well as for having the intelligence and initiative necessary for having acquired that knowledge. Knowing more than one previously did, especially if what one has just learned is particularly important, is almost universally regarded as a matter of personal progress. It is almost universally agreed that one of the principal marks of an advanced society, one of the principal criteria by which it is to be regarded as highly civilized, is the comparatively large amount of knowledge, particularly important knowledge, that it has acquired, recorded, made available to individuals and groups both within and beyond its boundaries, and, where appropriate, constructively applied.

There are certain unusual circumstances under which one might be led to reflect, if not altogether with conviction, that "I wish I hadn't known that" or "I would have been better off if I hadn't known that." But these special cases do not count against our general association of knowledge with progress. The expression "You know too much" is aptly associated with gangsters, secret police in military dictatorships, and other venal types. There is a maxim to the effect that a little knowledge can be a dangerous thing, but the focus of the maxim is more on the limits of the knowledge in question than the knowledge per se; besides, a maxim taken out of context can be a dangerous thing, too. Of course, there are many people who have a vested interest in restricting the acquisition and dissemination of knowledge and in keeping people as ignorant as possible, at least with respect to a defined area of knowledge; although there are special circumstances when it is morally acceptable or even morally obligatory to keep certain people from knowing a specific thing, people who restrict the acquisition and dissemination of knowledge in order to further their own narrow interests or because they arbitrarily assume that those over whom they have power are unfit to cope with knowledge are generally enemies of the progress that we associate with amelioration.

The defender of technology can associate technology's vital role in the advancement of personal and social knowledge with technology's contribution to the advancement of freedom. That in a sense is easy enough to do because we ordinarily associate knowledge not only with progress in general but with freedom in particular. Another familiar maxim teaches that knowledge is power; to the extent that knowledge is enabling, it makes us freer. Especially noteworthy is the contribution that knowledge makes to the enhancement of the kind of freedom that follows upon the enlargement of options available to us. Any enhancement of our freedom of choice renders our newly acquired knowledge dangerous, particularly to those who seek to maintain their power over us. It is not only the acquisition and dissemination of factual information that contributes to freedom and progress for individuals and societies, but also the acquisition and dissemination of ideas, insights, and theories. Here the advancement of knowledge is to be conceived as the advancement of understanding rather than merely as the collection and transmission of factual information. It may be worth recalling at this point that for Aristotle and other philosophers in the classical humanist tradition, the highest good—happiness in its most profound sense—is the contemplative life; it is reflection on the highest objects of thought, not merely the attainment of empirical or practical or technical knowledge, though these are valuable in and of themselves and help to make the contemplative life possible. We do not have to agree with Aristotle and other intellectualist types, but it is useful anyway to remember that the "wise" person or "sage" has traditionally been regarded in most cultures as someone who has done considerably more than accumulate a great number of facts to store in his memory, or even develop a very large number of skills. It is also useful to remember that there are fanatics who believe that relatively little is worth knowing and that getting people to attain this extremely important understanding, and to remain committed to this understanding in an abiding act of faith, is so spiritually important that it may require promoting ignorance about many other things. Thus, to take the most obvious example, there are diametrically opposed interpretations that can be given to the New Testament promise, "And ye shall know the truth, and the truth shall make you free."[30]

The overwhelming majority of critics of technology maintain that they too believe in the importance of knowledge; and most of them are being honest when they say so. As many of them recognize, a case can be made for the position that on balance technology, or at least technology in the last fifty years, has tended to restrict knowledge and foster ignorance. For example, Terri Toles-Patkin speaks with a disarming bluntness of what she takes to be technology's contribution to the "imbecilization of culture," that is, "a process by which people come to depend so heavily on technology to conduct their everyday lives that they become slowly but systematically stripped of their fundamental intellectual integrity, initiative and human dignity."[31] Toles-Patkin elaborates this position by referring to such consequences of recent technologies as the "deskilling" of individuals and the fragmentation of information but is most disturbed by the ease of accomplishment with which technology enables people to attain things.[32] "The ultimate imbecilization involves getting something for nothing, achievement without pain."[33]

There are points worth making here, but we should be careful not to blow them out of proportion, for the truth is that there have been plenty of "imbeciles" in every society from the beginnings of recorded history; and sophisticated technologies have not turned most people in our society into "imbeciles." Certainly you and Toles-Patkin and I represent proof that it is possible to have lived in the age of "high tech" without having been stripped of one's intellectual integrity, initiative, and human dignity; moreover, people have always depended heavily on technology, and they always will. The ever-increasing amount and complexity of technology parallel to some extent the ever-increasing amount and complexity of knowledge in general. When we look around, our gaze can easily become fixed on shallow, indolent, bigoted, "imbecilic" types; and it is easy to be offended by their very existence, especially if we have reason to believe that they are doing a great deal of harm or are enjoying life much more than hard-working, hard-thinking folks like Toles-Patkin are. Reaching for a readily available explanation, we may seize upon the theory that there is something unique in the anticulture of our society that is largely to be blamed for all this "imbecilization." As it must be something new, it is most likely the new technology, or particular new technologies such as television, or the technological "mentality." We should let go of the theory, all the more swiftly if we have seized upon it in a spirit of condescension or resentment.

The distorting effect of nostalgia needs to be checked. We may look back to the cultural glory of ancient Greece and wonder why there is no Aeschylus, Thucydides, Pericles, or Plato now; but the world of Plato was largely inhabited by nitwits and their manipulators, a state of affairs of which the wise Plato was keenly aware and to which he gave considerable attention in his writings.[34] We may look back to the High Middle Ages, an "age of faith," when the temporal institutions of the Western world were to an unsurpassed degree under the stewardship of men antagonistic in principle to all forms of hedonism, materialism, and venality, men who gave the world great universities and splendid cathedrals; but we cannot afford to forget the superstition, stupidity, and malice of a time just as fittingly symbolized by the senseless Crusades, which managed to gather many of history's most unscrupulous yet most manipulable blockheads. We may long for a revival of the spirit of the Renaissance, but for every Leonardo or Pico della Mirandola there were ten thousand manipulable dolts whose character defects have been etched for us with enduring sharpness in the pages of Desiderius Erasmus's *Praise of Folly* and Niccolò Machiavelli's *The Prince*.[35] The sublime Age of Reason has left us with memories of some exquisitely reasonable human beings; but one of the most reasonable of all, Spinoza, despite being one of history's most courageous and most eloquent defenders of democracy, could not refrain from observing that "the fickle disposition of the multitude almost reduces those who have experience of it to despair, for it is governed solely by emotions, not reason: it rushes headlong into every enterprise, and is easily corrupted either by avarice or luxury."[36] This was a man, after all, who witnessed the political assassination of his friends, good people, by a frenzied mob that had been manipulated by evil operators; he knew a great deal about "imbeciles" long before the invention of motion pictures, television, and computer games.

Mumford, impelled to convey to us the bleak news that "our inner life has become impoverished,"[37] puts part of the blame for our contemporary predicament on the technological optimism of Francis Bacon, a figure who conceivably has been the target of more defamatory rhetoric by antitech-nologists than anyone else in history.[38] In Mumford's view, the influential Bacon "turned his back upon religion and philosophy and art and pinned every hope for human improvement on the development of mechanical invention"[39] but did not have the foresight to realize that "the humaniza-tion of the machine might have the paradoxical effect of mechanizing humanity."[40] However, the achievement of Bacon can be judged quite differently. Mumford takes Bacon to have made merely "a few expiatory gestures of piety,"[41] but Bacon's *theological* defense of technology can now be seen as being as profound as it was ground-breaking.[42] More to the point, despite what may now be perceived as his excessive emphases on the empirical and inductive—emphases that were quite expedient and neces-sary in his day—Bacon was an authentic intellectual concerned above all with the advancement of learning;[43] he was a bold critic of both superstition and obscurantist academic metaphysics. His protechnological agenda was presented in the context of a broad educational philosophy that was historically important not only in freeing thinkers from their commitment to a moribund Scholasticism but in expediting the transition from the intellectual program of Renaissance humanism to the intellectual program of the Age of Reason. Thus, as Hans Jonas has pointed out, it is no coincidence that Bacon, even more than Leonardo, was able to anticipate the alliance of technology and *science*;[44] in Bacon's mind, there would always be an indissoluble correlation of knowledge, technology, and pro-gress.

As you read these printed lines in a book, thereby utilizing technologies more powerful in their distinctive way than the most advanced computer technology,[45] this Baconian correlation should be more obvious than it was to Mumford; but the educational and epistemological import of a wide array of technologies is worth considering. Focusing on information technologies, Paul Levinson has noted five distinct (though overlapping) ways in which technology contributes to the growth of human knowledge and ultimately to cosmic as well as cognitive evolution:

- All technologies are material embodiments, and thus more or less durable records of ideas that have survived some test with external reality;

- Telescopes, microscopes, and similar technologies extend external experience, and thus the generation of knowledge in areas inaccessible to the naked senses;

- Computers enhance the operation of our internal cognitive faculties themselves, fostering the generation of knowledge from huge quantities of experience which might otherwise have overwhelmed our unaided mental capacities;

- Speech, writing and similar media facilitate the criticism and dissemination of knowledge by transmitting information or representations via abstraction, a process especially hospitable to the communication of abstract concepts, and perhaps even responsible for their existence; and

- Photographic and image-and-sound producing media transmit representations of external reality with little or no abstraction, enabling widespread criticism and dissemination of representations with very high degrees of correspondence to aspects of external reality as directly perceived by the senses.[46]

This lucid and comprehensive survey of a variety of ways in which technology has contributed to the growth of knowledge and to forms of social, cultural, and personal progress is plainly the product of a mind that has benefited greatly from a culture that has not been rendered utterly ineffectual by any effects of "imbecilization." Despite its limitations, as in its arbitrary characterization of *all* technologies as material embodiments, it would surely have pleased Aristotle and Bacon, who would likely have inferred that the author's inner life is far from impoverished.

It would appear that most antitechnologists, and certainly most religious and aesthetic antitechnologists, normally are not as favorably impressed as people like Levinson are by all this knowledge to be acquired through such instruments as telescopes, microscopes, computers, and image-and-sound producing media. It would also appear that they do not remember as well as people like Levinson do that technologies are valuable records of *ideas* or that something like writing is as much a technology as the things that they blame for dehumanizing us. However, more is at stake here than just narrow judgment or poor memory. Pamela McCorduck, who usefully compares the cultural significance of the computer in the twentieth century with that of the printing press in the fifteenth century, notes that both technologies (which were in fact "less the result of a singular breakthrough than of an evolving set of technologies"[47]) were to a great degree "stoutly resisted by the established, centralized powers, who soon found themselves overtaken. Those established powers were forced to adopt the new technology and tried, too late, to control it."[48] While we must avoid responding to antitechnologist arguments with *ad hominem* ones, it is appropriate for us to note that insecure religious, political, and cultural leaders have been known throughout history to worry a great deal about the threat posed to their authority and influence by the liberating and enlightening effects of new technologies (and new forms of experience and culture) that cause spectacular surges in the accessibility of fresh information, ideas, and perspectives. This fear, which is often quite reasonable from the standpoint of naked prudence, frequently results in reactionary polemic and other reactionary undertakings by the leaders themselves, by their agents in religious, educational, artistic, and media institutions, and by "loyal" supporters who have been led to worry about the impact of radical cultural change on their own insecure circumstances.

We thus return to a recurrent theme of our inquiry; although there is indisputably considerable truth to the contention of recent antitechnologists that certain technologies developed in recent years pose distinctive problems of kinds that were not known in the past, the affinities between recent and earlier technologies can also be very revealing. There is an exceedingly long tradition of antitechnology, particularly (though certainly not exclusively) on the part of conservative religionists; and while there are many motives underlying antitechnological rhetoric, one of the most persistent has been the type of fear associated with reactionary sentiment. Indeed, as McCorduck has observed, despite the differences between the fifteenth century and our own century, "fear is fear," and we would be "arrogant" to imagine that the fears of people in our own time are more profound than the fears of people in earlier times.[49] There are even remarkable affinities between the reactionary spirit of certain contemporary religious antitechnological arguments and the reactionary spirit of the ancient religious attack on philosophy, logic, and "reason" epitomized by the derision of Socrates in Aristophanes's *Clouds*.

New technologies can bolster as well as undermine established authority. Leo Marx overgeneralizes when he suggests, "Since the state often seems to be the only institution capable of controlling technology, increases in technological power tend to be followed by increases in state power."[50] Nevertheless, it is evident that many new technologies, owing in part to their magnitude or complexity, require or at least invite control by those who have primary access to the resources of large, established political, ecclesiastical, business, and academic institutions. As McCorduck points out, the liberating and enlightening effects of new technologies have been achieved partly because of the initial failure of established cultural powers to appreciate the positive value to them of these technologies. Social critics have had good reason to worry about the centralization of power over new technologies and about the role of new technologies in increasing the centralization of power, but the salient issue on this level is the centralization (or distribution) of power rather than the consequences of technology as such. This issue is, of course, one of the central issues in social and political theory, and religionists have taken all kinds of stands on it, with respect to both the distribution of power in the state and the distribution of power in their own particular community of religious believers. We may note in relation to this matter that one of the most important of the immediate social consequences of the development (in the ancient Near East) of the fundamental technology of *writing* was that "it confirmed the power of the priests through the trained scribes."[51] Whether such confirmation of priestly power should be seen *on balance* as having expedited or hindered social, cultural, and personal progress—or human progress itself—over a *specific* period of time is obviously a question open to debate. In any case, with the passage of the millennia, literacy skills have spread and spread—owing in large part to the development of new information technologies—so that today countless millions possess them; it would be a great error to underestimate the contribution that they have made to intellectual and moral progress by undermining primitive superstition and undercutting the "authority" of those who prosper by fostering superstition.[52]

THE DESIRABILITY OF PROGRESS

Concentrating on some very important ways in which technologies have contributed to progress through the enhancement of freedom and knowledge, we have considered positive aspects of technology that religious antitechnologists generally undervalue. However, the appraisal of technology that has emerged in these pages is itself one-dimensional, having been developed with the specific purpose of putting those positive aspects in bold relief. Technologies have inhibited as well as promoted the growth of happiness, freedom, and knowledge; and there are any number of concerns in addition to happiness, freedom, and knowledge that an individual might want to factor into her equation when evaluating the overall relevance of technology to progress in a particular context. Given that there are any number of subjective factors that might enter into a general assessment of technology, we have to accept that antitechnologists and protechnologists will always be with us; and as it happens, there are things that we can learn from them. If we are really to arrive at a "wide view" of technology, then we should keep in mind that almost any new technology has both positive and negative effects and that its very newness is a major source of both.[53]

It is also only fair to remember that culpability for bad technology, the misuse of technology, and excessive confidence in technology should be widely allocated. Theodore Roszak has suggested that "the role of the technical expert in our society is analogous to that of the old tribal shaman . . . in the sense that both are deferred to by the populace at large as figures who conjure with mysterious forces in mysterious ways."[54] The typical technical expert does not demand or expect such deference and is apt to be rather uncomfortable with it. More to the point, the "populace at large" is not consistently deferential; quite to the contrary, it makes all sorts of demands on technical experts in the marketplace and elsewhere, and most technical experts are keenly aware of their dependence on the values, attitudes, and whims of consumers, clients, taxpayers, and voters. Much ado has been made by antitechnologists of the rise of technocracy,[55] but the ordinary technologist only very rarely rises to a very high position of political authority. More often than not, such a person finds herself to be an "accessory" in a social project, with the major decision-making power left to politicians and professional bureaucrats, technical experts of a very special kind.[56] In the "private" sector, the ordinary technologist has a much better chance of getting to the top, but even there decision-making power is largely concentrated in the hands of business executives whose attention is usually fixed on the proverbial bottom line. The technical expert puts her expertise at the service of politicians, bureaucrats, and business executives, and thus she cannot be held entirely blameless for the negative consequences of the bad projects in which she freely participates; but she did not create the corrupt or incompetent political and business leaders to whom she so often finds herself having to answer. Then again, the high profile that certain forms of technology sometimes enjoy—or rather *endure*—is partly a function of widespread disappointment with other areas of culture. Even Mumford admits that any mechanization of humanity in recent years has been as much a consequence of the recent "aridity" of traditionally spirit-nourishing forms of culture as of any protechnologist agenda.[57] The rise of material technology can at times be seen to be directly related to the corruption and deterioration of established religious institutions.

We need not embrace a thoroughgoing technological determinism, or even a quasi-deterministic model like Ellul's, to recognize that technological development inevitably proceeds in large measure as a result of its own momentum. This is perhaps partly because, as Veblen maintains, there is an "instinct of workmanship" that is one of the most basic of human instincts. This instinct, Veblen believes, "brought the life of mankind from the brute to the human plane, and in all the later growth of culture it has never ceased to pervade the works of man."[58] Even without acknowledging the existence of such an instinct, however, we can see that despite their considerable nostalgia for the way "things" used to be, and their frequent avowal that they are pretty much satisfied with "things" the way they are, most human beings want "things" to get better and are interested in contributing to making "things" better. Moreover, they are regularly mindful of the fact that this or that thing could be bigger, faster, more efficient, easier to manage, and so forth. The technological agenda of an individual or society is determined to a great degree by rudimentary awareness of these perpetual possibilities. Yet as "things" become bigger, faster, or whatever, they often become more complex, more demanding, more challenging, or more pervasive, and they force individuals and societies to adapt in ways that they had not anticipated would be necessary and now may have good reason to regret. Such considerations have induced antitechnologists and others to ask questions about the suitability of "technological progress" as an ideal; and some observers have gone further and expressed serious concerns about whether we should be striving for "progress" at all.

The idea that progress itself is not a sound ideal for societies, cultures, or individuals may seem to be counterintuitive. How, one might wonder, can a thoughtful, vital human being or society not aspire to be both better and better off and to see "things" improve? How can an individual not wish to see his loved ones and friends better off, and how can an ethical person not be willing to contribute in any way to the advancement of his fellow citizens and of humanity? A good way of trying to understand the view of the reflective person who is not convinced that we should be striving for progress is to consider his uneasiness about how the term *progress* is used by many people who advocate the realization of an ideal that they call by this name. Discerning philosophers from Plato and Aristotle to Nietzsche and Wittgenstein have commonly observed that words are tricky phenomena that tricky people habitually use in especially tricky ways; and most of the people who worry about the pursuit of "progress" believe that the term *progress* is often used in an especially tricky way.

In his *Grammar of Assent*, John Henry Newman, one of the most influential nineteenth-century religious critics of liberalism, explicitly singles out *progress* as one of those "political and religious watchwords" that are manipulatively employed by promoters of some dubious cultural agenda and then adopted by naive partisans who have little understanding of their significance.[59] He tells us that such words "in the mouths of conscientious thinkers, have a definite meaning, but are used by the multitude as war-cries, nicknames, and shibboleths, with scarcely enough of the scanti- est grammatical apprehension of them to allow of their being considered in truth more than assertions."[60] Cardinal Newman is not merely interested here in the study of language; a Roman Catholic apologist, he sees many of those in his society who stress the need for "progress" as enemies of the church and its age-old traditions. Thus he wants his readers to understand that much of the vague, fashionable talk in his society about "progress" is a consequence of efforts by cunning propagandists to manipulate naive people so that they will acquiesce to the subverting of the church's cultural influence in their society.[61] Newman's observation is not simply of histori- cal interest; his point could just as well be made by many cultural conser- vatives of our own day. Newman is also astute in recognizing that his "liberal" rivals appreciate the emotive force of a pro-word like *progress* and its serviceability as a device for making their own cultural agenda more appealing. (Newman himself was one of the greatest masters of such manipulative techniques.)

Using a mode of expression that was popular in philosophical circles some years ago, we might say that *progress* is normally a term strong in "emotive" meaning but rather weak in "descriptive" meaning;[62] and many people who worry about progress as an ideal are troubled by the practical consequences of this aspect of the term *progress*. They recognize how important it is that in any specific context we try to determine, as far as we can, precisely what it is that is being identified with "improvement" or "getting better." They caution us not to be lured into allying ourselves with people who have a largely hidden agenda for cultural change. Religious antitechnologists and others who are disturbed by what they see as the abandonment of life-sustaining religiocultural traditions may feel that many of those who idealize something that they call "progress" consider the departure from tradition as ameliorative in its own right. It is probably the case that many promoters of "progress" are not so much concerned with something positive and concrete as they are with experimenting with change. Such experimentation may have beneficial consequences, but it is unlikely that most people who uncritically endorse a progress-oriented cultural program would be comfortable with the realization that they have been unwittingly associating themselves with a cultural philosophy essen- tially committed to change for its own sake and the undermining of tradition.

Not all religious critics of technology disapprove of the pursuit of progress, but virtually all of them worry about the antitraditional attitude implicit in many protechnological arguments about the value of progress.

Almost all religionists in the Western world attach enormous importance, at least in theory, to what they take to be the traditional spiritual foundations of Western (or global) culture; and they would be justified in believing, as indeed most religious antitechnologists do, that the defender of technology is obliged to think as clearly as possible about where she stands with respect to the effect of technology on those cultural foundations. Specific traditions may in fact no longer be culturally invigorating; but protechnologist defenders of "progress" are under some obligation to speculate intelligently about what the effects of new technologies are likely to be on those traditions that remain culturally invigorating.

However they may appraise the relation of technology to genuinely ameliorative "progress," observers will generally acknowledge that technology is closely linked to *change*; and a heightened respect for (or tolerance of) change ordinarily brings with it an increased willingness to depart from tradition and the "ways of the past." There is in fact more than a little wisdom in Milan Kundera's observation that technology is "organized forgetting."[63] Still, it would be wrong for the antitechnologist to assume that when most defenders of technology talk about technology's contribution to progress, they are "really" only thinking about technology's contribution to change. For one thing, it may be proper to characterize change as something that is to some extent valuable in itself. The desirability of change may also be understood in relation to the pursuit of happiness, freedom, wisdom, and other major ideals, and more narrowly in relation to such specific objectives as escaping monotony, having access to new or different options, and having access to fresh perspectives.

Critics of technology "as such" and the technological "mentality" could certainly argue that technologists and admirers of technology, at least this century, have generally attached too much importance to a distinctive and independent ideal of "technological progress" and too little importance to technology's contribution to more basic (and perhaps more traditional) forms of progress involving the realization of ideals such as happiness, freedom, and wisdom. They could argue along these lines that while producing something that is bigger, faster, and so forth represents *in itself* a certain "technological progress," it is not necessarily a contribution to the more important *intrinsic* forms of "improvement" and "getting better" that are of concern to people whose attention is properly fixed more on genuine ends than on instruments. They would certainly be right to observe that a bigger or faster instrument does not necessarily make its user happier, freer, or wiser, even if the ability to produce it represents a distinctive form of "technological progress." (This last point is effectively conveyed in the slogan, "Small is beautiful."[64]) I would not deny that there are technologists and admirers of technology who seem to assign too much importance to a distinctive sort of "progress" that is represented by the capacity to produce instruments that, regardless of their value or the possible or probable consequences of using them, are "better" simply in the sense of being superior with respect to such criteria as size and speed. However, this is not as great a concession as the antitechnologist might take it to be. Without dwelling on the subjectivity that enters into my own appraisal of how much importance should be attached to one ideal as opposed to another ideal—or to one form of progress as opposed to another form—I shall observe that the larger part of this chapter has attempted to show how antitechnologists have generally undervalued technology's role in the realization of basic, traditional ideals such as happiness, freedom, and wisdom. Besides, the critic of technology is not justified in assuming that the *typical* technologist, admirer of technology, or user of technology does not assign enough importance to the realization of basic, traditional ideals, or to the pursuit of forms of progress other than "technological progress" narrowly construed, or to the possible or probable uses to which a new technology will be put, or to the *practical* relevance of such criteria as size and speed in *specific contexts*. It is not sufficient for the critic of technology to believe that such a case could be made; the critic of technology is obliged to make it. A point of a rather different kind needs to be kept in mind as well. The individual who assigns a great deal of importance to "technological progress" narrowly construed has very frequently been shown to have been right to believe that advances in this area would eventually be put to constructive uses that were not initially envisioned. Such advances may have been put to destructive uses as well, but in that regard they are not much different from advances in "basic research" or "pure science" that have gone on to be applied in unexpected ways. In any case, even technologies (and forms of culture) that are almost universally respected have been applied in destructive ways.

Whatever her estimation of the value of particular traditions, the historian of culture should be able to see that any form of "progress," whether genuinely ameliorative or not, not only challenges the status quo but, if not effectively restrained by conservative forces, eventually results in the integral transformation of a society. This should be especially clear in the case of "progress" related to technology, whether "technological progress" narrowly conceived or the progress toward the realization of basic, traditional ideals that is fostered by technology. According to S. Lilley, "Each society in youth encourages the advance of technology, but as the technological level rises, the society fails to keep pace with it, until there comes the breaking point at which the old society is transformed into one that is again fit to push technology to greater heights."[65] There is almost surely some overgeneralization in this contention, but still there are many obvious examples of the historical process that Lilley has described. Something that needs to be affirmed in opposition to dogmatic and reactionary traditionalism—and not all people properly characterized as "traditionalists" are dogmatic or reactionary—is that the integral transformation of a society brought about as a result of technological and other changes is not necessarily a bad thing. Indeed, it may in most cases be a rather splendid thing, something that imparts greater significance to the concept of civilization.

It is not always easy to distinguish between an authentic respect for tradition and a fear of change, and while people often feign the former in order to conceal the latter, there would not be much point in feigning the latter to conceal the former. Just as societies can have difficulty keeping pace with the rise in the technological level, so too can individuals and groups within a society. Thus it is hardly surprising that so many people feel threatened by technological change. Often they have very good reason to worry. The development of new technologies can initially result in substantial loss of control, and some individuals, groups, and societies adapt to cultural changes much less easily and less successfully than others. Nostalgia for times when one had mastery over familiar cultural phenomena and a corresponding sense of security is commonly accompanied by a vague desire to return to the "simple" life. Sophisticated thinkers who develop elaborate arguments in defense of returning to the simpler ways of the past (as, for example, Jean-Jacques Rousseau, Henry David Thoreau, and Leo Tolstoy)[66] normally encourage some return to "nature," which is implicitly or explicitly contrasted with technology and the realm of human works. In the Western monotheistic tradition, the idea of a return to nature is often closely linked to nostalgia for a lost Eden.[67]

As sophisticated as they may fancy themselves, most people have irrational as well as reasonable fears about future technology. Antitechnologist intellectuals, preachers, and activists are not the only cultural leaders who know that there is an audience that will respond affirmatively to appeals to its insecurity. Steven L. Goldman, who has undertaken a study of the image of technology in motion pictures, writes that "given the persistent popular association of science and technology with social progress and personal well-being, it is startling to discover that in films since the mid-1920s they have been depicted largely negatively."[68] Although there have been a few laudatory films, such as *The Story of Alexander Graham Bell* and *Breaking the Sound Barrier*,[69] far more have been negative, and one may call to mind such classic examples as *Metropolis*, *Modern Times*,

Dr. Strangelove, and *A Clockwork Orange*.[70] Of special interest is how the charming and immensely popular fantasy, *E.T.*, "triggered a series of films in which scientists or technologists are depicted as heartless or so committed to solving a technical problem that they are blind to its moral dimension."[71]

Some scholars have observed that at its most ameliorative—and its most obviously ameliorative—progress poses distinctive problems of a psychological nature. Nicholas Rescher draws our attention to a "fundamental paradox of progress: progress produces dissatisfaction because it inflates expectations faster than it can actually meet them."[72] Emmanuel Mesthene offers the example of how new forms of mass communications technology have been responsible for a great deal of social and international unrest by raising expectations faster than political institutions can deal with them.[73]

Despite such concerns, social theorist Robert Nisbet is convinced that "no single idea has been more important than, perhaps as important as, the idea of progress in Western civilization for nearly three thousand years. Other ideas will come to mind, properly: liberty, justice, equality, community, and so forth. I do not derogate from any of them. But this must be stressed: thoughout most of Western history, the substratum of even these ideas has been a philosophy of history that lends past, present, and future to their importance."[74] The idea of progress that Nisbet has in mind here is that "mankind has advanced in the past—from some aboriginal condition of primitiveness, barbarism, or even nullity—is now advancing, and will continue to advance through the foreseeable future,"[75] and Nisbet traces its development starting with the works of Hesiod and Aeschylus.[76] We need not endorse Nisbet's extraordinary appraisal of the idea's historical importance. Indeed, we may question his precise characterization of the idea, but his remarks raise a crucial consideration: progress is not only to be understood and valued in terms of its relation to such basic, traditional ideals as happiness, freedom, and wisdom, but is itself a basic, traditional ideal in terms of which other such ideals are themselves understood and valued.

Few people now accept the idea, associated by Mumford with the nineteenth century, that progress can be understood as "a single line without goal or limit."[77] The century of antibiotics, automobiles, and air conditioners is also a century of unprecedented genocide, exploitation, and pollution (although genocide, exploitation, and pollution all have an exceedingly long history). The technology that is utilized to bring us to new highs is also involved in our descent to new lows. Progress thus seems to be inevitably reflected in a shadow of retrogression. Critics of technology and progress will not let us forget these things, which surely need to be remembered. Nevertheless, spiritual vision is not only a protection against technology and progress but a way of invigorating them. Nisbet has concluded from his historical investigations that "only . . . in the context of a true culture in which the core is a deep and wide sense of the *sacred* are we likely to regain the vital conditions of progress itself and of faith in progress—past, present, and future."[78] This position is compatible with authentic respect for both technology and progress. But if there is to be a modus vivendi between religious spirituality, technology, and progress, religious attitudes and institutions will themselves have to be adaptable. Articulating this point as positively as he can, Mesthene writes that "if religious innovation can provide a meaning orientation broad enough to accommodate the idea that new technology can be creative of new values—or can serve to enhance or provide new content for old values—a long step will have been taken toward providing a religious belief system adequate to the realities and needs of a technological age."[79]

A religious person's understanding of the relations of religion, technology, and progress depends in large measure on his theological orientation. A religious believer who dwells on the theological theme that human beings are in a sinful state as a result of the "fall" of the first man is far more likely to regard technological endeavor and the striving for progress as vain than a religious believer who regards sermonizing about original sin as patently ridiculous. Those who believe in the inerrancy of Scripture are apt to be rather more resistant to certain kinds of technological change than those who are committed to historical method in Scriptural criticism. Of course, the atheist or agnostic will normally dismiss outright any explanation and appraisal of technology and progress that she sees as being based entirely on theological dogmas. Authentic dialogue concerning technology and progress is possible between people with different theological positions, between people of different religious faiths, and between religious believers and atheists, agnostics, secular humanists, and materialists. But it is usually the case in such dialogue that the participants realize at some point that their fundamental disagreements are disagreements with respect to theological positions. Now, most people have either very little respect for theological analysis or very little patience for it, and the vast majority of those remaining are not adept at it. In addition, many people profess to believe things that they do not wholeheartedly believe. This is particularly true in the domain of religion, which is an important reason why religious undercommitment has always been, and will always be, most people's principal paradigm of hypocrisy.[80] Cognizance of this peculiar situation can pose motivational problems for someone confronted with ostensibly "spiritual" perspectives on technology and progress; it can be disconcerting to find oneself having to respond to aggressively articulated positions that one is convinced one's partner in dialogue does not really hold.

Antitechnologist Alan R. Drengson challenges those who see technology as capable of solving all the problems that it creates, and looks askance at the final state of the "technological fix," which is a matter of "applying technology to cure the problems of the lower levels of technology."[81] Troubled by what he sees as the mechanization of the self that has been developing in recent years as a result of the excessive emphasis placed on technology, Drengson insists that only a "spiritual discipline" can reverse this trend.[82] However, do we not need to worry also about the spiritual fix and about religion's capacity to solve all the problems that *it* has created?

Albert C. Leighton, who has written about the mule as a cultural invention, makes reference to a difficult situation in which the ancient Israelites found themselves: "The ancient Israelites were forbidden by law to breed mules. Their attitude is exemplified in Leviticus 19:19, 'Thou shalt not let thy cattle gender with a diverse kind.' Consequently, the Israelites had to obtain their mules from other peoples. Ezekiel 27:14 says that the best mules are obtained from Togarmah (Armenia or Cappadocia)."[83] This simple case study sheds light on some of the complex relations obtaining between religion, technology, and progress as well as on related issues concerning tradition, theology, adaptation, and hypocrisy.

Throughout the centuries, spiritual descendants of these ancient Israelites have with terrible frequency found themselves in the infinitely more difficult situation of having to witness sophisticated technologies being put to use to torture and murder their loved ones. When one speaks with certain survivors of the Holocaust, one cannot help but be intensely moved by their deep religious faith and their respect for the traditional ways of their spiritual ancestors; and when one speaks with some of these same survivors, and with other survivors as well, one may be overwhelmed by the fact that despite what they have been through, these people retain an abiding belief in human progress and perfectibility. One will also find that in spite of their direct experience with the technological horrors of concentration camps, many Holocaust survivors who believe in the possibility of social progress have considerably more confidence in technology than in religion, whether that religion be a religion of no personal relevance to them, the religion that could not save loved ones faithful to it, or the very strange religion of those who persecuted them and their loved ones—or condoned or excused the persecution—because of ancient religious hatreds.

NOTES

1. Aristotle, *Nicomachean Ethics* 1094a.
2. Ibid., 1095a.
3. Ibid. 1095a–1100a.
4. Ibid., 1176a–1179a.
5. See, for example, John Stuart Mill, *Utilitarianism* (1863).
6. See, for example, Friedrich Nietzsche, *Beyond Good and Evil* (1886).
7. Nicholas Rescher, "Technological Progress and Human Happiness," in *Unpopular Essays on Technological Progress* (Pittsburgh, Pa.: University of Pittsburgh Press, 1980), 5.
8. Ibid., pp. 4–5.
9. Ibid., p. 19.
10. Ibid.
11. Ibid., p. 21.
12. Ibid.
13. See, for example, Deuteronomy 11:1–32.
14. Cf. Jay Newman, *On Religious Freedom* (Ottawa: University of Ottawa Press, 1991), 7–18, 30–33.
15. Ibid., ch. 2–3.
16. Ibid., pp. 7–8.
17. Peter C. Hodgson, *New Birth of Freedom: A Theology of Bondage and Liberation* (Philadelphia: Fortress Press, 1976), 10.
18. Ibid., pp. 8–10.
19. Exodus 20:2. Cf. Newman, *On Religious Freedom*, 41–42.
20. Cf. D.S.L. Cardwell, *Turning Points in Western Technology: A Study of Technology, Science and History* (New York: Science History Publications, a division of Neale Watson Academic Publications, 1972), 1.
21. Ivan Illich, *Tools for Conviviality* (New York: Harper and Row, 1973), xxiv.
22. Ibid., p. 12.
23. Friedrich Georg Juenger [Jünger], *The Failure of Technology*, trans. not identified (Chicago: Henry Regnery, n.d.), 74.
24. Cardwell, *Turning Points in Western Technology*, 2.
25. J. Mark Thomas, "Are Science and Technology Quasi-Religions?" *Research in Philosophy and Technology* 10 (1990): 95.
26. Ibid., p. 101.
27. Carl Mitcham, *Thinking Through Technology: The Path between Engineering and Philosophy* (Chicago: University of Chicago Press, 1994), 6.
28. Richard A. Peterson, "Technology: Master, Servant, or Model for Human Dignity?" *The Philosophy Forum* 9, nos. 3–4 (1971): 209.
29. Emmanuel G. Mesthene, *Technological Change: Its Impact on Man and Society* (Cambridge, Mass.: Harvard University Press, 1970), 50.
30. John 8:32.

31. Terri Toles-Patkin, "The Imbecilization of Culture," *Bulletin of Science, Technology and Society* 8, no. 5 (1988): 519.

32. Ibid., pp. 519–23.

33. Ibid., p. 521.

34. See, for example, Plato, *Republic* 555b–562a.

35. Desiderius Erasmus, *Praise of Folly* (1511); Niccolò Machiavelli, *The Prince* (1515).

36. Benedict de Spinoza, *A Theologico-Political Treatise* (*Tractatus Theologico-Politicus*) (1670), trans. R.H.M. Elwes (1883) (New York: Dover, 1951), 216.

37. Lewis Mumford, *Art and Technics* (New York: Columbia University Press, 1952), 10.

38. Ibid., pp. 4–5.

39. Ibid., p. 4.

40. Ibid., p. 5.

41. Ibid., p. 4.

42. Cf. Mitcham, *Thinking Through Technology*, 284–85.

43. Cf. Francis Bacon, *The Advancement of Learning* (1605).

44. Hans Jonas, "Seventeenth Century and After: The Meaning of the Scientific and Technological Revolution," in *Philosophical Essays: From Ancient Creed to Technological Man* (Englewood Cliffs, N.J.: Prentice-Hall, 1974), 74.

45. Cf., for example, Marshall McLuhan, *Understanding Media: The Extensions of Man* (New York: New American Library, 1964), ch. 9 ("The Written Word: An Eye for an Ear"), 16 ("The Print: How to Dig It"), 18 ("The Printed Word: Architect of Nationalism").

46. Paul Levinson, "Information Technologies as Vehicles of Evolution," *Technology in Society* 6, no. 3 (1984): 203.

47. Pamela McCorduck, *The Universal Machine: Confessions of a Technological Optimist* (New York: McGraw-Hill, 1985), 21.

48. Ibid., p. 23.

49. Ibid., p. 20.

50. Leo Marx, "Technology and the Study of Man," in W. Roy Niblett, ed., *The Sciences, the Humanities, and the Technological Threat* (London: University of London Press, 1975), 4.

51. A. Sommerfelt, "Speech and Language," in Charles Singer, E. J. Holmyard and A. R. Hall, *A History of Technology*, Vol. 1: *From Early Times to the Fall of Ancient Empires* (Oxford: Clarendon Press, 1954), 102.

52. Cf. McCorduck, *The Universal Machine*, 26–28.

53. Cf. Mesthene, *Technological Change*, 26.

54. Theodore Roszak, *The Making of a Counter Culture: Reflections on the Technocratic Society and Its Youthful Opposition* (Garden City, N.Y.: Doubleday, 1968), 260.

55. See, for example, Roszak, *The Making of a Counter Culture*, p. 5.

56. Cf. Mario Bunge, "Can Science and Technology Be Held Responsible for Our Current Social Ills?" *Research in Philosophy and Technology* 7 (1984): 20.

57. Mumford, *Art and Technics*, 5.

58. Thorstein Veblen, *The Instinct of Workmanship* (1914) (New York: W. W. Norton, 1964), 37.

59. John Henry Newman, *An Essay in Aid of a Grammar of Assent* (1870) (Notre Dame, Ind.: University of Notre Dame Press, 1979), 53–54. Newman makes this point in the course of his discussion of "profession" as a "notional assent."

60. Ibid., p. 54. Cf. Jay Newman, *The Mental Philosophy of John Henry Newman* (Waterloo, Ont.: Wilfrid Laurier University Press, 1986), ch. 2, esp. pp. 48–58.

61. Cf. Jay Newman, *The Mental Philosophy of John Henry Newman*, ch. 1., esp. pp. 29–34.

62. Cf. Charles L. Stevenson, *Ethics and Language* (New Haven, Conn.: Yale University Press, 1944).

63. Milan Kundera, *The Book of Laughter and Forgetting* (Harmondsworth, England: Penguin, 1983), 235–36. Cf. David E. Cooper, "Technology: Liberation or Enslavement," in Roger Fellows, ed., *Philosophy and Technology*, Royal Institute of Philosophy Supplement, no. 38 (Cambridge: Cambridge University Press, 1995), 16.

64. E. F. Schumacher, *Small Is Beautiful* (New York: Harper and Row, 1973).

65. S. Lilley, *Men, Machines and History*, revised and enlarged ed. (New York: International Publishers, 1965), 324. The original passage is italicized.

66. Cf. Leo J. Moser, *The Technology Trap: Survival in a Man-Made Environment* (Chicago: Nelson-Hall, 1979), 209.

67. Ibid.

68. Steven L. Goldman, "Images of Technology in Popular Films: Discussion and Filmography," *Science, Technology, and Human Values* 14, no. 3 (1989): 275.

69. Ibid., p. 288.

70. Ibid., pp. 276–88.

71. Ibid., p. 276.

72. Rescher, "Technological Progress and Human Happiness," 19.

73. Mesthene, *Technological Change*, 33.

74. Robert Nisbet, *History of the Idea of Progress* (New York: Basic Books, 1980), 4.

75. Ibid., pp. 4–5. The original passage is italicized.

76. Ibid., pp. 13–21.

77. Lewis Mumford, *Technics and Civilization* (New York: Harcourt, Brace, 1934), 429.

78. Nisbet, *History of the Idea of Progress*, 357.

79. Mesthene, *Technological Change*, 62.

80. See Jay Newman, *Fanatics and Hypocrites* (Buffalo, N.Y.: Prometheus, 1986), esp. ch. 3.

81. Alan R. Drengson, "The Sacred and the Limits of the Technological Fix," *Zygon* 19 (1984): 271.

82. Ibid., p. 272.

83. Albert C. Leighton, "The Mule as a Cultural Invention," *Technology and Culture* 8 (1967): 46.

Technology as a Religious Endeavor

RECONCILING TECHNOLOGY AND RELIGION

There can be little doubt that most cultural critics and observers who have been called here by the name of *religious antitechnologists* would object to being classified as such. They would maintain that they fully appreciate the essential goodness of some technologies as well as certain positive aspects of technology per se. They might also contend that it is misleading to characterize them as primarily *opposing* something—technology—when they are placing emphasis, in a positive way, on spiritual or existential concerns, such as human freedom and dignity, whose importance they believe to have become somewhat obscured as a result of contemporary fascination with sophisticated forms of technology. However, while they qualify their criticism of technology in various ways, these cultural critics and observers are clearly concerned with *general* aspects and consequences of technology and not only with aspects and consequences of individual technologies; and they rarely even bother to pretend that they are offering a balanced appraisal of technology, for the tone (and not merely the conclusion) of their analysis of technology is decidedly negative. The label of "antitechnologist" may at times be severe, misleading, and perhaps rhetorically manipulative; but it usefully enables us to distinguish a certain type of critic or observer from other writers and speakers on technology and culture whose program is both narrower and less censorious.

Though the typical religious critic of technology devotes a great deal of attention to revealing and explaining ethical and social problems precipitated by technology, he is not merely a moralist or social reformer but a religionist who almost certainly believes that there is some close and significant connection between religion, morality, and social reform. A person's understanding of the relations between religion, morality, and social reform is influenced by any number of subjective factors; nevertheless, at least as far back as Plato's Socratic dialogue, the *Euthyphro*, wise thinkers have been able to make a forceful case for the position that religious reflection and moral reflection can be usefully separated on some level. Most religious critics of technology will grant this point, even while holding that the purely secular moralist or social reformer fails to appreciate important basic relations between religion, morality, and social reform. That they will grant the point is evident in part from the fact that they regularly criticize technology and technologies with arguments that are not overtly based on theological assumptions and are clearly meant to appeal to practical reason rather than religious piety. Still, the religious critic of technology rarely if ever sees his misgivings about technology as largely irrelevant to his religious commitment. Even when his argument is meant to appeal to a confirmed unbeliever, he almost surely remains convinced that his understanding of certain dangers posed by technology has something important to do with holding a religious, spiritual world view rather than a materialistic or nihilistic one. More often than not, religious antitechnology has an apologetic dimension and carries along with it the position, explicit or implicit, that contemporary technology-related crises are in great part the result of the loss of spiritual vision and the decline of traditional religious attitudes, values, and institutions in our culture.

We saw in Chapter 3 that technology's contribution to kinds of progress or amelioration of which we may reasonably expect most religionists to approve could well be far greater than the religious antitechnologist recognizes; and as technology contributes greatly to the enhancement of, say, types of freedom and knowledge that even the religious antitechnologist himself considers intrinsically valuable, the religious antitechnologist's case would appear to be fundamentally flawed. To the extent that technology contributes significantly to the realization of ideals that religion itself aims at realizing, technology would appear to be a collaborator of religion that is cooperating rather than competing with it.

However, on another level technology could now be seen as an even more dangerous cultural rival of religion, for the religionist might now have reason to worry about the practical cultural observer's concluding that technology may be an adequate *substitute* for religion. Technology's very success in contributing to the realization of ideals such as freedom, knowledge, happiness, and peace—ideals that most defenders of religion see as historically associated with the traditional ethicosocial program of religion—may lead the practical observer to believe that technology is a proper successor to religion. She may believe that religion is no longer as necessary as it once was, if indeed it has ever been as necessary as its defenders have assumed it to be.

The religious critic of technology need not adopt a utilitarian, pragmatist, or functionalist conception of religion. She may elect to emphasize aspects of religion other than religion's capacity to contribute to the realization of such ideals as freedom, knowledge, happiness, and peace. She may stress the importance of what she takes to be religious *truth* or the personal *salvation* that can only be attained by means of a religious commitment. If she emphasizes concerns such as religious truth and personal salvation, the apologetic value of her criticism of technology largely evaporates. Open-minded listeners will recognize that whatever arguments she offers concerning technology's interference with freedom and other lofty but temporal values are of secondary importance at most, insofar as the real issue at stake now is whether a particular religious position should be accepted because it is true or a particular religious faith should be adopted because it can bring salvation of a kind that goes beyond fulfilment in earthly life.

Still, it is not enough for us to criticize the religious antitechnologist's position by showing that technology contributes significantly to the realization of ideals with which the religious antitechnologist sees technology as interfering. Whether the particular religious antitechnologists to whom we are replying are explicit or not in acknowledging aspects of religion that are important in their own right—apart from their general ethicosocial value—we need to give some attention to the matter of how technology is related to religion itself and not just to values that it may share with religion. We could, of course, respond to religious antitechnology on this level by attempting to establish that religion is not as deserving of respect as the religious critic of technology contends (or assumes). Although such a response would be appropriate under certain circumstances, this inquiry is not a suitable place for it; the general assessment of religion, or even a particular religion, is a complex matter involving metaphysical, epistemological, mystical, historical, cultural, sociological, psychological, and ethical considerations. In any case, a more direct as well as more conciliatory response is to attempt to establish that technology is essentially *compatible* with traditional religion. We could then, if we wished, enhance our response by showing that in important ways technology is not merely compatible with traditional religion but is actually *useful* to it or even *required* by it. In showing that technology goes beyond being merely compatible with traditional religion, we would be showing that technology, in at least some of its forms, represents a kind of religious endeavor. That is the course that we shall now follow. Considering certain major paradigms of traditional religion, we shall reflect on ways in which technology can be seen to be at the very least compatible with the teachings and practices of those religions; and when appropriate, we shall reflect on ways in which technology can actually be construed, in keeping with the spirit of those faiths, as a kind of religious endeavor.

When we examine what would appear to be relevant passages of the sacred works of world religions, we often find that they are somewhat equivocal with respect to the matter at hand. When we examine what would appear to be relevant historical considerations, we find that they too are subject to various interpretations. Theological interpretation and historical interpretation involve many subjective factors. Hence, it would not be surprising to find a particular religious critic of technology—or any other particular individual, for that matter—to be thoroughly unconvinced by the points that will be raised in the remainder of the chapter. Moreover, I acknowledge that often it is not clear from the sources whether in a particular instance technology is being permitted, encouraged, or required. Nevertheless, the analysis that will now be presented, which is intended more as a specimen of a certain type of analysis than a definitive analysis, should enable us to move back at least a few more steps from the religious antitechnologist's austere position. More importantly, it should shed some light on the complex relations between religion and technology.

TECHNOLOGY AND RELIGION IN THE ANCIENT NEAR EAST

It would not be unreasonable for us to proceed directly to an examination of considerations related to the status of technology in the Western monotheistic tradition that is our basic concern in this study. However, it is useful to consider at least briefly the status of technology in some of the earliest known religions. These religions give us a special perspective on essential human nature; and just as Judaism exerted a major influence on the initial development of Christianity, Islam, and other world religions, Judaism itself was to some extent influenced by religious conceptions and religious tendencies that preceded it.

Philosopher James K. Feibleman, who is greatly impressed by the degree to which religion throughout history has been aided by technology,[1] has observed that "the accounts of the earliest religions show them to have been involved with technology."[2] Feibleman's use of the equivocal term *involved* is appropriate, for one should be exceptionally cautious in inter-preting the kind of evidence that is available in this area. "If the earliest remains are any testimony, then already with early man the burials were formal, and artifacts were essential ingredients in the practice of religion. The bodies had been decorated with red ochre and were protected inside caves by an arrangement of stones."[3] We cannot know with any certainty to what extent the technological procedures and products to which Feible-man is referring were required by religious practice, but they would seem to have been much more than merely permitted. We may also note that in our own time, many if not most of the people with whom we are personally acquainted, including confirmed unbelievers, still choose to have their loved ones receive a formal burial, and one in which stone and other artifacts are involved.

Feibleman tells us that "with the arrival of full-scale civilizations, technology continued to promote the cause of religion. The technology of writing, at first on stone . . . and later on slabs of clay in Sumeria and Ebla, and on strips of papyrus reed in Egypt, was responsible for holy books."[4] Feibleman's phrase "promote the cause of religion" should itself give religious antitechnologists an occasion for reconsideration of their posi-tion; but the salient point concerns the importance to religion of the technology of writing. We should not undervalue the oral tradition in religion, but even setting aside the consideration that speech and language can themselves be reasonably regarded as technologies,[5] we may fairly assume that most religious critics of technology would concede that the emergence of religious literature represented an enhancement rather than a diminution of religion. The advent of writing undoubtedly transformed ancient religions in many ways, but it also may have had a conservative effect. Thus, as noted in Chapter 3, the advent of writing "confirmed the power of the priests through the trained scribes."[6]

R. J. Forbes, a prominent historian of ancient technology, attaches great importance to the role of religion throughout history as a factor affecting the development of technology.[7] Forbes informs us that in both ancient Egypt and ancient Mesopotamia, the temple school, which provided the only institutional form of education, taught mathematics along with reli-gious mysteries.[8] Although the class of craftsmen and technologists quickly developed along separate lines from the scholarly, clerical caste,[9] the craftsmen and technologists, who must have been extremely skilled to have been able to produce such excellent work without the aid of sophisticated tools and machines,[10] would appear from ancient texts to have belonged to guilds that "were first of all religious organizations devoted to worship of the patron-god. Hence technical operations were still accompanied by religious rites and ceremonies."[11] Forbes also draws our attention to an example of the ancient relationship between religion and technology that is almost too obvious: "It was the religious beliefs of the Egyptians regarding the after-life which caused them to erect the monumental pyramids. The fact that the common people had to sacrifice their energies and labors for this kind of work tells us much about the role and position of the Pharaohs as god-king."[12]

The temple was an institution central to ancient Near Eastern civilizations, and its influence radiated out to all forms of culture within those civilizations. Given Jacques Ellul's association of the city with technology,[13] we should take special note of religion's role in the development of the first cities. Gordon Childe observes in this regard that at the heart of the urban revolution that transformed the ancient world was the emergence of the temple city in Sumer.[14] Although one could perhaps make a case for the position that the advent of cities in the ancient Near East had a negative impact upon religion, one could more easily argue that the city not only developed in accord with religious attitudes and priorities but contributed substantially to the institutionalization and promotion of the role of religion in social life as well as to the enhancement of religion as a form of experience and culture. In any event, technology, which made possible (and in turn was fostered by) urbanization, predates the advent of cities just as religion does. Ellul himself grants that technical activity is the "most primitive" human activity,[15] although he confuses the issue when he states that technique is "essentially Oriental" and first developed principally in the Near East.[16]

The Israelites' long captivity in Egypt obviously had an immense cultural influence upon them, and much of that influence has extended to modern Judaism. Seen from an anthropological perspective, Judaism can be understood as representing in large part the systematic rejection of ancient Egyptian conceptions and values, as, for example, Nietzsche's provocative observations on Judaism's distinctive "slave morality" indicate (despite verging on anti-Semitic caricature);[17] but the Israelites were also positively impressed by much that they encountered in Egypt. In no area is this more evident than in their fascination with technology—and with creativity, building, and the city. Ellul's characterization of this spiritually corruptive fascination also at times verges on anti-Semitic caricature.[18] Yet Ellul is right to direct our attention to a protechnological aspect of ancient Jewish culture, a dimension of the culture related to Israel's experiences in Egypt and one that is too often overlooked, in spite of its vivid embodiment in Hebrew Scripture. If we pay this dimension insufficient attention, we may leave ourselves vulnerable to accepting uncritically the view that the general attitude toward technology in Hebrew Scripture is encapsulated in its representation of labor as a curse.[19]

TORAH AND *TECHNE*

While holding that there are passages in Hebrew Scripture (such as the accounts of the transgressions of Adam and Eve and the builders of the Tower of Babel)[20] that manifest the persistent fear that human beings have of their urge to do more and know more,[21] Samuel C. Florman, who has little patience for the harangues of religious antitechnologists, is deeply impressed by what he takes to be the essentially positive attitude toward technology that is regularly revealed in Hebrew Scripture. Florman begins his brief but engaging survey of Scriptural texts by reminding us that in Hebrew Scripture, as in the Homeric epics of ancient Greece "we find ourselves in an ancient, barren landscape, where man-made objects are the subject of wonder and delight."[22] Florman points to the fond mention made in Hebrew Scripture of such technological products as vessels, couches, candlesticks, lamps, tents, robes, trumpets, harps, weapons, armor, anvils, and saws.[23] He points out that "buildings and cities were as important to the Hebrews as they were to the Greeks; the Bible is full of walls, towers, warehouses, palaces, and gates. The desert environment makes for a special attitude toward water; the references to fountains, pools, wells and gardens are wonderfully refreshing. Canals, irrigation ditches, and troughs for animals take on an aura of importance."[24] Florman also reminds us of the "love of materials" manifested in Hebrew Scripture, and he takes note of diverse materials mentioned therein, such as silver, precious stones, iron, cedar, olive wood, marble, and brick. Again, "the description of the building of Noah's ark is detailed and exact, and the specifications for building the tabernacle, and later for building and rebuilding the temple, are exquisitely precise, taking up several chapters at a stretch. An appetite for fine workmanship and beauty is evident in many passages."[25]

Florman does not pretend to be a theologian, but he understands what he has read in Hebrew Scripture well enough to be able to pronounce that

the awesome God of the Old Testament has instilled in men creative skills so that they can build his holy kingdom on earth. . . . The engineering impulse comes to man as a gift from God. Material enterprise is not to be shunned; it is to be pursued energetically with the service of God always kept uppermost in mind. The most worthy work is, of course, the building of tabernacles and temples and the bringing of offerings to the Lord. But technological effort directed toward prosperity for society is also considered worthy, if the prosperous society is to be devoted to virtuous purposes. Moses made it clear to the Israelites that they were being given a land of abundance.[26]

Florman's point is in fact endorsed by certain Christian theologians whose theological orientation is notably different from Ellul's. Bernard Morel, reflecting on key passages in the Book of Genesis, concludes that

man is not put upon earth simply in order to go on living, but in order to extend his power. . . . Human achievement is thus a sign of God's action in the world. Human information, or more accurately, the symbols through which this information is elaborated and communicated, have a religious significance. God takes human science and technology into account. He attaches a divine value to them in proportion as man is in his own image and likeness.[27]

In a similar vein, Egbert Schuurman writes that "too often it is forgotten that in the Bible technology, as in the building of Noah's ark, is a sign of salvation. The Bible teaches that God himself gives wisdom and insight to man for technology."[28] Schuurman,[29] as Florman does,[30] properly attaches great importance to the Torah's poignant description of the Divine inspiration of the great craftsmen, Bezaleel and Aholiab:

And the Lord spake unto Moses, saying, See, I have called by name Bezaleel the son of Uri, the son of Hur, of the tribe of Judah: And I have filled him with the spirit of God, in wisdom, and in understanding, and in knowledge, and in all manner of workmanship. To devise cunning works, to work in gold, and in silver, and in brass. And in cutting of stones, to set them, and in carving of timber, to work in all manner of workmanship. And I, behold, I have given with him Aholiab, the son of Ahisamach, of the tribe of Dan: and in the hearts of all that are wisehearted I have put wisdom, that they may make all that I have commanded thee.[31]

Furthermore, the serious student of Scriptural theology can hardly afford to overlook that large parts of Hebrew Scripture are given over to what amounts to detailed technological instruction, in which the children of Israel or particular Israelites are guided in exactly how to go about performing essential tasks, both sacramental and worldly. The reader of Hebrew Scripture is constantly reminded of the precision that one is obliged to bring to doing certain jobs and making certain objects. The Torah is often spontaneously associated by Jews and non-Jews alike with God's commandments and laws; but what is so often overlooked is the fact that the instruction provided in the Torah regularly takes the form of the master Creator-Craftsman's directing students and apprentices on how to perform tasks that for a variety of rather different reasons they find themselves required to perform. The Torah does not only legislate; it instructs. It shows those who will hearken to its teachings how to perform countless specific procedures, and of course, it provides general instruction on how to live life well in accordance with both natural desire and Divine purpose.

The Torah begins with the fundamental representation of God as Creator-Craftsman: "In the beginning God created the heaven and the earth."[32] The first chapter of Genesis gives an account of the Creator's crafting of light and firmament; dry land and seas; grass and fruit trees; heavenly bodies; every living creature that moves; and finally, the human being, created in God's "own image."[33] "And God saw every thing that he had made, and, behold, it was very good."[34] "And on the seventh day God ended his work which he had made; and he rested on the seventh day from all his work which he had made."[35] Scripture begins, conceptually and chronologically, with the representation of a Supreme Being that is not only supremely contemplative but supremely creative; and though it tells us that God rested on the seventh day, it makes clear that the Divine labor brought satisfaction to God, who reflected on the goodness of the Divine creation.

God is regularly characterized throughout Hebrew Scripture in terms of moral attributes, as in this awesome description at Exodus 34:6–7: "The Lord, The Lord God, merciful and gracious, longsuffering, and abundant in goodness and truth, Keeping mercy for thousands, forgiving iniquity and transgression and sin." But this image of a merciful and gracious God is not to be conceived apart from the image of God as the master Creator-Craftsman ever-concerned with the Divine creation, and most especially with that which has been created in God's own image. Thus, in one of the Books of the Prophets, a merciful Creator is heard chastising the petulant Jonah: "Thou hast had pity on the gourd, for the which thou hast not laboured, neither madest it grow; which came up in a night and perished in a night: And should not I spare Nineveh, that great city, wherein are more than sixscore thousand persons that cannot discern between their right hand and their left hand; and also much cattle?"[36]

As one reads through the Pentateuch, one encounters numerous instances of Divine instruction, many of which can be seen to be prototypes of much subsequent technological guidance. In certain unforgettable passages of the Torah, God's teaching is directly associated with God's craftsmanship. "And he gave unto Moses, when he had made an end of communing with him upon mount Sinai, two tables of testimony, tables of stone, written with the finger of God."[37] "And Moses turned, and went down from the mount, and the two tables of the testimony were in his hand:

the tables were written on both their sides; on the one side and on the other were they written. And the tables were the work of God, and the writing was the writing of God, graven upon the tables."[38]

In the Book of Exodus, there is an arresting juxtaposition of the Divine moral instruction epitomized by the giving of God's Ten Commandments with the lengthy and detailed technological instruction on the building of the Sanctuary. It is useful to contemplate the fact that what is conceivably the most powerful and most influential moral exhortation in world history is soon after followed by chapter after chapter of precise direction on how to make various objects of sacramental significance. The two forms of instruction have several features in common, but not the least important is their stress on doing what one is doing earnestly, carefully, and precisely. The emphasis on technological precision is evident in this representative passage from the Divine instruction on the proper crafting of the tabernacle curtains:

Moreover thou shalt make the tabernacle with ten curtains of fine twined linen, and blue, and purple, and scarlet: with cherubims of cunning work shalt thou make them. The length of one curtain shall be eight and twenty cubits, and the breadth of one curtain four cubits: and every one of the curtains shall have one measure. The five curtains shall be coupled together one to another; and other five curtains shall be coupled one to another. And thou shalt make loops of blue upon the edge of the one curtain from the selvedge in the coupling; and likewise shalt thou make in the uttermost edge of another curtain, in the coupling of the second. Fifty loops shalt thou make in the one curtain, and fifty loops shalt thou make in the edge of the curtain that is in the coupling of the second; that the loops may take hold one of another.[39]

We encounter passage after passage, page after page, and chapter after chapter of such technological instruction; and while being aware of the sacramental significance of the objects being described, we may also be struck by the sheer fascination with technology that the Supreme Being is conveying to humanity.

It is, to be sure, also noteworthy that the technological instruction in the second half of the Book of Exodus is temporarily but powerfully interrupted by the account of Israel's greatest apostasy, the crafting of the molten calf. Idolatry is the foremost Scriptural paradigm of technology gone wild; the making of a "graven image"[40] represents a rejection of God and of the spiritual context in which all human action and creation are ultimately to be rendered intelligible. Such overreaching technology represents not only vanity and infidelity in all their forms but the diminution of the essential dignity of human achievement:

And when the people saw that Moses delayed to come down out of the mount, the people gathered themselves together unto Aaron, and said unto him, Up, make us gods, which shall go before us; for as for this Moses, the man that brought us up out of the land of Egypt, we wot not what is become of him. And Aaron said unto them, Break off the golden earrings, which are in the ears of your wives, of your sons, and of your daughters, and bring them unto me. . . . And he received them at their hand, and fashioned it with a graving tool, after he had made it a molten calf: and they said, These be thy gods, O Israel, which brought thee up out of the land of Egypt.[41]

The great sin sinned by the people was a matter of their having transferred their reverence from God to an object of their own making. The idol is a product of human technology; and it indicates that human fascination with human powers and human creations has become so excessive that people believe that they can now do without the spiritual context in which human activity has hitherto been rendered meaningful. The religious antitechnologist is warranted in seeing any quasi-religious reverence for human powers and human creations as akin to the idolatry described at Exodus 32. This chapter of Scripture does demarcate certain bounds of acceptable technology. The amoral technician or any other human agent who has unlimited confidence in (or unlimited reliance upon) human creations is in a way rejecting God and vainly attempting to substitute human creations for God. However, the sin of the people described in Exodus 32 was an extremely specific and extremely grave one. It was not simply a matter of general fascination with technology. After Exodus 32, detailed technological instruction is resumed; and in the course of the Scriptural narrative, human creations again become the subject of wonder and delight.

JUDAISM AND TECHNOLOGY

Judaism, an ancient but living faith notable for both its rich tradition and its rich diversity, has continually confronted challenges posed by new technologies. It would not be entirely fair to reproach Christian theologians such as Ellul for concentrating almost exclusively on Hebrew Scripture in their approach to the distinctiveness of the culture of Jews and Judaism. However, those who are open to a broader, more sympathetic, and more accurate understanding of Jewish culture can see that Judaism's approach to technology has also been conditioned by rabbinic scholarship, Midrash and Talmud, Jewish philosophy, Jewish mysticism, and the historical circumstances of Jewish communities and the Jewish people. Of course, it has been greatly affected by alien cultural influences and by the new technologies themselves. Contemporary Jewish scholars and teachers must work as hard as ever at reconciling the demands of an authentic Judaism with the demands of the latest technologies. To an outsider, it might seem strange to see a Hasidic Jew in full beard and traditional garb being so comfortable with the most sophisticated computer or telecommunications technology. There is no idolatry here; Hasidim and other Orthodox Jews have never ignored the need for a modus vivendi between traditional ways and new technologies, although they have retained more respect for certain traditions than their theologically liberal brethren. Yet liberal as well as traditionalistic Jewish believers still regularly grapple with theological and practical problems precipitated by new technologies such as organ transplantation.

The Jews could not have survived as a people with a culture if they had not remained faithful to certain elements of the distinctive world view reflected in the spiritual teaching of the Torah; but even had they not been subjected to relentless persecution, they could not have survived as a people over the course of so many centuries had they not recognized the need for their culture to be adaptable to certain conditions of each successive phase of modernity. One cannot fully understand the relations of Judaism and technology without an appreciation of the basic importance of the conceptual framework established by the Torah, but neither can one fully understand them without taking into account post-Scriptural Jewish thought and experience, even though such thought and experience have been substantially shaped by that ancient framework.

David Novak helpfully draws the attention of students of religion and technology to one of the many famous disputes between the school of Rabbi Hillel and the school of Rabbi Shammai. This dispute centered on whether "vessels"—manufactured things, including machines—must cease working on the Sabbath. That the two great schools had to debate the issue is powerful evidence in its own right that Hebrew Scripture in itself does not provide all the insight necessary for a comprehensive Jewish theology of technology. In this case, as so often, mainstream Jewish tradition has sided with the plain good sense of the school of Hillel. It has acknowledged, in Novak's words, that "automatic technology need not be stopped for the Sabbath as long as it does not require human attention on the Sabbath, as long as it permits its makers and even its attendants to transcend it."[42] Obviously, this view has had momentous practical implications for observant Jews.

Mainstream Jewish theology enables its followers to take a more generous view of human accomplishments than does the kind of Christian theology that Ellul and others have embraced. Abba Hillel Silver, a Jewish scholar who has emphasized the distinctiveness of Judaism, points with characteristic directness to a crucial distinction between the two theologies: "The idea that man needs to be 'saved' either from the toils of life or from some Original Sin or from the prison house of matter . . . is not part of Judaism. . . . Nor does it [Judaism] accept the doctrine of man's corrupt origin."[43] Cognizant though they may be of the failings of human beings, committed Jews generally remain bewildered by, and unsympathetic to, the severe interpretation that Christian thinkers like Ellul place upon the passages in the Book of Genesis dealing with the "fall of man." Human beings and their works, as such, are simply not *offensive* to mainstream Jewish theologians in the fundamental way that they are to many Christian theologians.

Still, it would be misleading to characterize Judaism and Jewish culture as essentially protechnological. Even without dwelling on the lessons of the Tower of Babel and the molten calf, or the countless temptations to assimilation that their people have encountered, those endeavoring to be loyal to an ancient faith cannot help but be somewhat ambivalent with respect to much that is new and modern. Also, a certain condescension toward human creations is implicit in the importance that most world religions, including Judaism, attach to the superhuman or "transcendent" source and sanction of religious teaching. As important as prophets are in a prophetic religious tradition such as that of Judaism, they are seen by orthodox believers as intermediaries rather than creators, agents who have received revealed truth from on high and passed it on to humanity. However humanistic it may be in other ways, traditional Judaism is assuredly not humanistic in the sense of regarding human beings as the supreme authorities of the cosmos or the creators of the most important phenomena. Lest Jews forget that even the greatest of the prophets can at most *transmit* sacred wisdom, the Torah draws attention to Moses' grave error in the desert, the sin of not sanctifying God in the eyes of the children of Israel.[44] According to this understanding, human creations cannot be deserving of the highest reverence; recognizing the glory of the Torah or indeed any Divine creation requires a concomitant appreciation of the limitations of even the most magnificent human creations. In addition, as many other lofty religions and philosophies do, Judaism sharply contrasts the eternal and immutable with the ever-changing world of transient phenomena so vividly epitomized by the constant replacement of old technologies with new ones.

The matter at hand is not purely theological, however. When we move from theological considerations to anthropological and philosophical ones, we may well be struck by the problematic status of the Torah itself and of all the ostensibly sacred, revealed, and prophetical works of all world religions. Since the Enlightenment, and especially since the nineteenth century, it has become increasingly common for students of religion, including those who have a deep respect for the historical and continuing importance of religion as a form of experience and culture, to assume that the sacred works of all cultures are themselves essentially human creations. Conceived of in this way, sacred works are themselves cultural products, and they are also in a sense the result of a distinctive form of technology. In the last chapter of this inquiry, we shall give due consideration to the sense in which religion itself may properly be regarded as a kind of technology.

CHRISTIAN THEOLOGICAL PERSPECTIVES ON TECHNOLOGY

Christianity is in important ways an outgrowth of Judaism, and while it represents both a synthesis of Jewish and non-Jewish conceptions and a radical transmutation of some of those conceptions, most Christian theologians have in their general approach to technology remained fairly close to Christianity's Jewish roots. Christians take Hebrew Scripture to be the Old Testament of their Bible, and while they interpret Hebrew Scripture in terms of New Testament teaching, they often regard its outlook on issues as authoritative, particularly those issues on which the New Testament is silent or equivocal. Christian theologians concerned with technology routinely focus on passages in the Book of Genesis; the views of Morel and Schuurman may be recalled in this regard. In surveying Christian theological views on technology,[45] David J. Hawkin draws attention to relevant passages in Genesis and underscores the special importance of the verses beginning at Genesis 1:26:

And God said, Let us make man in our image, after our likeness: and let them have dominion over the fish of the sea, and over the fowl of the air, and over the cattle, and over all the earth, and over every creeping thing that creepeth upon the earth. So God created man in his own image, in the image of God created he him; male and female created he them. And God blessed them, and God said unto them, Be fruitful, and multiply, and replenish the earth, and subdue it: and have dominion over the fish of the sea, and over the fowl of the air, and over every living thing that moveth upon the earth.[46]

Hawkin tells us that "this text is by far the most important in the whole debate about the relation of technology to Christianity, for commentators almost universally take it to mean that God hands over his creation to the human being, who thus enters into a partnership with God and 'finishes' or 'completes' the work of creation."[47] Hawkin also takes note of the notorious complexity of interpreting this text.[48]

There are, nevertheless, distinctive features of the Christian tradition that have influenced Christian theological attitudes toward technology. One, Mumford points out, involves the role played by contempt for the body in preparing the way for the development of the machine.[49] There has never been anything corresponding to this phenomenon in mainstream Judaism. Another such feature, which we touched on earlier, is the historical influence of a new attitude toward labor in the medieval monasteries, an influence especially manifest in early Protestantism. The statutes of the monasteries often prescribed manual labor, which gradually came to acquire "religious significance and real dignity."[50] Later, "during the Reformation, work and the execution of vocational duties underwent a clear increase in valuation."[51] On the other side of the ledger must be entered, for example, the influence of the frequent anxiety and periodic paranoia of reactionary ecclesiastical leaders who have seen the emergence of new technologies as a threat to their temporal power. In the High Middle Ages, this temporal power reached a scale that could not have been conceived earlier. Although the temporal power of ecclesiastical leaders has generally waned since the pontificate of Innocent III, there is a recurrent nostalgia in certain ecclesiastical and political circles for the days when popes and bishops had the power to disrupt technological advancement at will for whatever motive. We may note, by way of example, that in our own time critics of the Roman Catholic hierarchy's action against contraceptive technologies regularly complain, occasionally with some degree of fairness, about self-serving ecclesiastical overreaching into the secular political domain. The fact remains, however, that in spite of the illiberal spirit of the Inquisition and the Index that has been apparent in the Roman Catholic hierarchy's responses to technological programs of various sorts, the church's overall attitude toward technology has never been essentially negative. Maxine Singer, who points to the church's historical ambivalence toward both science and technology, reminds us that the same church that dragged Galileo before its Inquisition is patron of the Pontifical Academy of Sciences, an institution that has had commendable predecessors.[52] Of course, the medieval church made an unparalleled contribution to the advancement of technology with its establishment of universities. When we think of the medieval universities, great faculties of theology and arts may immediately come to mind. Yet some of the earliest universities, particularly in Italy, were committed to ground-breaking research and training in medicine and other technical fields.

In Chapter 1, we noted in passing some prominent Christian thinkers who qualify in some sense as protechnological in their general outlook. The Jesuit theologian Wilhelm E. Fudpucker, who cites these thinkers in his own defense of technology, writes that "the idea that there is any inherent opposition between religion and technology founders on two brute facts: the historical reality that one particular religion, namely Christianity, has been the sponsor of modern technology; and the sociological truth that technology is creating a world which is manifestly more and more Christian."[53] Fudpucker is actually putting forward not "brute facts" but disputable empirical claims. The first would appear to undervalue, among other things, ecclesiastical antitechnological tendencies, technological underdevelopment in Latin America, and the congruence of a sociopolitical agenda for technological growth with certain traditional Chinese and Japanese religious world views. The second is even bolder in light of the widespread view of many Christians and non-Christians alike that the world is becoming less and less Christian with the passing of time. However, it is undoubtedly true that a notably high proportion of the modern world's technologically most advanced nations can be found in those parts of the world historically associated with Christendom. It is also true that the development and application of old and new technologies have in important ways, if not necessarily on balance, contributed to making the world "more Christian" in the sense of being closer to what the founders of Christianity wished it to become.

If Christian antitechnologists have trouble grasping this last point, that may be in part because of their attachment to arbitrary and misleading imagery. Anthropologist Margaret Mead, judging that "most young Americans tend to find absurd any attempt to juxtapose the historic Christian doctrine and our cybernetic age,"[54] suggests that

even today, most Christians find more vivid and appealing the image of the soup kitchen for the victims of poverty or earthquakes or floods or war than they do the plans made by the World Health Organization for the prevention of epidemics or by the Food and Agriculture Organization for an adequate world food supply. Christian compassion, on the part of the fortunate, and Christian resignation, on the part of victims of tribulation, still prevail as the true expressions of Christian giving.[55]

There may be some speculative overgeneralization in these comments, but Mead has put her finger on a crucial point. If Christians and other religionists have difficulty in appreciating the extent to which the development and application of technologies represent religious endeavors—or integral components of religious endeavors—that may be in part because spontaneous imagery has led to their uncritically retaining narrow paradigms of that in which religious endeavor consists. Other things being equal, Christians still have reason to admire the individual who is prepared to make personal sacrifices so that the poor can be served in soup kitchens. However, if Christians become so captivated by this image that it becomes their fundamental paradigm, they may lose sight of the religiousness of, say, those nutritional scientists, engineers, and bureaucrats whose Christian commitment manifests itself in facilitating the provision of food to thousands or millions in economically disadvantaged societies. The nutritional scientist's relationship with those that she serves may lack the personal contact that marks the relationship between the soup kitchen volunteer and those that he serves. But the fact that the nutritional scientist works in the background does not render her service any less valuable, any less noble, or any less religious; indeed, on one level, the fact that she remains unknown to those that she serves—people who probably do not even realize that they have a debt to nutritional scientists and other technologists—renders her Christian charity nobler than that of the volunteer who is at least present to witness a smile and receive a word of thanks.

Extending this point, we may consider that the religionist who does not take advantage of the most efficacious technology available may to some degree be morally and religiously irresponsible. I grant that we need to allow for subjective factors in judgment, existential aspects of commitment, and a wide range of individual differences. Nevertheless, there are many people who simply have not strived hard enough to cultivate those qualities— imaginativeness, adaptability, resourcefulness, courage, patience, and so on—necessary for determining what constitutes, and then doing, the best that they can do to serve their fellows in a particular context. Every day lives are lost and sufferings multiplied because people who are in a position to do great good *feel uncomfortable* with a certain technology and are unable or disinclined to exploit it at a critical moment.

When one clings uncritically to arbitrary images that result in certain narrow paradigms of religious giving and religious responsibility, it becomes difficult to see the efforts of professed believers participating in apparently ameliorative technological programs such as those identified by Mead as representing an authentically religious endeavor; but it also becomes difficult to see the Divine spirit at work in such efforts. One is then left with an especially troublesome version of an age-old theological problem. Most religious antitechnologists, concerned as they are with cultural criticism and cultural reform, are given to deploring the forsaking of God and to urging a return to God. Yet even those religious antitechnologists who have drifted toward determinism, or who for other reasons are reluctant to pass sweeping moral judgment on their fellows, tend to offer little in the way of explanation of the *withdrawal* of God. In a comprehensive analysis of some facet of the relationship between God and humanity, theologians almost inevitably find themselves obliged to address the problem of theodicy. The theological antitechnologist is confronted with the special problem of having to account for why God would allow individuals such as the compassionate, resourceful, and religiously committed nutritional scientist to carry on their work in the mistaken belief that their technological endeavor is morally and religiously sound.

It is unfair to demand of theological antitechnologists that they do a more satisfactory job than other theologians of handling the notoriously impenetrable problem of theodicy, and it is unrealistic to expect that they will be able to do so. However, by devaluing technological efforts and achievements, theological antitechnologists are passing up a precious opportunity to see the Divine spirit at work in the world. Some religious protechnologists have taken hold of that opportunity. Carl Mitcham, commenting on the protechnological outlook of the Roman Catholic engineer Friedrich Dessauer, notes that viewing technological invention and the technological transformation of the world as a participation in Divine creation provides Dessauer with a context within which the question of technological progress becomes one of theodicy.[56] A related view, and a very influential one, is that of the Roman Catholic scientist Pierre Teilhard de Chardin, who, in spite of his well-known difficulties with his ecclesiastical superiors, is properly regarded as an authentic Christian visionary and one of the most important Christian voices of this century. At the heart of Teilhard's vision is "a God who not only creates but animates and gives totality to a universe which he gathers to himself by means of all those forces which we group together under the name of evolution. Under the persistent pressure of Christian thought, the infinitely distressing vastness of the world is gradually converging upwards, to the point where it is transfigured into a focus of loving energy."[57] Technology's place in this evolution is significant. "[G]eneral technology is not merely a sum of commercial enterprises, a mechanical dead-weight on our shoulders, but rather the sum of processes combined reflectively in such a way as to preserve in men the state of consciousness which corresponds to our state of aggregation and conjunction."[58] Teilhard contends that through technology, evolution is "making a fresh bound" and "becoming reflective."[59]

The protechnological ardor of Christian thinkers like Teilhard, Dessauer, and Fudpucker pales beside that exhibited in John C. Kimball's 1869 tribute to machinery in the Unitarian *Christian Examiner*. Historian John F. Kasson tells us of Kimball's view that as inventors "endured their own metaphorical crucifixions," they "carried on the work of Jesus, who had himself been a mechanic as His Father was an inventor. In invention lay religion. The progress of technology and Christianity were inseparably linked."[60] There was indeed no doubt in Kimball's mind that machinery was a "gospel-worker."[61] Kimball's hyperbole is no less preposterous than that displayed in religious antitechnological diatribes, but if Kimball has lost all sense of proportion by concentrating on Jesus' importance as the prototypical inventor-mechanic, he has indirectly drawn our attention to some noteworthy attributes of Jesus. The Jesus that is encountered in Gospel is less a philosophical thinker given to abstract reflection than a practical moral teacher who does good deeds and performs miracles. Moreover, despite his learning and insight, he stands apart from the class of priests, scribes, and sages; the reaction that he elicits in this regard is striking:

And when the sabbath day was come, he began to teach in the synagogue: and many hearing him were astonished, saying, From whence hath this man these things? and what wisdom is this which is given unto him, that even such mighty works are wrought by his hands? Is not this the carpenter, the son of Mary, the brother of James, and Joses, and of Judah, and Simon? and are not his sisters here with us? And they were offended at him.[62]

Christian protechnologists can be heartened by the New Testament characterization of Jesus both as a carpenter and as one who impresses by his ability to fashion "mighty works" with his "hands" even while offending those who resent him as an upstart far removed, by vocation as well as social class and temperament, from the cultural elite of his people.

Though Christianity would thus appear to offer abundant opportunity for regarding a great deal of technology as religious enterprise, it also, as Judaism does, demarcates certain bounds of acceptable technology. A version of Hebrew Scripture has been incorporated into the Christian Bible (and actually makes up the larger part of that Bible), and thus the Torah's representation of idolatry as the principal paradigm of iniquitous technology maintains some of its basic force. In addition, for Christianity, any technological application that violates a central ethical principle of Hebrew Scriptural teaching is still to be seen as sinful. However, certain changes in emphasis are noteworthy. While idolatry is still perceived negatively in the New Testament,[63] it no longer is regarded therein with the deep abhorrence with which it is regarded in Hebrew Scripture. It is regarded as foolish but as a less appropriate object of criticism than, say, hypocrisy is. Furthermore, by concentrating on the *spirit* of the moral teaching of the Torah—and treating all of the Torah's commandments as instrumental in relation to love of God and love of one's neighbor[64]—the New Testament replaces the numerous specific prescriptions of Hebrew Scripture with a general exhortation to act on the basis of charity. These changes in emphasis, which are partly the consequence of classical Greek cultural influences, represent to some degree a reflection of Christianity's devaluation of the things of "this world," including material phenomena and earthly desire. With its soteriological emphasis, Christianity from one perspective can be seen as regarding technology, along with natural phenomena and all other things of "this world," as ultimately not particularly important. "Love not the world, neither the things that are in the world."[65] "For what is a man profited, if he shall gain the whole world, and lose his own soul? or what shall a man give in exchange for his soul?"[66] Christian antitechnologists are undoubtedly right to argue that the Christian world view requires one to fix one's attention on the realm of the spiritual; but Christian critics of technology tend to be arbitrarily selective in disparaging technology while being tolerant—and often approving—of so many other things of "this world." To the extent that its focus is on the spiritual, Christian teaching can hardly be seen as subordinating human creations to, specifically, the physical embodiment of the person or any other aspect of the natural world. Indeed, a Christian theological argument to establish the importance of respect for nature will of necessity have to rely largely on passages from the Old Testament.[67]

HAWKIN'S THEOLOGICAL CRITIQUE OF CHRISTIAN PROTECHNOLOGY

David Hawkin, in examining the relation of technology to Christianity, stresses the value of considering technology within the context of a general theological understanding of modernity. He obliquely acknowledges the protechnological implications of the sophisticated approaches to modernity taken by the Lutheran theologians Friedrich Gogarten[68] and Dietrich Bonhoeffer;[69] reminds us that the Bible may permit technology (and not discourage it) even if it does not encourage technology;[70] and observes that "a deterministic pessimism is simply not congruent with God's gift of freedom."[71] However, in the final analysis Hawkin sides with the religious antitechnologists. "Those Christians who believe that the ancient wisdom of Christianity is not fundamentally at odds with the assumptions of the technological enterprise would do well to ponder the sombre fears of Grant and Ellul."[72] In Hawkin's view, "our technological society is simply not in accord with Christian ideals of charity and justice,"[73] and "it is in the proliferation of nuclear weapons that we see most clearly the hallmark of our age."[74] Hawkin associates modern technology with the "liberal concept of freedom," which, along with its "concomitant values efficiency, mastery, and utility" has led to "economic inequality, pollution, and depersonalization."[75] He sees Christian theology as capable of helping us to achieve the radical change of attitude needed for reversing this trend.[76]

Hawkin is also critical of the view that the Bible encourages technology.[77] He sees the basic argument in defense of this position as "neatly summarized" by Harvey Cox in an article in which Cox maintains that "the cultural impact of biblical faith provides a necessary precondition for technology."[78] Hawkin concedes that Cox may be right in seeing the doctrine of creation in the Book of Genesis as having eliminated an important obstacle to technological development—the animistic conception of nature—but he questions Cox's assumption that there is a causal connection between the doctrine of creation and the rise of technology.[79] Surveying passages from the early chapters of Genesis, Hawkin challenges Cox's theological view that the Bible attributes special worth to human work, and he reminds us of the key passage in which labor is characterized as a curse.[80] While granting that Cox is justified in seeing the Bible's rejection of fatalistic and cyclical conceptions of history as imparting a distinctive meaningfulness to human action, Hawkin questions Cox's assumption that the Bible links humanity to God's creativity in such a way as to encourage technological development.[81] In criticizing this assumption, Hawkin suggests that it ignores the fact that the "real fruition" of technology has been "limited to the last few hundred years," that is, in the period after Christianity was "culturally dominant."[82]

Hawkin, a conscientious theological scholar who appreciates the need to offer his readers more than romantic wailings, understands that there is an important Christian protechnological outlook that the serious Christian critic of technology is obliged to confront. Hawkin does not take long to dismiss the "basic" religious protechnological argument that he sees, with some justification, as having been neatly summarized in Cox's article. Yet he wisely acknowledges that all that he can provide is a dissenting view.[83] He is clearly aware of subjective factors that influence theological interpretation, and he knows that standing behind Cox are powerful minds like Gogarten and Bonhoeffer whose earnest reflections are not to be taken lightly. In spite of his respect for Ellul, he makes a point of explicitly distancing himself from deterministic pessimism of the kind with which Ellul periodically flirts. It is instructive to consider how such a conscientious scholar can line up on the antitechnological side and find himself unable to conceive of technology as an authentically religious endeavor.

First there is the matter of Hawkin's concern with modernity. In placing so much emphasis on the importance of considering technology within the context of a general theological understanding of modernity, Hawkin is left undervaluing the importance of considering it within other contexts. As Ellul does, Hawkin sometimes makes an explicit distinction between "modern" technology and technology as such;[84] yet he also characterizes technology as the concrete manifestation of modernity,[85] and at times he makes broad observations about the technological "enterprise"[86] and technology itself. Thinking back to issues considered in earlier chapters, we can see that the concept of modernity is not as clear as Hawkin believes (and thinks that he has established),[87] and that the affinities between "modern" and earlier technologies are greater than Hawkin allows. In following Ellul and Grant in decrying the spiritual impoverishment of our "technological age,"[88] Hawkin loses sight of the sense in which every age is a technological age as well as being "modern" in relation to earlier ages. (Ironically, at one point Hawkin himself properly criticizes Cox for ignoring pre-Biblical technology.)[89] Besides, Christianity itself, like every other living religion, is not merely a repository of ancient wisdom but an institution that organically develops—in large measure because of its need to respond effectively to technological change and other aspects of each ensuing "modernity"—and even begets new world views, secular as well as religious.

When Hawkin makes the sweeping judgment that our society—"technological" or otherwise—is simply not in accord with Christian ideals of charity and justice, our first response should be that the matter at hand is not so "simple." Our second response might be that few if any societies have been in accord with those lofty Christian (and transcultural) ideals; and certainly the society of the High Middle Ages that Hawkin takes to be one in which Christianity was "culturally dominant" does not stand out for its realization of such ideals. There is, to be sure, much to deplore in our society, and we are all under some obligation to speak out against (and in other ways oppose) callousness and injustice in our society. Yet while I admit that on some days I am inclined to share Hawkin's negative appraisal of our society, the fact is that we have seen in recent years many remarkable advances in charity and justice. We may wonder whether Hawkin has given sufficient credit to, say, massive efforts to provide food, education, technology, and other aid to peoples in remote places whose misery has historically been ignored; participation in new forms of international organization devoted to the promotion of global peace, prosperity, and respect for the rule of law; bold and often successful attempts to combat entrenched varieties of racism, sexism, homophobia, exploitation of children, and kindred evils that until very recently were tolerated and frequently promoted by most leaders of world religions and their followers; and fruitful efforts to reduce colonialism and foster democracy in places where it has never existed. It may be that sometimes such endeavors have been possible *despite* the influence of corruptive technologies; and it is clear that some of these endeavors have had little to do with technology. Still, it is significant that it was possible for them to be undertaken, cultivated, and extended in our "technological society." Even more notable is the role that technology actually has played in some of them.

Here, of course, Mead's point about imagery may come to mind. Joseph Gremillion, a participant in a 1975 "interreligious peace colloquium," has written of the powerful impact made on him by a conference presentation by Norman Borlaug, who drew the attention of the audience to technological as well as ethical problems that need to be confronted in dealing with the global food crisis. Borlaug talked about priorities, but he also talked about the need to increase grain production and about the key importance of fertilizer.[90] Gremillion tells us that as he listened to Borlaug, he "saw that it is healthy for religious leaders to learn about the things of the world from lay experts of high competence. The striking lesson comes through that while feeding the hungry is a simple religious imperative, it is not a simple undertaking. Technology and economics, ideology and political will, inner motives, religious and cultural values, all enter it. It's a complex business, feeding the one human family."[91] Perhaps it is as complex in its own way to determine how much the work of people like Borlaug should count in an assessment of whether our "technological society" is in accord with Christian ideals of charity and justice. Mead's point may again come to mind when Hawkin announces that it is in the proliferation of nuclear weapons that we see most clearly the hallmark of our age. We do not all see the "hallmark" of our age as Hawkin and Ellul do, and many of us do not see our age as having any hallmark at all. No reasonable person would deny that the proliferation of nuclear weapons should be a public concern of the first order; and perhaps most people would grant that the proliferation of nuclear weapons is, like idolatry, a primary instance of technology gone wild. But Hawkin is surely wrong in believing that a nuclear weapon is clearly the principal paradigm of modern technology. If he took the trouble to ask around in the university cafeteria, church social hall, or local shopping mall, Hawkin would undoubtedly find that for many people the "hallmark" of our "technological age"—or rather, the principal paradigm of new technology in our society—is the computer, while for others it is the birth control pill. It would not be "clearly" unreasonable for people to point alternatively to, say, television, automobile travel, exploration in outer space, vaccination and the widespread elimination of infectious disease, or electric lighting.

Some of these technologies have notable religious applications or significance. For example, the computer and television have been effectively employed to disseminate the "good news" of Christianity and other religious teachings;[92] the Scriptural importance attached to the struggle against infectious disease is evident in several passages, most notably in the Torah's detailed instruction on the response to leprosy;[93] and the development of electric lighting may bring to mind the central importance of the invention of light in the doctrine of creation in the Book of Genesis.[94] The antitechnologist's fixation on nuclear weapons also calls for closer consideration. When Ellul first put forward his most influential antitechnological ideas, the threat to humanity posed by nuclear weapons loomed much larger in the consciousness of most people than it does today. Hawkin's analysis has been put forward over thirty years later, and much has changed since the 1950s, particularly in people's attitudes. We should never take lightly the threat posed by nuclear weapons, and I am prepared to grant that people generally should take that threat more seriously than they do. Still, there are all sorts of reasons why most people are not as obsessed with the nuclear threat as they once were (and as some antitechnologists still are). Though thousands upon thousands of people have been killed in countless wars, skirmishes, and terrorist attacks all over the globe since the end of World War II, a nuclear bomb has not been employed in warfare for over fifty years. In recent years we have seen great strides made in nuclear disarmament, the calming of relations between the nuclear superpowers, and the redirection of nuclear technology from military to peaceful applications. The fact is that most people in our society worry more about their car, television, or computer breaking down than about a nuclear bomb being detonated somewhere even accidentally. Perhaps they are being foolish and irresponsible, but maybe they are making a prudent and realistic assessment of their situation. Furthermore, the leader of the American people who sanctioned the use of nuclear weapons against the Japanese in World War II is remembered more fondly by most Americans (and many non-Americans) than most of his successors are. With respect to the religious dimension, it is worth remembering that during the Cold War, many people in the "free world" saw nuclear weapons as a defense against godless communism. Furthermore, the number of people who have died as a result of nuclear weapons is very small in comparison with the number who have died, even just in recent decades, because of ingrained religious hatreds.

Hawkin is not at all clear about what he means by the "liberal concept of freedom" or why he believes that it is closely tied to modern technology. However, it is surely a caricature of liberalism to associate it with efficiency, mastery, and utility rather than with, say, autonomy, individualism, and antiauthoritarianism;[95] and when Hawkin assigns the blame for economic inequality, pollution, and depersonalization to liberal conceptions, he is not so much a proponent of postliberal theology as a reactionary crank. He may be right in believing that a certain kind of Christian theology can help people to achieve the radical change of attitude needed for sociocultural reform, but it has usually been theological and political liberals, not conservatives, who have been at the forefront of our society's attacks on economic inequality, pollution, and depersonalization.

Hawkin makes some acute criticisms of the version of the "basic" religious protechnological argument that Cox offers in his article. He knows, however, that Cox has provided in this short piece what is at best a neat summary of a complex position. Despite his penchant for sensational overstatement, Cox is prepared to qualify some of his bolder claims just as Ellul is. Thus, in a more recent work Cox, though still critical of religious antitechnology,[96] predicts confidently that "the postmodern world will also be one in which the exaggerated claims made for science and technology will be modulated."[97] Hawkin also knows that theology, even at its most scholarly and most disciplined, is more a humanistic than a scientific form of inquiry, one that generates interpretations and perspectives of more or less value rather than definitive solutions to empirical problems. Hawkin's interpretation and perspective are valuable in part because they enable us to see that there is more to the relation of technology to Christianity than the ardent Christian protechnologist would have us believe. There is always a danger, however, that in advocating one's own interpretation one will misrepresent as well as undervalue alternative ones. In the article that Hawkin criticizes, Cox is not as careful as he could be, but he does touch upon issues that are worth considering more closely. Hawkin is right to observe that Christian protechnologists like Cox need to temper their enthusiasm when they speculate about certain "necessary preconditions" and "causal connections," but Hawkin is a sophisticated enough thinker to understand that the complexity of causation does not render it unreal.

THE ALLEGED RESPONSIBILITY OF WESTERN RELIGION FOR DESTRUCTIVE TECHNOLOGY

It is, in fact, a specific allegation with respect to the causal influence of Biblical faith in encouraging technology and a protechnological attitude that has probably elicited more controversy in recent years than any other academic thesis concerning the relations of religion and technology. I refer to the position of Lynn White, Jr., that mainstream Christianity, having promoted a world view that led to a certain technological thrust in the West, is largely responsible for the environmental crisis now facing humanity.[98] White concentrated on those passages in the Book of Genesis, alluded to earlier, in which man is seen as having been given "dominion" over the rest of Divine creation. White was not offering anything new when he argued that there is a causal relationship between the historically dominant Biblical world view and the development of a certain kind of protechnological agenda; as we have seen, this basic position goes back at least as far as Max Weber. But in addition to focusing attention on newly fashionable academic concerns about environmental ethics, White adopted a rather judgmental stance toward Holy Scripture that was bound to exhilarate many secularist scholars, offend many conservative religious scholars, and perturb many liberal religious scholars. Though White held that biblical faith is indeed protechnological, his argument could hardly give much comfort to religious protechnologists like Cox. On the other hand, despite his criticism of technology gone wild, White was undermining the position of religious antitechnologists like Ellul, for in White's view traditional Western religious faith was to be seen not as the cure for the technological sickness but as its principal cause.

Over twenty years after the publication of White's article, Frank R. Harrison III noted testily that White's view and similar views had come to "dominate discussions of technology and religion" and to "set the boundaries for both the types of questions that can be raised . . . [and] the permissible responses."[99] Harrison regretted this situation, which "distracts many thinkers from considering far deeper problems of which a multitude of religious and technological crises in the Western world are only symptomatic."[100] Ironically, Harrison then went on to offer his own critical analysis of the theses that he believed had already received too much attention.[101]

White's critics have undoubtedly been right to note that he is not an especially sophisticated theologian. White's views have come under attack not only by Christian theologians but by Jewish theologians, some of whom may have been upset by the earnest, well-meaning White's unintentional suggestion, little more than a generation after the promotion of Nazi ideology, that the Jewish world view had led to the pollution of the planet. In a fairly typical critical response to views like White's, the Jewish scholar Mark Swetlitz challenges the particular interpretation that advocates of such views have placed on the opening chapters of Genesis. He insists that these advocates have been wrong to infer that the world view promoted in these chapters "gives human beings the permission to plunder, without limit, the natural environment in order to satisfy human needs."[102] Swetlitz assures us that comments and reflections by Jewish scholars throughout Jewish history unequivocally reject such a reading of the Scriptural passages in question, and in fact emphasize the importance of respect for nature.[103]

It might well appear, however, that the main issue here is really historical rather than theological. Although he drifted somewhat imprudently into theological territory, White was basically reflecting as an academic historian. His primary concern was not what God or ancient prophets meant to teach but rather how generations of believers have acted on the basis of their interpretation of what they take to be Divine guidance. Hence, religious antitechnologists could conceivably look favorably upon White's analysis to the extent that it confirms their own suspicion that many believers, earnest or otherwise, have been careless in their interpretation of Scripture.

However, a genuine theological problem still arises. It would be bad form for someone like White to criticize God or great prophets for being morally shortsighted; but we are not really letting Judaism and Christianity off the hook when we attribute the contemporary environmental crisis and other crises resulting from technology gone wild to careless interpretation of Scripture. Judaism and Christianity are not simply to be understood in terms of what God and ancient prophets "really meant"; they are cultural phenomena, and in a sense technological phenomena, and they are in large measure—if not entirely—what human beings have made them. Moreover, the critic of these Western religions may well be moved to reflect, with Nietzsche, that the God of Jews and Christians "seems incapable of clear communication."[104] As almost every teacher and student realizes, being a competent teacher involves more than having insights worth conveying; it involves being able to communicate them clearly and effectively.

In any case, while theological and historical interpretations are not beyond criticism, they involve types of subjectivity that do not figure significantly in ordinary empirical judgment. Thus they are not so easily refuted. This point applies as much to a view like White's as it does to the view that White sees as having had such adverse consequences. Whatever the weaknesses in his argument, White has been helpful in focusing our attention on the possibility that at least one chain among the complex causal connections between Western monotheism and technology involves technology as a *deleterious* religious endeavor. To be able to grant even this possibility is to have access to a fresh perspective on certain limitations of both religious antitechnology and religious protechnology. Of course, the religious traditionalist may well want to conclude that all that is needed in the way of response is a more profound theological understanding of the relevant Scriptural passages. But a radical or adventurous mind may wonder whether Judaism and Christianity are worthy or even capable of rehabilitation.

In an essay that he came to reject because of its misunderstanding of what the technological society really is,[105] George Grant reflects that "there is need of a public religion, yet it is unclear what that public religion should be."[106] What candidates might a religious antitechnologist in the West be seriously prepared to consider? Seyyed Hossein Nasr speaks glowingly of the authentic Muslim's love of nature and Islam's conception of humanity's obligation to nurture and care for the ambience in which it plays the central role.[107] Nasr generally attributes technological abuses in the Islamic world to the corruptive influence of Western ideas and practices: "In fact, the Islamic world is not totally Islamic today, and much that is Islamic lies hidden behind the cover of Western cultural, scientific, and technological ideas and practices emulated and aped to various degrees of perfection, or rather one should say of imperfection, by Muslims during the past century and a half."[108] Probably a more promising candidate would be one of the Eastern religions, for as Harold Coward has observed, "Eastern traditions propose an intimate interconnectedness between humans and nature. They challenge the dominant Western view of a strong qualitative difference between humans on the one hand and animals and plants on the other."[109] Taoism might well be the prime candidate, with its emphasis on *wu-wei*, non-ego-centred behavior in harmony with the *tao*.[110] As David Kinsley observes, Taoist texts offer *wu-wei* as an alternative to the Confucian model that emphasizes the need to develop culture and impose a human order on the natural environment; for the Taoist, human nature and the world are "just fine" the way they are, and we should rejoice in them rather than seek to improve and develop them.[111] Taoists go well beyond Ellul in their disapproval of the complications and refinements of city life, and stress the importance of cultivating rapport with the nonhuman world.[112] Some critics of technology gone wild have turned with respectful interest to North American aboriginal religious perspectives, which, despite their differences, share "a belief in the environment as composed of different peoples manifesting the one divine spirit" and "a genuine respect for the welfare of all forms of nature within the environment."[113]

We have good reason to believe that such major religious antitechnologists as Nicolas Berdyaev, Emil Brunner, Gabriel Marcel, Eric Gill, Jacques

Ellul, and Dietrich von Hildebrand would not have endorsed the institutionalization of Islam, Taoism, or a North American aboriginal religion as the public religion of their society, even if they could have been persuaded—which is extremely unlikely—that such a move would stem the tide of dehumanization engendered by the technological "mentality." Though some of them were willing to say a kind word about a particular dimension of a faith very different from that of their ancestors, I doubt that any of them could be induced to abandon Christianity even on the level of personal commitment. Their confidence in Christianity can hardly be questioned. Thinking back to other religious critics of technology whose views we touched upon in Chapter 1—Langdon Gilkey, George Blair, Jean Ladrière, Brent Waters, Rudolf Allers, J. Mark Thomas, and David Schrader—we may reasonably speculate that most of them could not seriously entertain the possibility that the Christian faith is beyond rehabilitation. Indeed, even White's controversial article ends by holding up as an appropriate role model that venerated Christian figure, St. Francis.[114]

There are, of course, Christian communities whose aversion to modern technologies is manifested in their daily life. Not far from where I live in Ontario, members of Mennonite communities manage to get on with their lives without electricity or automobiles. The leading spokesmen for religious antitechnology may admire such people on some level, but for the most part they have not gone very far toward adopting the life-style of Mennonites. They have undoubtedly enjoyed their trips to the country, where they have been able to get away for a while from the daily stresses of their demanding academic and ecclesiastical vocations. But unlike my Mennonite neighbors, these antitechnologists have reconciled themselves to being at ease with refrigerators, radios, and taxis. That is not necessarily because they are undercommitted to their religious or antitechnological world view. The more germane consideration is that they are people who are not much confused about their religious identity; whether Orthodox, Roman Catholic, Lutheran, or Calvinist, they know where they stand, they know from whence they came, and they are pretty sure where it is that they will loyally remain. It is usually clear from their writings that if they have been prepared to countenance anything in the way of "public religion," it has been a religion compatible if not identical with their own. The speculations of Lynn White, Jr., or of sterner critics of the dominant traditional Western religious world view, cannot shake their conviction that the solution to the problem of dehumanization engendered by the technological mentality is to be found in a return to the faith of their ancestors.

Most of the enlightened religious thinkers of our day contend that what is needed for cultural reform is not a "public religion" that will inevitably degenerate into something repressive and dehumanizing; instead, a healthy pluralism in society would allow for the cooperation of earnest, intelligent, benevolent individuals committed to a wide range of world views, secular as well as religious. I can endorse this position even though I am mindful of how inconsistent it is with the traditional attitude of religionists that their own faith is the best faith and something that they should promote. We have reached a stage in the development of world religions and cultures when authentically religious individuals, committed to spiritual values, are more or less obliged to recognize that authentic faith brings with it the ability to respect what is noble in faiths very different from their own. Has the development of this understanding of the value of religious and cultural pluralism only been possible *despite* the processes of dehumanization at work in the "technological society"? Has it perhaps been possible in some measure because sophisticated communications technologies have allowed us to know our "neighbors" well enough to try to "love" them?

NOTES

1. James K. Feibleman, *Technology and Reality* (The Hague, The Netherlands: Martinus Nijhoff, 1982), 181–84.
2. Ibid., p. 181.
3. Ibid., pp. 181–82.
4. Ibid., p. 182.
5. See, for example, A. Sommerfelt, "Speech and Language," in Charles Singer, E. J. Holmyard and A. R. Hall, eds., *A History of Technology*, vol. 1: *From Early Times to the Fall of Ancient Empires* (Oxford: Clarendon Press, 1954), ch. 4.
6. Ibid., p. 102.
7. R. J. Forbes, "Mesopotamian and Egyptian Technology," in Melvin Kranzberg and Carroll W. Pursell, Jr., eds., *Technology in Western Civilization*, vol. 1: *The Emergence of Modern Industrial Society: Earliest Times to 1900* (New York: Oxford University Press, 1967), 45.
8. Ibid., p. 29.
9. Ibid.
10. Ibid., p. 44.
11. Ibid.
12. Ibid., pp. 45–46.
13. Jacques Ellul, *The Meaning of the City*, trans. Dennis Pardee (Grand Rapids, Mich.: William B. Eerdmans, 1970), esp. 1–146, 171.
14. Gordon Childe, "Early Forms of Society," in Charles Singer, E. J. Holmyard and A. R. Hall, eds., *A History of Technology*, vol. 1: *From Early Times to the Fall of Ancient Empires* (Oxford: Clarendon Press, 1954), 44–49.
15. Jacques Ellul, *The Technological Society* (1954), trans. John Wilkinson (New York: Knopf, 1964), 23.

16. Ibid., p. 27.

17. See, for example, Friedrich Nietzsche, *The Genealogy of Morals* (1887), Essay 1, sec. 7.

18. Cf. Ellul, *The Meaning of the City*, 23–146, esp. pp. 23–28.

19. Genesis 3:17–24. Cf., for example, Friedrich Rapp, *Analytical Philosophy of Technology*, trans. Stanley R. Carpenter and Theodor Langenbruch, Boston Studies in the Philosophy of Science, vol. 63 (Dordrecht, The Netherlands: D. Reidel, 1981), 95.

20. Genesis 11:1–9.

21. Samuel C. Florman, *The Existential Pleasures of Engineering* (New York: St. Martin's Press, 1976), 75.

22. Ibid., p. 110.

23. Ibid.

24. Ibid.

25. Ibid.

26. Ibid., pp. 111–12.

27. Bernard Morel, "Science and Technology in God's Design," in Hugh C. White, Jr., ed., *Christians in a Technological Era* (New York: Seabury Press, 1964), 87.

28. Egbert Schuurman, "A Christian Philosophical Perspective on Technology," in Carl Mitcham and Jim Grote, eds., *Theology and Technology: Essays in Christian Analysis and Exegesis* (Lanham, Md.: University Press of America, 1984), 113.

29. Ibid.

30. Florman, *The Existential Pleasures of Engineering*, 111–12.

31. Exodus 31:1–6.

32. Genesis 1:1.

33. Genesis 1:3–27.

34. Genesis 1:31.

35. Genesis 2:2.

36. Jonah 4:10–11.

37. Exodus 31:18.

38. Exodus 32:15–16.

39. Exodus 26:1–5.

40. Cf. Exodus 20:4.

41. Exodus 32:1–4.

42. David Novak, "Technology and Its Ultimate Threat: A Jewish Meditation," *Research in Philosophy and Technology* 10 (1990): 61.

43. Abba Hillel Silver, *Where Judaism Differed: An Inquiry Into the Distinctiveness of Judaism* (New York: Macmillan, 1956), 183.

44. Numbers 20:1–12.

45. David J. Hawkin, *Christ and Modernity: Christian Self-Understanding in a Technological Age*, SR Supplements vol. 17 (Waterloo, Ont.: Wilfrid Laurier University Press, 1985), 80–93, 106–16.

46. Genesis 1:26–28.

47. Hawkin, *Christ and Modernity*, 110.

48. Ibid., p. 111.

49. Lewis Mumford, *Technics and Civilization* (New York: Harcourt, Brace, 1934), 35.

50. Friedrich Klemm, *A History of Western Technology* (1954), trans. Dorothea Waley Singer (New York: Charles Scribner's Sons, 1959), 64.

51. Rapp, *Analytical Philosophy of Technology*, 95.

52. Maxine Singer, "Vatican City State: The Pontifical Academy of Sciences," *Technology in Society* 13, no. 4 (1991): 427–32.

53. Wilhelm E. Fudpucker, "Through Christian Technology to Technological Christianity," in Carl Mitcham and Jim Grote, *Theology and Technology: Essays in Christian Analysis and Exegesis* (Lanham, Md.: University Press of America, 1984), 53.

54. Margaret Mead, "Introduction," in Hugh C. White, Jr., ed., *Christians in a Technological Era* (New York: Seabury Press, 1964), 12.

55. Ibid., p. 14.

56. Carl Mitcham, *Thinking Through Technology: The Path between Engineering and Philosophy* (Chicago: University of Chicago Press, 1994), 110. Cf. Friedrich Dessauer, "Technology in Its Proper Sphere," a translation of an excerpt from Dessauer's *Philosophie der Technik* (Bonn, Germany: Friedrich Cohen Verlag, 1927) in Carl Mitcham and Robert Mackey, eds., *Philosophy of Technology: Readings in the Philosophical Problems of Technology* (New York: The Free Press, 1992), 317–34.

57. Pierre Teilhard de Chardin, "Reflections on Happiness" (1943), in *Toward the Future*, trans. René Hague (New York: Harcourt Brace Jovanovich, 1975), 127–28.

58. Pierre Teilhard de Chardin, "The Place of Technology in a General Biology of Mankind" (1947), in *Activation of Energy*, trans. René Hague (London: Collins, 1970), 159.

59. Ibid., p. 161.

60. John F. Kasson, *Civilizing the Machine: Technology and Republican Values in America, 1776–1900* (New York: Grossman Publishers, a division of the Viking Press, 1976), 153.

61. Ibid.

62. Mark 6:2–3. But cf. Matthew 13:55: "Is not this the carpenter's son?"

63. See, for example, 2 Corinthians 6:16.

64. Matthew 23:34–40. Cf. Leviticus 19:18, Deuteronomy 6:5.

65. 1 John 2:15.

66. Matthew 16:26.

67. Cf. Hawkin, *Christ and Modernity*, 115–16.

68. Hawkin, *Christ and Modernity*, 80–83. Cf. Friedrich Gogarten, *The Reality of Faith*, trans. Carl Michalson et al. (Philadelphia: Westminster, 1959).

69. Hawkin, *Christ and Modernity*, 84–85. Cf. Dietrich Bonhoeffer, *Letters and Papers From Prison* (London: S.C.M. Press, 1951).

70. Hawkin, *Christ and Modernity*, 116.

71. Ibid., p. 120.

72. Ibid. Cf. pp. 85–93.

73. Ibid., p. 119.

74. Ibid.

75. Ibid., p. 116.

76. Ibid.

77. Ibid., pp. 108–16.

78. Harvey Cox, "The Christian in a World of Technology," in Ian G. Barbour, ed., *Science and Religion: New Perspectives on the Dialogue* (New York: Harper and Row, 1968), p. 262. Cf. Hawkin, *Christ and Modernity*, 106.

79. Hawkin, *Christ and Modernity*, p. 106. Cf. Cox, "The Christian in a World of Technology," 262–63.

80. Hawkin, *Christ and Modernity*, 106–7. Cf. Cox, "The Christian in a World of Technology," 263–64.

81. Hawkin, *Christ and Modernity*, 107–8. Cf. Cox, "The Christian in a World of Technology," 264–65.

82. Hawkin, *Christ and Modernity*, 108.

83. Ibid., p. 116. Cf. p. 85.

84. Ibid., p. 116.

85. Ibid., p. 109.

86. Ibid., p. 116.

87. Ibid., pp. 94–95.

88. Ibid., pp. 117–20.

89. Ibid., pp. 106, 159.

90. Norman Borlaug, "Production and Technology," in Joseph Gremillion, ed., *Food/Energy and the Major Faiths* (Maryknoll, N.Y.: Orbis, 1977), 17–24. The volume is based on presentations to the First Interreligious Peace Colloquium in Bellagio, Italy, in 1975.

91. Joseph Gremillion, "The Facts of the Food/Energy Crisis" (Introduction to Session One), in Joseph Gremillion, ed., *Food/Energy and the Major Faiths*, 9.

92. Cf., for example, Jay Newman, *Religion vs. Television: Competitors in Cultural Context*, Media and Society Series (Westport, Conn.: Praeger, 1996), ch. 3.

93. Leviticus 13–14.

94. Genesis 1:3–4: "And God said, Let there be light: and there was light. And God saw the light, that it was good: and God divided the light from the darkness."

95. Cf., for example, Jay Newman, *On Religious Freedom* (Ottawa: University of Ottawa Press, 1991), ch. 5.

96. Harvey Cox, *Religion in the Secular City: Toward a Postmodern Theology* (New York: Simon and Schuster, 1984), 39–41.

97. Ibid., p. 189.

98. Lynn White, Jr., "The Historical Roots of Our Ecologic Crisis," *Science* 155 (1967): 1203–1207. See also Lynn White, Jr., *Medieval Religion and Technology: Collected Essays* (Berkeley: University of California Press, 1978).

99. Frank R. Harrison III, "The Judeo-Christian Tradition and Crises in Contemporary Technology," *Research in Philosophy and Technology* 10 (1990): 103.

100. Ibid.

101. Ibid., pp. 103–18.

102. Mark Swetlitz, "A Jewish Commentary on the Religious Origins of Technological Civilization," *Research in Philosophy and Technology* 6 (1983): 197–98.

103. Ibid., pp. 198–204. Cf. Katharine Temple, "Doubts Concerning the Religious Origins of Technological Civilization," *Research in Philosophy and Technology* 6 (1983): 190–92.

104. Friedrich Nietzsche, *Beyond Good and Evil* (1886), trans. Walter Kaufmann (New York: Vintage Books, 1966), sec. 53.

105. George Grant, *Technology and Empire* (Toronto: House of Anansi, 1969), 43.

106. George Grant, "Religion and the State," in *Technology and Empire* (Toronto: House of Anansi, 1969), 59.

107. Seyyed Hossein Nasr, "Islam and the Environmental Crisis," in Steven C. Rockefeller and John C. Elder, eds., *Spirit and Nature: Why the Environment Is a Religious Issue* (Boston: Beacon Press, 1992), 92. Cf. pp. 89–92.

108. Ibid., p. 87.

109. Harold Coward, "Religious Responsibility," in Harold Coward and Thomas Hurka, eds., *Ethics and Climate Change: The Greenhouse Effect* (Waterloo, Ont.: Wilfrid Laurier University Press, 1993), 48.

110. Ibid., pp. 54–57.

111. David Kinsley, *Ecology and Religion* (Englewood Cliffs, N.J.: Prentice-Hall, 1995), 80.

112. Ibid., 81.

113. Coward, "Religious Responsibility," 57. Cf., for example, Jerry Mander, *In the Absence of the Sacred: The Failure of Technology and the Survival of the Indian Nations* (San Francisco: Sierra Club Books, 1991).

114. White, "The Historical Roots of Our Ecologic Crisis," 1207.

Religion, Technology, and Culture

RELIGION AS A KIND OF TECHNOLOGY

It should be clear by now, if it was not from the start, that technology can be usefully viewed as "compatible" with religion by some significant criteria of compatibility. In fact, at least with regard to the forms of religion that are apt to be most familiar to most readers of this study, the term *compatible* does not do complete justice to the ways in which technology can be properly regarded as a genuine religious endeavor. Still, if we are to attain something that qualifies as a philosophical understanding of relations between religion and technology, we need to move on to a more abstract level of analysis. Given the point at which we find ourselves in the inquiry, we may conclude that the most prudent transition to this more abstract level of analysis would be to consider the reasonableness of regarding religion, at least in its most familiar forms, as itself a kind of technology.

Early in the inquiry, it was assumed that readers of this study have working conceptions of religion and technology based on their own experience and reflection. With respect to the idea of technology, it was necessary in time to proceed to conceptual clarification, which took up much of Chapter 2. No comparable clarification has been provided for the idea of religion; discussion of this notoriously complex idea would likely be superficial in a study of this size and scope and would probably be more of a distraction than an aid to understanding. In the course of discussing particular religious phenomena, I have tried to avoid the underhanded imposition of a dogmatic theory of the nature of religion. However, it may be impossible to avoid arbitrary presuppositions in such a discussion. Since more of these are surely on the way, I must beg your indulgence and ask that you make whatever allowances necessary in order for you to benefit from whatever is of value in the perspectives being recommended.

It undoubtedly would perplex most speakers of our language to hear religion characterized as a form of technology, and their perplexity can generally be explained in terms of the specific paradigms of religion and technology that these people have derived from images related to their personal experiences, conversations, reading, and so on. Accordingly, when a person has responded peevishly to the suggestion that religion can be usefully conceived of as a kind of technology with the blunt comment that "I can't see how praying for world peace is anything like playing a computer game," we need first to show him the limitations of his paradigms. We can then go further and show him that praying for world peace does in fact have important features in common with playing a computer game.

The idea that certain if not all religious phenomena can be helpfully regarded as technological or technical phenomena is at least implicit in various philosophical reflections on technology. For example, Alexander S. Kohanski in developing his philosophy of technology tells us that he understands by technology "not just the electric media of communication or highpowered instruments of production and distribution of material goods, but also all forms of social, political, even cultural and religious organized life, which are being administered by a variety of mental as well as physical contrivances."[1] Kohanski not only draws our attention to "techniques used in . . . the organization of religious institutions."[2] He reminds us that if we undervalue mental contrivances in relation to physical and material ones, we will be stuck with narrow paradigms of technology such as the electric communications media. James K. Feibleman points out that "both tools and skills are required for art, religion, and philosophy as much as for economics and politics,"[3] and José Ortega y Gasset, mindful of the preoccupation in the West with material technology, observes that "human life is not only a struggle with nature; it is also the struggle of man with his soul. What has Euramerica contributed to the techniques of the soul? Can it be that in this realm it is inferior to unfathomable Asia?"[4]

An awareness of the technological character of religious phenomena has sometimes been unintentionally conveyed in analyses that attempt to contrast religion with technology. Consider the contrast that Richard Deitrich, a devotee of Paul Tillich's theology of culture, sets up here between artifacts of technology and artifacts of religion:

The obvious artifacts of technology are tools, machines, electronic devices, etc.; the knowledge is scientific (i.e., derived by the scientific method); and the technique is utilization of causal relationships regarding energy and matter.

The obvious artifacts of religion are cathedrals, statuary, sacred books, etc.; the knowledge is non-scientific (i.e., instinctual, common-sensical, traditional, revealed, emotive, conscience-derived, etc.); and the technique is utilization of relationships not derived from energy nor inherent in matter.[5]

It is striking from the start that Deitrich associates religion as much as technology with "artifacts." (His doing so is all the more impressive when one bears in mind Carl Mitcham's carefully considered view that *technology* may best be defined as "the making and using of artifacts."[6]) However, almost everything Deitrich says can be interpreted in such a way that it undermines the very contrast that he is trying to establish. His paradigms of "artifacts of technology" are limited, but more importantly, the phenomena that he picks as his paradigms of "artifacts of religion" are themselves more obviously technological products than most other religious phenomena that he might have cited. When Deitrich writes of cathedrals and statuary, he unintentionally reminds us of Aristotle's two principal examples of products of *techne*: the products resulting from building[7] and sculpture.[8] Furthermore, the production of a cathedral or a statue may on several levels involve tools, machines, electronic devices, scientific knowledge, and utilization of causal relationships regarding energy and matter. (And the crafting or use of a simple tool may involve instinctual and traditional forms of understanding that are quite different from the "scientific method" as such.)

Deitrich's reference to the status of sacred books is even more revealing. In Chapter 3, we took note of the immense historical importance of the book as a technological product. The book, whether sacred or profane, developed from the germinal technologies of the spoken word and the written word;[9] combined with later technologies such as print and automation,[10] it took on whole new dimensions of cultural influence. While the emergence and evolution of the sacred book as a cultural phenomenon undoubtedly has much to do with instinctual, commonsensical, and traditional forms of cognition, as a book—in the most important senses of that term—it is at least as fittingly regarded as an "artifact of technology" as any machine or electronic device, and it can conceivably be regarded as the tool par excellence. Moreover, to fail completely to appreciate the scientific understanding that has gone into any book's "production"—on a number of conceptual levels—is to reveal oneself as bound to a puerile epistemology.

In the prophetic traditions of Western monotheistic faith, the sacred book is no mere *outgrowth* of "religion as such." It is close to the heart of those traditions. Sacred literature is also close to the heart of other long-established world religions. A sacred book is associated by believers with God's (or some other higher force's) preeminent communication with humanity; for them, it is revealed truth, revealed code, true prophecy, and the Word. To believers, their living faithfully by its teachings and directions is to some extent what fundamentally distinguishes them from savages, pagans, barbarians, secularists, and deluded people from strange cultures who naively believe that *their* religious community's special book is sacred. In our own society, familiar phrases have been institutionalized in everyday language: "The Good Book," "The Holy Book," "People of the Book," and so on. Even acerbic critics of the long-established world religions acknowledge the enormous cultural importance of so accessible a cultural, sociopolitical, intellectual, and psychological tool, one that has been used to create innumerable other tools. As for the answer to the question of who produced the sacred book and the higher cosmological truth and higher moral teaching that it communicates to humankind, for the believer, "It's in the Book," if perhaps in some arcane, mystical, symbolic way that defies explanation in the language of mere mortals. For the believer, the sacred book has marks of Divine inspiration, though its transcendent source may also be grasped by some other form of cognition. Some reflective people associated with a religious community may not be able to accept the idea that the sacred literature of their community has such a transcendent source; yet even they may want to be counted with the believers, and they will insist that this sacred literature is somehow special and different from "ordinary" human creations.

We need not dwell on the sacred book alone. Technology—the field of productive technique, skill, method, procedure, and the like—can be helpfully regarded as the context of every aspect of religion, for every aspect of religion is, at least when considered from a certain perspective, concerned with some form of production. If this production is not something physical or material, then it may be a condition, a state of affairs, or a way of understanding. A physician or amateur healer endeavors to make use of her practical knowledge to produce a state of health in her patient's body. Likewise a priest or lay religionist who prays for rain or world peace is concerned with correct application of those techniques and skills that will make his world better by some standard and will produce something that does not presently obtain. Those who pray, like those who heal, are no less drawing on art or technology—on *techne*—because their techniques and skills will not result in the production of something material like a book, statue, or building. In the New Testament, those who would learn how to live well and be saved come to Jesus the teacher in much the same spirit as those who would be healed come to the Jesus who makes the lame walk and the blind see:[11] "Lord, teach us to pray."[12]

There is, of course, a vast social scientific literature devoted to the analysis of religion as a form of culture and experience. When anthropologists, sociologists, and social psychologists explain religious phenomena, they are required by the nature of their enterprise to treat these phenomena as human creations, or at least to treat them only to the extent that they can be regarded as human creations. Though they must acknowledge the importance of the believer's sense of the sacred, holy, or transcendent, and may be believers themselves, as social scientists they must set aside any purely theological considerations and concentrate on the human origins and functions of religious phenomena. The believer would be right to argue that social scientific perspectives necessarily ignore aspects of religious phenomena that can only be grasped humanistically, phenomenologically, or through mystical and other forms of personal experience that are not social scientifically and behavioral scientifically accessible. But a reflective student of religious phenomena can also appreciate how much is lost when one dismisses as "irrelevant" the analyses of those religious studies scholars who follow in the rich intellectual tradition of Max Weber,[13] Emile Durkheim,[14] and Georg Simmel.[15] These scholars do not point specifically to the value of conceiving religious phenomena as technological products. Yet in their emphasis on the development of religious phenomena as human responses to human needs, they make such a conception easier to comprehend.[16] Philosophers of religion and culture, with a long tradition of speculative metaphysics behind them, may be more accommodating to theological considerations. They may also increasingly find it appropriate to emphasize the human origins of religion and the practical needs that religious phenomena have been created to address. This tendency has been most pronounced in the writings of humanistic pragmatists such as William James and F.C.S. Schiller.[17] It is also notable in the work of philosophers as remarkably diverse in their world view, methodology, and program as Hans Vaihinger,[18] Henri Bergson,[19] Miguel de Unamuno,[20] R. G. Collingwood,[21] Ernst Cassirer,[22] and Kai Nielsen.[23] The philosophical conception of religious phenomena as human creations representing responses to practical human needs can actually be traced throughout the history of philosophy to the ancients, probably most markedly in the speculations of various Sophists.[24]

Although numberless religious phenomena have literally been created by hand, or by mechanical extensions of the hand—and here all kinds of sacramental objects and relics come to mind as well as sacred books, statuary, and religious edifices—at least as interesting are those that have been created entirely by the brain, mind, or soul. The term *technology* often calls to mind the making of objects by means of the hands, but in technology the hands are at the service of the brain, mind, or soul. Having grasped that point, one should eventually be able to recognize that there are "artifacts," "tools," and other characteristic products of human activity that do not require the work of the hands at all. Yet given the paradigms and imagery to which one finds oneself bound, one may require considerable time to arrive at this recognition. The confusion that is possible in this regard is well illustrated by a couple of statements by Oswald Spengler, a highly eccentric philosopher of technology whose work is out of favor. With characteristic assertiveness, Spengler writes at one point, "What is man? And how did he come to be man? The answer is—through the genesis of the hand."[25] This provocative announcement is not quite compatible with the oracular insight with which Spengler had embarked on his philosophical approach to technology: "If, then, we would attach a significance to technics, we must start from the *soul*, and that alone."[26]

In Chapter 4, we took note of the memorable passages of the Torah in which it is described for us how the moral teaching of the Decalogue was physically as well as intellectually transmitted to the prophet who had been chosen by God to be the agent of his people and of all humanity. We observed that in these passages God's moral teaching, in the form of directions on how to lead the good life in communion with God and neighbor, is directly associated with God's craftsmanship. God is depicted here as the supremely creative figure, the Creator. God's creativity, too, is conceptually associated with God's craftsmanship. (Whatever God's ultimate purposes—which transcend all human powers of understanding— God has set for Himself certain standards: "And God saw every thing that he had made, and behold, it was very good."[27]) Now, according to Scripture, in transmitting the Decalogue God did not only speak to Moses and all Israel amid thunder and lightning. The commandments were written down for Moses and Israel with the "finger of God." Moses is depicted as physically carrying in his hand two stone tablets representing the "work of God," the "writing of God."[28] This Scriptural account of a key moment in the moral enlightenment of humanity is obviously of great theological and anthropological import, but it is also of philosophical interest.

Religious iconography, even in awkward Hollywood treatments, invariably captures at least some of the symbolic power of the account: the inspired Moses, "whom the Lord knew face to face,"[29] is depicted as coming down from Sinai not only with profound moral insights in his mind but with consecrated material objects of the highest order conceivable. The supreme splendor of the tablets has nothing to do with the material out of which they are made—stone—but is derived from the fact that they manifest in a very special way the personality of the Creator. Specifically, they manifest the wisdom and compassion of God who is providing a unique form of guidance to the creatures created in God's image so that they can freely realize a potential dignity that they have not been able to conceptualize "on their own." At their particular stage of moral and intellectual development, the Israelites, having only recently been freed from bondage, needed to be able to see with their own eyes what God had made for them with His own hand. It was not even enough for them to have heard the Divine Voice amid thunder and lightning. They needed to be brought to realize that God was not another tyrant who was out to browbeat them and bend them to His will. Rather He was the One who had fashioned for them a wondrous gift that would ameliorate their lives more than any other creation. They needed to be brought to grasp that these stone tablets that Moses brought down from Sinai were immeasurably greater than a golden calf, or all the gold in Egypt, or all the pyramids and other visible products of the world's most advanced and most awe-inspiring technology. What God had made for them was not simply some tablets of stone but a moral code that would free them from a bondage ultimately far more limiting than that which they had endured in the land of Egypt. This code was to be the instrument—the "tool"—by which they would rise from a condition of slavery to a condition of dignity, and by which all humanity would rise to a new order of civilization. The imagery of Divine technology is very rich here. To kings and pharaohs, these stone tablets would seem inconsequential in comparison with the precious metals and precious stones that filled their palaces and temples; but to the Israelites in the desert, these stone tablets that God had made for them were to be understood as vastly more precious than gold and emerald, for they represented God's direct teaching in the palpable form of a gift. God had made a code for His people and for humanity; God had fashioned for them, both as individuals and as a community, a new way of understanding themselves, and their destiny, and their relations with their fellow human beings; God had crafted for them a system of concepts and ideas that would transform their vision of their circumstances and would enable them to attain a dignity and meaningfulness in the cosmos that transcend pleasures, riches, and honors. God had not merely spoken to them, or commanded them; He had made something for them, something that would enable them to grasp what it really is in which the true greatness of a creation, of a product, consists.

The Israelites were thus led to understand better what the wisest among them already had come to realize; the "highest" creations, human or Divine, are not material at all. They are created by mind and only capable of being apprehended by mind. Even material products, from utensils to royal palaces, derive a special ontological status from the role played by the mind in conceiving them and bringing them into existence; but the greatest creations of all are those that can be apprehended by the mind alone. The Hebrew sages, like the greatest spiritual teachers of ancient Greece and ancient Asia, vividly conveyed to humanity some sense of the shallowness of materialism. Their God could not be visibly depicted in a drawing, painting, or statue. He could only be apprehended by the mind, although He was no mere abstraction.

One could, of course, carry this analysis further and see God—the idea of God—as the greatest product of ancient Jewish technology. The crafting and communicating of this idea, and of the complex network of metaphysical and moral ideas that it has brought with it, would clearly represent a *techne*, a knowledge of how to make things that has been vastly more influential than the technology that has resulted in pyramids or computer chips. The Egyptians and other great peoples of the ancient Near East all had their gods, but one may surmise that the ancient Jewish sages realized that it would not be enough merely to adapt earlier religious conceptions to accommodate the cultural needs of their people. What was needed, they may have sensed, was a commanding new vision,[30] at once simple and complex, concrete and abstract, particular and universal.

Many religious traditionalists, and some progressive religious thinkers as well, would disapprove of this layer of analysis. Yet it is quite compatible with the spirit of the utilitarian, pragmatist, functionalist approach to religion that is regarded as both reasonable and properly appreciative of religion in many of the most sophisticated intellectual circles, including theological ones. For those individuals who authentically believe that the human being was created by God in God's image, the position that God was created by human beings in a refined version of their own image will appear, if not outright blasphemous, then at least sadly indicative of the arrogance and narrowness of vision of a certain type of secular humanist. Those reactionary religious antitechnologists who are committed to a theology that systematically denigrates human accomplishments may be reminded of an old pattern: ingratitude and disloyalty to God, denial of God, and the illusion that mere mortals can make their own god. The molten calf and all other idols having proved to be wholly inefficacious, those scoffers who cannot bear to believe in God—and resent the faith of those who can believe—have an alternative strategy; they can say that

whatever religion has constructively accomplished is a result of the beneficent action in the world of the "God" that human beings *made* with their
own minds and their own language.

With regard to technology as such, a certain irony should not be lost on
us. We have seen that the sages of ancient Israel had an ambivalent attitude
toward human creations. That they markedly limited respect for those
creations is reflected to some extent in their refusal or inability to conceive—or to *admit* that they could conceive—of the core cultural force of
the Jewish religious tradition, the Torah, as the creation of mere mortals,
even mortals as wise as themselves or as wise as those symbolized in their
lore by Abraham and Moses. Whatever the ancient Jewish sages could
conceive, they must surely have believed that the stiffnecked rabble[31]
would settle for nothing less than a "revelation" from "above"; these slaves
and descendants of slaves would not put up for long with the teachings of
a moral philosopher turned moral legislator, but they might listen in time,
or at least from time to time, to the message of an inspired prophet. How
ironic it would be if the invocation of the superhuman and "transcendent,"
so intense an expression of lack of confidence in the ability of human beings
to create by themselves an adequate foundation for communal experience
and culture, were itself in the final analysis a particularly imposing indication of the ingenuity of human technology.

There is an attenuated variant of this analytical perspective that would
be acceptable to many religious traditionalists as well as many progressive
humanists and tough-minded social scientists. It could be plausibly argued
that it was not God, or the idea of God, that was the greatest product of
ancient Jewish technology but rather a way of understanding God, or at
the very least, a way of understanding "ultimate" reality. A world view, a
Weltanschauung, of this gravity and impact is a technological product to be
treated with great respect, regardless of whether or not God exists, or
whether or not it makes sense to think of God's existence or nonexistence
as something that can be "known." Even a traditional religious believer
may hold that while the ancient Israelites were themselves instruments in
the historical unfolding of God's plan for humanity, the noblest people
among them possessed intellectual, communicative, and artistic powers
rendering them uniquely suitable for the creative articulation of a way of
understanding that would serve untold generations of Jews and non-Jews
as an extraordinarily effective tool. This tool would enable them to organize
their experiences and to contribute to the meaningful realization of ideals
that they have sensed they cannot fully comprehend.

Despite all the antitechnological ranting about the culturally destructive values underlying technicism and the "technological society," the fact

remains that the values inherent in technologies are generally indicated by the roles that the technologies have been designed to perform. However, technologies can be put to uses for which they were not initially designed. That is one of the most important reasons why technology is such a progressive cultural force. Religion today still performs many of the roles that it performed in ancient times. However, it no longer performs certain roles that it once performed, and it now performs certain roles that it did not perform long ago. In this regard it is not so different from the simplest and most commonplace artifacts; but perhaps I am being misleading, for it may be more appropriate to regard religious phenomena in their most basic form *as* simple and commonplace artifacts. Every so often, people and peoples dramatically enhance them and put them to remarkable new uses. Yet these religious phenomena were performing vital roles in the age when flint arrowheads represented "state-of-the-art" technology in their own cultural sphere; and some of those roles they are still called upon to perform.

Of course, defenders and critics of particular religious phenomena, and of religion generally, are quite right to strive to make reasonable evaluations of their continuing (and historical) value; and even if it were not right, many of them would do it anyway. In any case, in explaining how religion and religious phenomena can be regarded as "technological," my aim has not been to reveal the most fundamental and most important truth about religion but to consider a type of perspective that contributes to our understanding and appreciation of both religion and technology and of some of their more abstract relations. Religion is a very complex form of experience and culture. To attain deep insight into its nature and importance, one would have to go well beyond regarding it as a kind of technology. Moreover, there are times in human affairs, both personal and communal, when it is prudent not to look very closely at religion but rather to accept it as we find it and to incorporate it into our reflection and our activity to whatever extent we conscientiously can. In this respect, religion is again much like other technologies. Michael Polanyi has offered the example of a tennis player, who should not look at the tennis racket when playing. Polanyi's lesson that "any skillful performance is paralyzed by attending focally to its tools"[32] applies to religion and religious phenomena just as much as to the tools that Polanyi actually had in mind.

THE COMMON FIELD OF RELIGION, CULTURE, AND TECHNOLOGY

Whatever value there may be in considering religion as, among many other things, a kind of technology, it is plain that talking about religion in this way will make most speakers of our language somewhat ill at ease. They may be prepared to concede, after reflection upon the themes outlined above, that there is a sense in which religion can be appropriately characterized in this way; but even then, given the paradigms and images that they are accustomed to associating with the terms *religion* and *technology*, they may still feel that to classify religion as a kind of technology is to "stretch a point" and to employ language in a misleading, manipulative, or cumbersome way. The paradigms and images that people ordinarily associate with terms in everyday language are to be treated with respect; they greatly influence our understanding and use of the terms, and language is, after all, primarily a means of communication.

One would generally encounter considerably less resistance to the assertion that religion is a form or aspect of culture. In many contexts in everyday language, the term *culture* is yet more equivocal than the terms *religion* and *technology*. In addition, some of the paradigms that many people in our society regularly associate with *culture*, such as watching a performance of a classical ballet, do not appear on the surface to have much more in common with religious rites than certain common technologies do. However, there are many people, especially university educated people, who regard it as "obvious" that religion is a form or aspect of culture.

In the last hundred years, most philosophers of culture and other humanistic cultural theorists, partly as a result of the influence of cultural anthropologists, have come to regard religion as one among several basic forms of culture. For example, in his *Essay on Man*, Cassirer has a chapter on myth and religion along with chapters on language, art, history, and science;[33] and in *Speculum Mentis*, Collingwood offers a chapter on religion to go along with chapters on art, science, history, and philosophy.[34] (We may note that in these two major works, technology is not considered as a distinct form of culture in its own right apart from its relation to art and science.) Yet this attitude toward religion, so common nowadays among both humanistic and social scientific scholars, and also to be found among many a woman and man "in the street," would have troubled the many people in earlier societies who took for granted the *priority* of religion, not so much in its relation to other "forms" of culture, but in relation to culture itself.

Even in recent years, those cultural theorists and cultural critics disturbed by the "decline" of religion in communal life have often been moved to observe either that religion is more central to culture than art, science, and other forms of culture are; that religion is the essence of culture; or that religion transcends and encompasses culture. Many of these observers are not entirely clear about the precise relations of religion, culture, and the various "forms" of culture, but they feel the need to express their conviction that religion should be treated as more than just one of several basic aspects of culture. For example, the reactionary poet T. S. Eliot insists that no culture can appear or develop except in relation to a religion.[35] He asks whether the culture and religion of a people "are not different aspects of the same thing: the culture being, essentially, the incarnation (so to speak) of the religion of a people."[36] While recognizing that people in modern Western societies tend to regard religion as only an aspect of life, Eliot suggests that there is at least a sense in which it would be fitting to regard a religion as the *whole* way of life of a people, a way of life that is also its culture.[37] Protestant theologian Paul Tillich, though critical of the tendency of many fellow theologians to depreciate culture in its secular forms, insists that "religion is not a special function of the human spirit."[38] Thus efforts to reduce religion to the status of a special sphere among others within culture have resulted in the "tragic estrangement of man's spiritual life from its own ground and depth."[39] In Tillich's view, "religion is the substance of culture, culture is the form of religion."[40] Although these remarks of Eliot and Tillich are rather vague and debatable, they express feelings and concerns that are undoubtedly shared by most religious antitechnologists and other religious cultural critics.

There are many activities in which we are regularly engaged that cannot sensibly be regarded as "religious," even if their precise character is to some extent the result of determining factors related to religious elements in their historical context. Watching a performance of a classical ballet, performing an experiment in a chemistry laboratory, participating in a debate about the company pension plan, and playing a card game may all have religious connections of one or another sort, and at times such connections may be significant, but it normally is fitting to categorize such activities as instances of secular rather than religious culture. As important as we may consider religion in our own lives or in our society in general, the vast majority of us would acknowledge that most activities in which human beings are engaged are not specifically religious in any but an extremely attenuated sense. Also, there have been many people, reflective and otherwise, who have held that religion, involving as it does irrational, prescientific, and superstitious modes of thinking, is on balance no longer a constructive form of culture, and that there should be continuing efforts to minimize its cultural influence.

One reason why disagreements about the precise relations of religion, culture, and the various "forms" of culture could never be satisfactorily resolved is that underlying them are even more fundamental disagreements about the nature of culture itself. In their detailed 1952 study of concepts and definitions of culture, the anthropologists A. L. Kroeber and Clyde Kluckhohn cited 164 definitions of *culture*, and they acknowledged that the list could go on considerably.[41] In the last decade or two, with cultural theory very much in academic fashion, new definitions of *culture* have been devised on a daily basis, and manipulative definitions of *culture* now seem to be flying across the scholarly and pseudoscholarly literature in all directions. All this is sufficiently discouraging to make one wonder whether the term can be usefully employed at all; but the fact that so many people feel the need to clarify or shape the concept of culture is itself a confirmation of the importance and irreplaceability of the concept.

For the record, we may note that Kroeber and Kluckhohn have provided their own "scientific" definition of *culture* as "a set of attributes and products of human societies, and therewith of mankind, which are extrasomatic and transmissible by mechanisms other than biological heredity, and are as essentially lacking in sub-human species as they are characteristic of the human species as it is aggregated in its societies."[42] This complex definition may irk or intimidate some readers accustomed to using the word *culture* regularly in nonscientific chat, and there are many contexts, particularly in humanistic discourse, when this definition would be misleading. Nevertheless, if one examines it phrase by phrase, one should be able to appreciate the earnest effort of the authors to be precise and comprehensive; and I have drawn attention to this particular definition partly out of respect for the work of dedicated scholars who took the trouble to draw up and reflect upon a catalog of 164 different definitions.

I shall not be contributing yet another definition to the list, but I cannot afford to be quite as evasive as I have been with respect to the terms *religion* and *technology*, for I need to propose certain things about culture in order to make my points about the relations of religion, technology, and culture; so I shall now indicate some features of culture that I deem to be of special relevance. Although they do not constitute a definition of *culture*, they offer a particular perspective on culture, and I shall try to present them as undogmatically as possible.

The basic feature of culture that should be of interest to us here is that it involves things that have been created and promoted by human beings in the expectation that those things may be appropriated or taken up by other human beings. The use here of the consummately vague term *things* is intentional, for I am not only thinking of ballets and religious rites but of political institutions, environmental conditions, and flint arrowheads. Cultural products, as the Kroeber-Kluckhohn definition neatly indicates, are normally contrasted with purely *natural* products. They are also normally contrasted with those human products that are not shared or expected to be shared by other people. Though the term *products* may immediately bring to mind material objects, I suggest that it is also proper according to the conventions of ordinary language to regard as cultural products all of the following: ideas and theories, modes of perception and action, techniques and methods, services, rites and customs, and institutions. These things are all "produced" in some sense by human beings, and they can be appropriated or taken up by other human beings in some way. The class of cultural products can thus be seen as including creations as diverse as those in the spheres of fine art, industrial art and technology, philosophical and historical explanation, religion, science, social work, politics, economics and business, and education.

The distinction between the cultural and the natural is crucial for our purposes. Granted, as Feibleman has observed, "What humans make is a rearrangement of nature, and so the artificial is not to be set off from the natural as though opposed to it but considered rather a special subdivision of it."[43] This subdivision is very special indeed, at least to human beings or to a Creator who fashioned them in His image. Consider in this regard the difference, for example, between an outcrop of stone and a statue made of stone.

Another feature of culture that is of interest to us here is that cultural products are normally intended as ameliorative. Anthropologists and other social scientists tend now to employ the term *culture* in a primarily descriptive way, but traditionally the term has typically had normative force, and it still carries that force in most humanistic discourse. *Culture* is derived from a French term that is in turn derived from the Latin *cultura*, a derivative of the term *cultus*, which was associated by the Romans with cultivation, particularly agriculture. According to humanistic scholar Giles Gunn,

From the beginning, culture has always been associated with processes of nurture. Deriving from the Latin word *cultura* (from the root *colere*, "to protect, cultivate, inhabit, or honor with worship") the earliest uses of culture always linked it to natural processes of tending and preservation. But by the early sixteenth century, cultural processes of natural preservation had been extended to human nurture, and before long were transferred from the particular domain of individual experience to the more abstract level of general or collective experience.[44]

We must not confuse the meaning of a term with its etymology or history, but there is a crucial point to be extracted from this analysis: there is a long and fundamental tradition of associating culture with human creations or products intended to nurture and ameliorate (rather than simply with human creations or products as such). According to this understanding, an authentic cultural product is normally created and subsequently promoted in order to improve in some sense both the condition or circumstances of its creator or promoter—whether that be a person or a group—and, more importantly, the condition or circumstances of other human beings for whose interests the creator or promoter has a specific concern. Culture in its primary and chief sense involves nurture of various kinds: cultivating, sustaining, caring for, looking after, bringing up, and so forth. By extension, it involves generally ameliorating the condition or circumstances of fellow human beings by making available to them a wide variety of creations or products—only some of which are material objects—that when appropriated or taken up will enhance the quality of their lives.

The historical association of culture with human creations produced in the course of efforts at amelioration is evident in many definitions of *culture*. A typical example of this normative conception of culture is F. R. Cowell's definition of *culture* as "that which, being transmitted orally by tradition and objectively through writing and other means of expression, enhances the quality of life with meaning and value by making possible the formulation, progressive realization, appreciation and the achievement of truth, beauty, and moral worth."[45] Perhaps more impressive because of its conciseness and longevity is a 1791 dictionary definition of *culture* as "the art of improvement and melioration."[46] There are numerous definitions of *culture*, of course, that focus on other aspects of culture; and as was noted above, social scientific definitions of *culture* have tended to be primarily descriptive. So for example, *culture* is now often employed by social scientists (and those influenced by them) to refer simply to the distinctive way of life of a particular community or people. Still, Kroeber and Kluckhohn, though themselves anthropologists who for their own vocational purposes settle upon a "scientific" definition of *culture*, acknowledge that the term *culture* not only began by definitely containing the idea of betterment or improvement but still retains this meaning today in many usages, both popular and intellectual.[47]

What has just been said about certain salient features of culture according to a traditional understanding of the phenomenon may seem trivial and obvious, or doctrinaire and manipulative, or just plain obscure. Yet one may find it easier to catch the drift of this analysis when we move on now to consider the relation of technology to culture. It should not be hard to understand why so many scholars and casual observers find it fitting to regard technology as one more among several basic forms of culture. Technology has not, over the centuries, received the same degree of attention from philosophers of culture that religion, fine art, science, philosophy, and other forms of culture have received. One may well be struck by the fact that major philosophers of culture such as Dilthey and Nietzsche have not taken it seriously as a subject for detailed discussion.[48] Still, perhaps again partly as a result of the influence of cultural anthropologists, it has been much more common in recent years for philosophers of culture and other cultural theorists to take for granted technology's important place alongside other forms of culture that ordinarily come more quickly to mind. Here one may think back to some of the recent literature on philosophy of technology surveyed in Chapter 2.

However, it is indeed interesting that there has arisen in the philosophical and semi-philosophical literature on technology a disagreement about the *priority* of technology that directly parallels the disagreement about the priority of religion that we considered above. At the very outset of our investigation, we considered certain statements by important philosophers of culture that express the view that technology is in a sense more important and more fundamental than other forms of culture. You may recall Veblen's contention that in the growth and current maintenance of culture, the facts of technological use are "fundamental and definitive";[49] and Ortega y Gasset, you may remember, was convinced that "man begins where technology begins."[50] Certain protechnological authors that we have considered almost seem to be saying at times that technology rather than religion is the "essence" of culture, or even that technology transcends and encompasses culture. There would appear to be virtually no limit to the assertions that might be made for technology vis-à-vis culture, at least if we are to judge by these extraordinary speculations by Willem H. Vanderburg:

Technology is often thought of as a means to accomplish human ends. Although obviously true to some extent, this is only part of the picture. Technologies and techniques also mediate relationships, thus constituting intermediaries between human beings, or between them and anything in their environment. This reduces the role of traditional culture and helps to illuminate how Technique can come to replace or supersede culture as the foundation of social ecology.[51]

Bold claims made for technology vis-à-vis culture have been duly noted by critics. Philosopher Joseph Margolis feels it necessary to remind us that "culture is both the context of technology and the genus of which the technological cannot be more than a determinate species."[52] There is no theme more central to Lewis Mumford's vast corpus of writings on "technics" than his repeated contention that it has been a grave mistake of cultural theorists to overemphasize the temporal and conceptual priority of the human being as toolmaker at the expense of the fundamental importance of the human being as nontechnical symbol-maker.[53]

But how justified can it be to exclude symbol-making from the field of "technics" or technology when human beings *make* symbol systems just as they make flint arrowheads? Was there not real value in the typology of the classical Greek philosophers of culture that treated all forms of *techne*, from the most symbolic works of fine art to the most utilitarian works of industrial art, as having enough in common to be usefully subsumed under the same category of intellectual virtue? Is there not a sense in which technology and culture are basically the same phenomenon?

Granted, the terms *technology* and *culture* are not interchangeable in everyday discourse or even in most humanistic and scientific discourse; and most people's paradigms of technology are plainly quite different from their paradigms of culture. Yet both technology and culture can be understood as ameliorative human production. They both represent the intelligent, disciplined effort of human beings, individually and in groups, to create, promote, and take up "things" that will not only improve the immediate condition of those involved on some level in the employment of those "things" but will also be capable—in at least an abstract sense—of ameliorating the condition of others, including descendants and other people in future generations. As for religion, though it may helpfully be conceived as either a form of technology or a form of culture, it can also be helpfully conceived as a systematic and comprehensive effort to ameliorate the human condition. As such it has something very fundamental in common with both technology and culture. Depending on how much one is intellectually and temperamentally inclined to expand or contract one's particular concepts of technology, culture, and religion, one may regard any of the three concepts as the most general and inclusive.

The particular concept among the three that one happens to regard as most general and inclusive is probably for most people a consequence of determining factors of whose relevance they are hardly aware: how they were educated, how important religion and technology were to them when they were impressionable young children, mass media influences, and so forth. However, for some people there are definite agendas at work here. For example, the professional cultural anthropologist or the poet or dramatist who is a confirmed atheist has committed herself to a world view and a mission in life that make it more difficult for her to regard culture as an aspect of religion than if she believed in a higher power. In contrast, a conservative religionist worried about the "decline" of religion in communal life has already invested a great deal of emotional cash in the view that religion is not just one of several aspects of culture alongside of technology, philosophy, and the like. The Victorian theologian J. C. Shairp, though he admired Matthew Arnold's prominent efforts to promote "culture," found it impossible for a man in his position to abide Arnold's having deprived religion of its priority: "[A]ssigning to religion a secondary, however important, place, this theory, as I conceive, if consistently acted on, would annihilate religion."[54] The applied scientist who is not given to much abstract reflection on religion or culture may seem rather noncommittal with respect to these issues of priority and generality. Yet when he has to compete for government or university research funds, his talk about the necessity of weighing the value of research endeavors by the ultimate criterion of "practical importance in everyday life" will reveal that this unwitting disciple of Herbert Spencer or John Dewey is able to summon up the requisite self-confidence. In his own way he has managed to convince himself that religious and cultural endeavors are in the last analysis merely secondary technologies.

In one of those quaint half-truths for which his bigoted critic, Charles Kingsley, made him legendary, John Henry Newman writes in *The Idea of a University* that a university is an institution in which an "assemblage of learned men, zealous for their own sciences, and rivals of each other, are brought, by familiar intercourse and for the sake of intellectual peace, to adjust together the claims and relations of their respective subjects of investigation."[55] Newman knew better. He realized that the university is in some ways a microcosm of society—or of "culture," as some would say—and that religionists must struggle there, as in the society at large, against those forces that would increase the influence of secular interests at the expense of traditional religious interests. Newman was convinced that many promoters of secular learning—including the applied sciences— are allies, intentional or not, of the "liberal" social reformers who are bent on subverting the influence of religion in university life and social life generally. He was quite explicit in making this point in his notoriously reactionary 1841 article in *The Times* in which he attacked Lord Brougham and Sir Robert Peel for promoting secular education.[56] When Newman went off to found his own Catholic university in Ireland, he made it crystal clear to the applied scientists there that the work that they were doing was *conceptually* subordinate as well as practically and administratively subordinate to the religious work of churchmen. The historian can see here what would later become a pattern in a basic kind of religious antitechnological argument.[57]

As a warrior in the struggle of religious traditionalists against the encroaching forces of secularist "liberalism," Cardinal Newman was not the sort of person who "for the sake of intellectual peace" would be prepared to sacrifice the principle of the sociocultural priority of religion. Compared to this ardent Victorian apologist, Christian antisecularists of our own century like Berdyaev and Ellul seem almost permissive. Nonetheless, Newman's talk about the peaceful adjustment of claims and relations invites consideration of the possibility that those cultural observers who are not tied to such specific agendas as those of Newman or the antireligious materialist (for example, the Marxist or Freudian) might be prepared to accept religion and technology—and perhaps culture itself—as equally fundamental phenomena, without one of them having to be conceded a conceptual priority. Perhaps many cultural observers and cultural critics, including those who are proreligious and protechnological, could even be brought to conceive of religion, technology, and culture as distinct but compatible ways of understanding the same essential phenomenon—the effort of human beings to ameliorate their condition, and that of fellow human beings, by means of the production or creation of things that they earnestly believe will make people better and better off. Like the expressions "evening star" and "morning star" in Gottlob Frege's famous example, "religion," "technology," and "culture" could then be regarded as referring to the same designated object but as having different senses. There would still be considerable scope for making distinctions in emphasis in accordance with popular usage; but there would also be new insight into the arbitrariness of popular usage.

For example, it might reasonably be argued that in much popular usage the terms *culture* and *religion* suggest the relative permanence of socially appropriated human creations, while the term *technology* suggests the relative transience of socially appropriated human creations. It is certainly the case that people talk about "the latest technology" in a way that they would not talk about "the latest culture" or "the latest religion." But we can see on reflection that technology is in fact not as transient as people so often assume; automobiles have replaced horse-drawn carriages, but we are still using fire to cook meat. Similarly, much common talk about "the Christian religion" obscures significant differences between early Christianity and the Christianity of our own day, as much common talk about "English culture" obscures major differences between the societies of Elizabeth I and Elizabeth II. It almost goes without saying that religion and culture can be progressive while technology can be conservative; but appreciating what religion, technology, and culture have in common may help us to get beyond those habits of popular usage that lead us to accept uncritically the association of religion and culture with the old and backward-looking and of technology with the new and forward-looking.

When we take the broad view of technology and religion indicated above, we are treating them not as forms or aspects of culture—alongside philosophy, science, history, and the like—but rather as the field of culture itself. What philosophers, scientists, and historians *produce* are themselves cultural products. In this sense, the creation of a philosophical, scientific, or historical treatise can itself be regarded as a technological endeavor—a matter of knowing how to make such a thing—or as a religious endeavor—performing a role that, whether or not one is aware of it, is ultimately meaningful only because of an underlying prerational commitment to a world view that allows for the meaningfulness of human endeavors. As important as philosophy, science, history, and the fine arts are in their own right, it would not make much sense to regard any of them as the field of culture itself; the fine arts represent a particular type of *techne*, and philosophy and science, as the classical Greek philosophers observed, are not *essentially* concerned with production or making at all; they are primarily forms of experience or understanding, as is history, too. It could be argued that religion is also essentially a form of experience or understanding, but such a position would undervalue the historical association of religion with the direct practical consequences of faith. Faith commitment *requires* a kind of productive activity in much the same way as a commitment to art does. Thus, it is important here not only to recognize certain close relations between religion, technology, and culture, but also to recognize that comparable relations do not hold between any of them and other familiar forms and aspects of experience and culture.

Even if one is not prepared to regard religion as a kind of technology, or technology as a religious endeavor, one ought to remain open to an appreciation of features that religion and technology share with each other and do not share with other forms and aspects of culture. For example, the dehumanization associated by critics of certain technologies with technological mechanization and automation significantly parallels the dehumanization associated by critics of certain religious institutions with arid ritualism. One would have to stretch one's analogy quite a bit to find anything comparable with respect to other familiar forms or aspects of culture. Again, recent criticism of technocracy directly parallels much traditional criticism of theocracy, whereas it is virtually inconceivable that a state could come to be dominated by scientists, historians, poets, or even (as Plato himself concedes)[58] philosopher-kings.

This final analysis of relations between religion and technology (and of their common relation to culture), focusing as it does almost entirely on abstract concepts, is sufficiently abstruse to invite the suspicion that it has little to do with the more practical concerns that were at least touched upon earlier in the inquiry. Such a suspicion is justified in part; and whenever an attempt is made to consider at length the philosophical dimensions of a cultural problem, there is a good chance that at some point the discussion will trail off into rarefied theoretical speculation of the kind that has made philosophy an object of ridicule since the time when the hapless Thales, gazing in wonder at the heavens, stumbled into a ditch. If we have not yet reached that point in this discussion, we are close enough. It is time to return to more concrete considerations, though this much can be said in defense of the abstract speculation in this section: if nothing else, it suitably completes the long argument—developed in stages throughout this study—intended to establish that religious antitechnologists generally have not looked deeply enough into the nature of either technology or religion. If they would, they would find that religion and technology are much *closer* than they realize, and on many levels. It also brings nearer to the foreground a theme that has been developed more politely and more modestly in the background, that practical individuals should be careful not to lose sight of the great practical importance of religion itself.

CONCLUDING PRACTICAL CONSIDERATIONS

Reflecting on the position outlined above that religion, technology, and culture can be helpfully conceived as representing the same essential phenomenon of ameliorative human production, one may wonder what value there can possibly be in blurring obvious distinctions between phenomena as manifestly different as religion and technology. Philosophical analysis has traditionally emphasized the value of drawing distinctions rather than blurring them. This emphasis is particularly apparent in the writings of the classical Greek philosophers, especially Aristotle, who sometimes seems to believe that understanding things is largely a matter of categorizing them. The distinctions that the ancient Greek philosophers have bequeathed to us have at times generated conceptual and practical difficulties. Yet some have clearly been enormously useful and others have become so much a part of our everyday thinking that it is almost pointless to attempt to evaluate them. Much can hang on distinctions considered in this inquiry, such as the classical distinction between *techne* and *episteme* or the distinction made by proponents of the "distinctiveness theory" who insist that "modern" technology is qualitatively different from earlier technology. Even when we feel compelled to challenge such distinctions, we can appreciate how they put key issues into focus. What value can there ultimately be in blurring a distinction, particularly such a useful and firmly established distinction as that between religion and technology?

Blurring distinctions can be revealing when it is done carefully, responsibly, and with a definite purpose in mind. To blur a distinction intentionally, especially a long-established one, is not to obliterate it but to draw attention to its not being as solid as we are accustomed to assume. The intentional blurring of a distinction can have beneficial consequences when it frees us from misleading paradigms and images and encourages us to avoid routine and unimaginative responses. Such blurring is not simply a matter of noting similarities between phenomena that have not been sufficiently appreciated nor even simply a matter of playing down differences that have been exaggerated; more specifically, it is a matter of drawing attention to the risks involved in exaggerating the importance of familiar differences. It can never be an adequate substitute for the drawing of useful distinctions; it can at best serve as a remedy for the abuse of distinctions.

A pertinent example involves the blurring of distinctions between religious faiths when the adherents of those faiths have been engaged in destructive forms of religious competition. One way in which interfaith dialogue has been helpful has been in enlightening members of antagonistic religious communities with respect to how much more they have in common than they previously recognized. There are, to be sure, substantial differences between Christians and Muslims and between Roman Catholics and Protestants. If we dismiss those differences as trivial, we do an injustice to each of these communities of believers, which rightly believes that there is something important and admirable about certain distinctive features of its world view and way of life. However, an effective starting point in getting these religious communities to back off from their tendency to demonize or otherwise view intolerantly the adherents of rival faiths is to remind them of shared beliefs, values, and attitudes that have been too often obscured in the heat of religious controversies and "holy" wars. Thus, it can at times do much good to blur the distinction between Christians and Muslims and to remind them that they share belief in one God, specific moral ideals, and a disapproval of materialistic conceptions of the person. Similarly, it can sometimes be helpful to blur the distinction between Roman Catholics and Protestants and to remind them that being Christian counts for more in some ways than being a particular kind of Christian.

This example is especially pertinent because sociocultural conflicts between those who are proreligious and those who are protechnological are often marked by the kinds of misunderstanding and contempt that enlightened people are accustomed to associating with religious and antireligious bigotry. Cultural competition is often salutary, and much of it is simply inevitable; and as beneficial as cooperation can be for all parties concerned, it is not always as beneficial as constructive competition.[59] Still, the competitive spirit needs to be properly channeled if it is not to manifest itself in destructive ways, and mutual respect is often of value in its own right.[60]

In comparing some of the individuals involved in controversies concerning religion and technology to garden variety religious and antireligious bigots, I may appear to be guilty of glaring overstatement as well as placing on the proverbial camel the straw of distinction blurring that has finally broken its back. Yet I maintain that similarities and parallels are worth considering here. Note, for example, how the response developed in this study to the position of religious antitechnologists mirrors the pattern of techniques that an educator might employ in trying to free someone from anti-Semitic attitudes.[61] Just as in Chapter 2 we considered in some detail the nature of technology (and its relation to *techne*), an educator might encourage the anti-Semite to take a much closer look at real Jews so that he could see that they are not fundamentally malevolent. At the same time, the educator might endeavor to expose the arbitrariness of the anti-Semite's generalizations ("All Jews are greedy"), paradigms (some Jewish investment bankers on Wall Street), and images (the Jew counting his shekels). Just as in Chapter 3 we considered the contributions of technologies to the realization of ideals promoted by world religions, the educator might draw the attention of the anti-Semite to some of the substantial contributions that Jews have made to the promotion of freedom, knowledge, and other goods. As in Chapter 4 we considered representative cases of how technology is compatible with or a manifestation of religious commitment, the educator might try to persuade the anti-Semite that the Jew, rather than typically being, say, a subversive secularist or a subverter of the state, is much more often a genuinely religious person and an authentic patriot. As in the first part of Chapter 5 we considered how religion can be helpfully conceived as a kind of technology, the educator might show the anti-Semite how much of the world view and way of life of which the anti-Semite himself approves—say, Christianity or Islam—represents an outgrowth of Judaism and an embodiment of core Jewish teachings. Finally, as in the middle part of this chapter we focused on the abstract identity of religion, technology, and culture, the educator might impress upon the anti-Semite the importance of those universals that on one level transcend all particularity, make brotherhood and sisterhood possible, and define the human community.

Knowledge or understanding is valuable for its own sake, and it is in a way its own reward. It also is of unlimited practical and instrumental value; and its being so is in great measure what technology is about. One important application of knowledge or understanding is in the promotion of tolerance. The virtue of tolerance, often confused nowadays with the vice of permissiveness, is something quite different from being inclined to accept what should not be tolerated. It also should not be confused with love or even genuine respect, but it is not inferior to these, only different. Tolerance is a great virtue because it is a disposition that involves properly accepting with forbearance and restraint all sorts of people and things that we fear, resent, or take offense about.[62] One cannot afford to be permissive if one is to be righteous; but if one is to avoid being *self*-righteous, one must strive for tolerance and humility, a virtue that perplexed many of the great philosophers but is precisely delineated in the sacred works of many world religions.[63] Cultural critics, particularly those who see themselves as imparting the teaching of traditional religion, need to be constantly aware of the danger of vitiating the pursuit of goodness by contaminating it with hypocrisy and conceit.[64] When they feel threatened and marginalized by secularist and antireligious cultural forces, religious leaders and other religionists often react by attempting to reclaim the high moral ground in their society. That they should do so is entirely understandable and in itself not a bad thing; there is often a vacuum in authentic spiritual and moral leadership in a society, and women and men of deep faith are legitimate candidates for filling it. However, special prudence and temperance must be exercised when taking upon oneself the mantle of prophet, defender of the faith, and shepherd to one's confused and wayward fellows.

Those who are given to excessive apprehension or indignation may be capable of being effective cultural critics, but they are not ideally suited to the role and have frequently proven themselves to be capable of doing considerable harm. Those who are unduly pessimistic, ambitious, or self-satisfied also have a way of disrupting traffic on the road up to the high moral ground. Anti-Semitism, anti-Catholicism, and other nefarious forms of religious and antireligious bigotry are never entirely out of fashion, either among the undereducated, the miseducated, or the ineffectively educated; and even among those who inhabit the loftiest precincts of "high" culture, it is still acceptable to seek guidance from those whose bigotry is casually dismissed as a minor eccentricity. Nevertheless, we have reached a stage in the development of civilization at which most people who want to retain a firm footing on the high moral ground think twice before discharging their resentment in attacks on the most conspicuous victims of historical religious hatred. For such people, technology is certainly a safer target.

However, while technology, the "technological society," and the "technological mentality" may appear to be wholly impersonal abstractions, they represent the personality and activity of flesh-and-blood human beings: technologists, their promoters, and their clients. The critic of "modern technology" as such is open to the very charge of dehumanization that he is given to hurling in many directions when he obscures the fact that current attitudes toward technology and technologies are a function of the beliefs and actions of real human beings.

As for the antireligious bigotry of protechnologists and others who are quick to dismiss all religion as maleficent superstition, it also may seem to be directed at a safe target, especially in an age when high-minded religionists freely acknowledge that they bear some of the guilt for the evils perpetrated by fanatical and hypocritical forerunners. Yet neither Voltairean satire nor Bismarckian *Kulturkampf* is likely to help us "moderns" to acquire a sounder vision of the relations of religion and culture. Bigotry is bigotry, whether exhibited by the pious or the skeptical. Moreover, those who deride all things religious not only do an injustice to authentically saintly individuals but naively and imprudently underestimate the staying power of many traditional religious beliefs, values, attitudes, and institutions.

The practical critic of bad technology may feel that the analyses in this investigation have skirted the main issue, which is that we and our fellows and future generations are sure to suffer greatly if public consciousness is not raised to an understanding of the urgent need to stem the tide of destructive technologies and bring about the disciplined regulation of dangerous technologies. No responsible person can ignore the importance of this issue, which, however, is not the issue that we have been addressing in this investigation. With due respect to zealous environmentalists and critics of dangerous biotechnologies, weapons technologies, and telecommunications technologies, we need to remember that once one becomes convinced that only the moral and cultural issues that concern her are deserving of consideration, she is well on the way toward the fanaticism and callousness that she rightly deplores in others. In any case, the focus of this inquiry has not been on technologies, or even on technology as such, but on religion and technology and their relations. Religionists and secularists alike are morally obliged to reflect on the evils and dangers of specific technologies, especially when their voices and votes can have a significant impact on social policy affecting the development of those technologies. In addition, men and women of faith may well have special obligations in this sphere that secularists do not. Antitechnology, religious or otherwise, is another matter, however; and even if we could eliminate all the bad technologies in the world, that in itself would not be enough to sustain us, physically or spiritually.

In its concern about arbitrary and misleading definitions, generalizations, paradigms, and images, this inquiry has been concerned with a rather different dimension of human ignorance, imprudence, and corruption. What happens in this order of human stupidity does, in fact, have enormous consequences for public consciousness about specific technologies—and specific religious phenomena—but the problems that we have encountered herein are not so easily addressed by legislation or "policy." The persistence of these problems throughout the centuries should discourage us from overconfidence in a quick fix, technological or otherwise.

What then is to be done? For a start, we must all draw to some extent on our influence to promote a situation in our own society and others whereby through farsighted decision making and the efficient division of labor, competent and committed individuals and groups will be provided with the encouragement, resources, and sociocultural power necessary for devising and instituting effective methods of correcting and preventing specific misapplications of religion and technology. We also have to use some of our influence to encourage leaders and other workers in education, religion, mass communications, and the various arts and technologies to work even harder than they already do toward enabling us to make more informed and more constructive appraisals of what is good and what is bad in the current state and the potential state of technological and religious development.

Professional technologists, who are increasingly required to devote themselves to narrower concerns and the acquisition of more specialized forms of knowledge, should be encouraged to listen to those religious and secular thinkers and educators who have made it their special vocation to examine and explain, as conscientious helpers rather than antagonistic cranks, the moral and cultural ramifications of specific technological projects. They should also be encouraged to take seriously the value to them, especially in preparing for their careers, of an adequate foundation in liberal education, including basic studies in the history and philosophy of religions. (Many technologists are in fact religious individuals; but being religious does not in itself provide them with adequate understanding of the relations of religion and technology.) In the *Apology*, Plato portrays Socrates as having had a deep respect for craftsmen—who he gratefully acknowledged knew many fine things which he did not—but as also regretting that their success in their own field had led them to believe mistakenly that they were "very wise in other most important pursuits."[65] The greatest Greek philosophers understood that we cannot reasonably expect the technical specialist to be a philosopher. Yet they underestimated the ability of the apprentice technologist to benefit from basic humanistic studies of general ethical and social issues. In particular, many technologists can be brought to appreciate, if they do not already, the historical and continuing practical cultural value of religion and to benefit from the analysis of what is, from a useful perspective, a "high" technology. In the process, they will come to understand better the difference between ameliorative activity and exploitative activity. This understanding will not only elevate their own work but will enable them to appraise more accurately the conscientiousness of the religionists whom they encounter in their professional and personal lives.

As for religious leaders and other religionists, those who are committed to the serious investigation of technology and technologies should continue to draw on their special insights to contribute to the constructive understanding of specific technologies and their consequences. They should communicate their ideas to technologists and the general public without rancor, condescension, or bombast. They should participate in genuine dialogue with technologists and others who are capable of enlightening them as well as being enlightened by them. They should be constantly mindful of the need for progress in religion; and they should perhaps pay special attention to what they can learn from technologists in various fields about providing their fellows with cultural products that are pleasing and accessible as well as ameliorative. They and all religionists should keep the faith and avoid debilitating forms of determinism, pessimism, hopelessness, and cynicism, even if such tendencies have been sanctioned by established theologies. They should have confidence that the higher Spirit in which they profess to believe will not abandon them. They should take heart in the realization that modern technology is not likely to lead to the the total annihilation or dehumanization of humanity when even thousands of years of corrupt religion have not had so dreadful a consequence.

Would a beneficent and omnipotent force allow humanity to destroy itself with its technology? Could such a force be so impatient with human striving as to be willing to see these creatures punished for their aspirations and adventures by being dehumanized or obliterated? Religious antitechnologists have been right to observe that humanity possesses technologies that have the power to destroy all life on earth; but this possibility represents a challenge not only to protechnological thinkers but to religious thinkers, ever patching up their tattered theodicies. Could the destruction of humanity be consistent with a Divine plan?

Countless people have given up on theodicy, theology, and religion itself, but none among them as yet appears to have sounded the note of inspiration and encouragement needed for sustaining humanity in a post-religious world. Theologians who insist on the essential vanity of human accomplishments hardly have anything more promising to offer. Forswearing confidence in the Divine and the human: what dismal prescriptions these are for creatures trying to maintain the conviction that life is meaningful and worth living.

What then is to be believed? Practical reflections having brought us back to theoretical ones, it would appear that the most important thing to be done is to settle upon a sound world view. In a free and pluralistic society, we can expect there to be ample disagreement as to what might qualify as a sound world view. Commitment to such a world view will inevitably be a matter of personal faith, involving many subjective factors. Still, we do not have to create a world view from scratch, for we have any number of sublime cultural products to take up, some authentically inspired. These tools for building a faith may help to save us yet, from determinism, pessimism, hopelessness, and cynicism. As we apply them, work with them, and integrate them into our experience and understanding and way of life, we may be awed not only by the grace that they have brought to our lives but by the even more imposing grace represented by the freedom and creativity of those who have participated in their development and transmission as well as by the freedom and creativity that we ourselves have been able to bring to their utilization, adaptation, and enhancement. Some of us will come to believe, with Emerson, that "there is a divine Providence in the world, which will not save us but through our own cooperation."[66]

NOTES

1. Alexander S. Kohanski, *Philosophy and Technology: Toward a New Orientation in Modern Thinking* (New York: Philosophical Library, 1977), 178.

2. Ibid.

3. James K. Feibleman, "Technology as Skills," *Technology and Culture* 7, no. 3 (1966): 320.

4. José Ortega y Gasset, "Man the Technician," in *Toward a Philosophy of History*, trans. not identified (New York: W. W. Norton, 1941), 161.

5. Richard Deitrich, "Paul Tillich and Technology: His Importance for Robust Science, Technology, and Society (STS) Education," *Bulletin of Science, Technology and Society* 10, nos. 5 and 6 (1990): 279.

6. Carl Mitcham, *Thinking Through Technology: The Path between Engineering and Philosophy* (Chicago: University of Chicago Press, 1994), 1.

7. Aristotle, *Nicomachean Ethics* 1140a.

8. Aristotle, *Metaphysics* 1013b.

9. Cf. Marshall McLuhan, *Understanding Media: The Extensions of Man* (New York: New American Library, 1964), ch. 8–9.

10. Ibid., ch. 16, 18, 33.

11. Luke 7:19–23.

12. Luke 11:2.

13. See, for example, Max Weber, *The Sociology of Religion*, trans. Ephraim Fischoff from the 4th German ed. (1922) (Boston: Beacon Press, 1964).

14. See, for example, Emile Durkheim, *The Elementary Forms of Religious Life*, 2d ed. (1915), trans. J. W. Swain (London: Allen and Unwin, 1976).

15. See, for example, Georg Simmel, *Sociology of Religion* (1905), trans. Curt Rosenthal (New York: Philosophical Library, 1959).

16. See, for example, Anthony F. C. Wallace, *Religion: An Anthropological View* (New York: Random House, 1966); John Milton Yinger, *Religion, Society and the Individual* (New York: Macmillan, 1957).

17. See, for example, William James, *Pragmatism* (New York: Longmans, Green, 1907), lecture 8; F.C.S. Schiller, "Faith, Reason, and Religion" (1906), in Reuben Abel, ed., *Humanistic Pragmatism: The Philosophy of F.C.S. Schiller* (New York: The Free Press, 1966), 256–74. Cf. Jay Newman, "The Faith of Pragmatists," *Sophia* 13, no. 1 (1974): 1–15.

18. Hans Vaihinger, *The Philosophy of "As If"* (1911), trans. C. K. Ogden (from the 6th German ed.), 2d ed. (London: Routledge and Kegan Paul, 1935).

19. Henri Bergson, *The Two Sources of Morality and Religion* (1932), trans. R. Ashley Audra and Cloudesley Brereton (New York: Henry Holt, 1935).

20. Miguel de Unamuno, *The Tragic Sense of Life* (1913), trans. J. E. Crawford Flitch (New York: Dover, 1954).

21. See, for example, Lionel Rubinoff, ed., *Faith and Reason: Essays in the Philosophy of Religion by R. G. Collingwood* (Chicago: Quadrangle, 1968).

22. See, for example, Ernst Cassirer, *Language and Myth*, trans. Suzanne K. Langer (New York: Harper and Row, 1946).

23. See, for example, Kai Nielsen, *An Introduction to the Philosophy of Religion* (London: Macmillan, 1982).

24. Cf. G. B. Kerferd, *The Sophistic Movement* (Cambridge: Cambridge University Press, 1981), ch. 13.

25. Oswald Spengler, *Man and Technics: A Contribution to a Philosophy of Life* (1931), trans. Charles Francis Atkinson (London: Allen and Unwin, 1932), 35.

26. Ibid., p. 9.

27. Genesis 1:31.

28. Exodus 31:18, 32:15–16.

29. Deuteronomy 34:10.

30. Cf. Friedrich Nietzsche, *Beyond Good and Evil* (1886), trans. Walter Kaufmann (New York: Vintage, 1966), sec. 248.

31. Exodus 32:9, Deuteronomy 10:16.

32. Michael Polanyi, "The Scientific Revolution," in Hugh C. White, Jr., ed., *Christians in a Technological Era* (New York: Seabury Press, 1964), 33.

33. Ernst Cassirer, *An Essay on Man* (New Haven, Conn.: Yale University Press, 1944), part 2.

34. R. G. Collingwood, *Speculum Mentis* (Oxford: Clarendon Press, 1924).

35. T. S. Eliot, *Notes towards the Definition of Culture* (London: Faber and Faber, 1948), 27.

36. Ibid., p. 28.

37. Ibid., p. 31.

38. Paul Tillich, *Theology of Culture*, ed. Robert C. Kimball (New York: Oxford University Press, 1959), 6.

39. Ibid., p. 8.

40. Ibid., p. 42.

41. A. L. Kroeber and Clyde Kluckhohn (with the assistance of Wayne Untereiner and appendices by Alfred G. Meyer) (1952), *Culture: A Critical Review of Concepts and Definitions* (New York: Vintage Books, 1963), 291.

42. Ibid., p. 284.

43. James K. Feibleman, "Technology as Skills," *Technology and Culture* 7, no. 3 (1966): 318.

44. Giles Gunn, *The Culture of Criticism and the Criticism of Culture* (New York: Oxford University Press, 1987), 6.

45. F. R. Cowell, *Culture in Private and Public Life* (London: Thames and Hudson, 1959), 105.

46. John Walker, *A Critical Pronouncing Dictionary* (1791).

47. Kroeber and Kluckhohn, *Culture: A Critical Review of Concepts and Definitions*, 283.

48. Friedrich Rapp, *Analytical Philosophy of Technology*, trans. Stanley R. Carpenter and Theodor Langenbruch, Boston Studies in the Philosophy of Science, vol. 63 (Dordrecht, The Netherlands: D. Reidel, 1981), 8.

49. Thorstein Veblen, *The Instinct of Workmanship* (1914) (New York: W. W. Norton, 1964), v.

50. José Ortega y Gasset, "Man the Technician," 117–18.

51. Willem H. Vanderburg, "Technology, Society, and Culture: A Framework for Understanding," *Technology in Society* 7, no. 4 (1985): 417.

52. Joseph Margolis, "Culture and Technology," *Research in Philosophy and Technology* 1 (1978): 27.

53. See, for example, Lewis Mumford, *Art and Technics* (New York: Columbia University Press, 1952), 16–17, 161.

54. J. C. Shairp, *Culture and Religion in Some of Their Relations* (3d ed.; Boston: Houghton Mifflin; Cambridge, Mass.: The Riverside Press, 1872), 89.

55. John Henry Newman, *The Idea of a University* (1853, 1858), Part 1, Discourse 5 (Garden City, N.Y.: Doubleday, 1959), 128–29.

56. John Henry Newman, "The Tamworth Reading Room" (1841) in *Discussions and Arguments on Various Subjects* (London: Basil Montagu Pickering, 1872), 254–305. This diatribe is incorporated into ch. 4 of the *Grammar of Assent* (1870).

57. John Henry Newman, *The Idea of a University*, Part 2, Lectures 7–10. Cf. Jay Newman, "Newman on Christianity and Medical Science," *Paideusis* 3, no. 2 (1988): 28–35; also Jay Newman, "Theology and Some Curricula," *Paideusis* 1, no. 2 (1988): 12–21.

58. Plato, *Republic* 592a–b.

59. Cf. Jay Newman, *Competition in Religious Life*, Editions SR no. 11 (Waterloo, Ont.: Wilfrid Laurier University Press, for the Canadian Corporation for Studies in Religion, 1989), esp. ch. 2.

60. Ibid., ch. 4.

61. Cf. Jay Newman, *Foundations of Religious Tolerance* (Toronto: University of Toronto Press, 1982), ch. 9.

62. Ibid., ch. 1.

63. Cf. Jay Newman, *On Religious Freedom* (Ottawa: University of Ottawa Press, 1991), 78–85.

64. Cf. Jay Newman, *Fanatics and Hypocrites* (Buffalo, N.Y.: Prometheus Books, 1986), ch. 3.

65. Plato, *Apology* 22c–d, trans. G.M.A. Grube in *The Trial and Death of Socrates* (Indianapolis, Ind.: Hackett, 1975), 26.

66. Ralph Waldo Emerson, "The Fugitive Slave Law" (1884), in Ralph Waldo Emerson, *The Portable Emerson*, ed. Carl Bode and Malcolm Cowley (New ed., Harmondsworth, England: Penguin Books, 1981), 557. This lecture, given in 1854, was originally published in the *Miscellanies* volume of Emerson's collected works.

Bibliography

Agassi, Joseph K. *Technology: Philosophical and Social Aspects. Episteme* series, vol. 11. Dordrecht, The Netherlands: D. Reidel, 1985.

Allers, Rudolf. "Technology and the Human Person." In *Technology and Christian Culture*, edited by Robert Paul Mohan. Washington, D.C.: Catholic University of America Press, 1960.

Angus, Ian H. *George Grant's Platonic Rejoinder to Heidegger: Contemporary Political Philosophy and the Question of Technology*. Queenston, Ont.: Edwin Mellen Press, 1987.

Arendt, Hannah. *The Human Condition*. Chicago: University of Chicago Press, 1958.

Aristotle. *Metaphysics*.

——— . *Nicomachean Ethics*.

——— . *Physics*.

——— . *Poetics*.

——— . *Politics*.

——— . *Rhetoric*.

Bacon, Francis. *The Advancement of Learning* (1605).

Ballard, Edward Goodwin. *Man and Technology: Toward the Measurement of a Culture*. Pittsburgh: Duquesne University Press, 1978.

Barbour, Ian G. *Ethics in an Age of Technology*. San Francisco: Harper Collins, 1993.

——— , ed. *Science and Religion: New Perspectives on the Dialogue*. New York: Harper and Row, 1968.

——— . *Science and Secularity: The Ethics of Technology*. New York: Harper and Row, 1970.

Benjamin, Walter. "The Work of Art in the Age of Mechanical Reproduction."
     In *Illuminations*. Trans. Harry Zohn. New York: Schocken, 1969.
Berbekar, Rosalia. "Hephaestus—The God We Love to Hate: The Lingering Pro-
     and Anti-Technology Debate." *Bulletin of Science, Technology and Society*
     8, no. 2 (1988): 172–82.
Berdyaev, Nicolas. *The Destiny of Man*. Trans. Natalie Duddington. London:
     Geoffrey Bles, 1955.
———. *The Fate of Man in the Modern World* (1935). Trans. Donald A. Lowrie.
     Ann Arbor: University of Michigan Press, 1961.
Bergson, Henri. *The Two Sources of Morality and Religion* (1932). Trans. R. Ashley
     Audra and Cloudesley Brereton. New York: Henry Holt, 1935.
Blair, George A. "Faith Outside Technique." In *Theology and Technology: Essays in
     Christian Analysis and Exegesis*, edited by Carl Mitcham and Jim Grote.
     Lanham, Md.: University Press of America, 1984.
Bonhoeffer, Dietrich. *Letters and Papers From Prison*. London: S.C.M. Press, 1951.
Borchert, Donald M., and David Stewart, eds. *Being Human in a Technological Age*.
     Athens: Ohio University Press, 1979.
Borgmann, Albert. *Technology and the Character of Contemporary Life: A Philo-
     sophical Inquiry*. Chicago: University of Chicago Press, 1984.
Borlaug, Norman. "Production and Technology." In *Food/Energy and the Major
     Faiths*, edited by Joseph Gremillion. Maryknoll, N.Y.: Orbis, 1977.
Brunner, Heinrich Emil. *Christianity and Civilisation*. 2 vols. London: Nisbet,
     1948–1949.
Bunge, Mario. "Can Science and Technology Be Held Responsible for Our
     Current Social Ills?" *Research in Philosophy and Technology* 7 (1984):
     19–22.
———. "The Five Buds of Technophilosophy." *Technology in Society* 1, no. 1
     (1979): 67–74.
———. "Technology and Applied Science." *Technology and Culture* 7, no. 3
     (1966): 329–47.
Cardwell, D.S.L. *Turning Points in Western Technology: A Study of Technology,
     Science and History*. New York: Science History Publications, a division
     of Neale Watson Academic Publications, 1972.
Cassirer, Ernst. *An Essay on Man*. New Haven, Conn.: Yale University Press,
     1944.
———. *Language and Myth*. Trans. Suzanne K. Langer. New York: Harper and
     Row, 1946.
Childe, Gordon. "Early Forms of Society." In *A History of Technology*, Vol. 1, *From
     Early Times to the Fall of Ancient Empires*, edited by Charles Singer, E. J.
     Holmyard, and A. R. Hall. Oxford: Clarendon Press, 1954.
Choe, Wolhee. *Toward an Aesthetic Criticism of Technology*. New York: Peter
     Lang, 1989.
Collingwood, R. G. *The New Leviathan*. Oxford: Clarendon Press, 1942.
———. *The Principles of Art*. Oxford: Clarendon Press, 1938.

_____ . *Speculum Mentis*. Oxford: Clarendon Press, 1924.

Cooper, Barry. *Action Into Nature: An Essay on the Meaning of Technology*. Notre Dame, Ind.: University of Notre Dame Press, 1991.

Cooper, David E. "Technology: Liberation or Enslavement." In *Philosophy and Technology*, edited by Roger Fellows. Royal Institute of Philosophy Supplement, no. 38. Cambridge: Cambridge University Press, 1995.

Coward, Harold. "Religious Responsibility." In *Ethics and Climate Change: The Greenhouse Effect*, edited by Harold Coward and Thomas Hurka. Waterloo, Ont.: Wilfrid Laurier University Press, 1993.

Coward, Harold and Thomas Hurka, eds. *Ethics and Climate Change: The Greenhouse Effect*. Waterloo, Ont.: Wilfrid Laurier University Press, 1993.

Cowell, F. R. *Culture in Private and Public Life*. London: Thames and Hudson, 1959.

Cox, Harvey. "The Christian in a World of Technology." In *Science and Religion: New Perspectives on the Dialogue*, edited by Ian G. Barbour. New York: Harper and Row, 1968.

_____ . *Religion in the Secular City: Toward a Postmodern Theology*. New York: Simon and Schuster, 1984.

_____ . *The Secular City*. New York: Macmillan, 1965.

Deitrich, Richard. "Paul Tillich and Technology: His Importance for Robust Science, Technology, and Society (STS) Education." *Bulletin of Science, Technology and Society* 10, nos. 5 and 6 (1990): 275–81.

Dessauer, Friedrich. *Philosophie der Technik*. Bonn, Germany: Friedrich Cohen Verlag, 1927.

_____ . "Technology in Its Proper Sphere" (translation of an excerpt from *Philosophie der Technik*, 1927). In *Philosophy of Technology: Readings in the Philosophical Problems of Technology*, edited by Carl Mitcham and Robert Mackey. New York: The Free Press, 1992.

Drengson, Alan R. "The Sacred and the Limits of the Technological Fix." *Zygon* 19 (1984): 259–75.

Durkheim, Emile. *The Elementary Forms of Religious Life*, 2d ed. (1915). Trans. J. W. Swain. London: Allen and Unwin, 1976.

Eliot, T. S. *Notes towards the Definition of Culture*. London: Faber and Faber, 1948.

Elliott, David and Ruth Elliott. *The Control of Technology*. London: Wykeham; New York: Springer-Verlag, 1976.

Ellul, Jacques. *The Meaning of the City*. Trans. Dennis Pardee. Grand Rapids, Mich.: William B. Eerdmans, 1970.

_____ . *Perspectives on Our Age: Jacques Ellul Speaks on His Life and Work*. Ed. William H. Vanderburg. Trans. Joachim Neugroschel. Toronto: Canadian Broadcasting Corporation, 1981.

_____ . *Propaganda: The Formation of Men's Attitudes*. Trans. Konrad Kellen and Jean Lerner. New York: Alfred A. Knopf, 1968.

_____ . "Statements by Jacques Ellul and Ivan Illich." *Technology in Society* 17, no. 2 (1995): 231–38.

———. *The Technological Society* (1954). Trans. John Wilkinson. New York: Knopf, 1964.

———. *The Technological System* (1977). Trans. Joachim Neugroschel. New York: Continuum, 1980.

Emerson, Ralph Waldo. "The Fugitive Slave Law" (1884). In *The Portable Emerson*, edited by Carl Bode and Malcolm Cowley. New ed. (1946) Harmondsworth, England: Penguin Books, 1981.

Erasmus, Desiderius. *Praise of Folly* (1511).

Feibleman, James K. *Technology and Reality*. The Hague, The Netherlands: Martinus Nijhoff, 1982.

———. "Technology as Skills." *Technology and Culture* 7, no. 3 (1966): 318–28.

Ferré, Frederick. *Philosophy of Technology*. Englewood Cliffs, N.J.: Prentice-Hall, 1988.

Florman, Samuel C. *The Existential Pleasures of Engineering*. New York: St. Martin's Press, 1976.

Forbes, R. J. *Man the Maker: A History of Technology and Engineering*. London: Abelard-Schuman, 1958.

———. "Mesopotamian and Egyptian Technology." In *Technology in Western Civilization*, vol. 1, *The Emergence of Modern Industrial Society: Earliest Times to 1900*, edited by Melvin Kranzberg and Carroll W. Pursell, Jr. New York: Oxford University Press, 1967.

Freud, Sigmund. *The Future of an Illusion* (1927). Trans. W. D. Robson-Scott (1953). Revised and newly edited by James Strachey (1961). Garden City, N.Y.: Doubleday, 1964.

———. *The History of the Psychoanalytic Movement and Other Papers*. Ed. Philip Rieff. New York: Collier Books, 1963.

Fudpucker, Wilhelm E. "Through Christian Technology to Technological Christianity." In *Theology and Technology: Essays in Christian Analysis and Exegesis*, edited by Carl Mitcham and Jim Grote. Lanham, Md.: University Press of America, 1984.

Giedion, Siegfried. *Mechanization Takes Command: a Contribution to Anonymous History*. New York: Oxford University Press, 1948.

Gilkey, Langdon. "The Religious Dilemmas of a Scientific Culture: The Interface of Technology, History and Religion." In *Being Human in a Technological Age*, edited by Donald M. Borchert and David Stewart. Athens: Ohio University Press, 1979.

Gill, David W. *The Word of God in the Ethics of Jacques Ellul*. American Theological Library Association monograph series no. 20. Metuchen, N.J.: American Theological Library Association and The Scarecrow Press, 1984.

Gill, Eric. *Christianity and the Machine Age*. London: Sheldon, 1940.

Gogarten, Friedrich. *The Reality of Faith* (1957). Trans. Carl Michalson et al. Philadelphia: Westminster, 1959.

Goldman, Steven L. "Images of Technology in Popular Films: Discussion and Filmography." *Science, Technology, and Human Values* 14, no. 3 (1989): 275–301.

———, ed. *Science, Technology, and the Theory of Progress.* Research in Technology Studies, vol. 2. Bethlehem, Pa.: Lehigh University Press; London and Toronto: Associated University Presses, 1989.

Gouldner, Alvin W. *The Dialectic of Ideology and Technology.* New York: Seabury Press, 1976.

Grant, George. "Justice and Technology." In *Theology and Technology: Essays in Christian Analysis and Exegesis,* edited by Carl Mitcham and Jim Grote. Lanham, Md.: University Press of America, 1984.

———. "Religion and the State." In *Technology and Empire.* Toronto: House of Anansi, 1969.

———. *Technology and Empire.* Toronto: House of Anansi, 1969.

———. *Technology and Justice.* Notre Dame, Ind.: University of Notre Dame Press, 1986.

Gremillion, Joseph. "The Facts of the Food/Energy Crisis." In *Food/Energy and the Major Faiths,* edited by Joseph Gremillion. Maryknoll, N.Y.: Orbis, 1977.

———, ed. *Food/Energy and the Major Faiths.* Maryknoll, N.Y.: Orbis, 1977.

Gunn, Giles. *The Culture of Criticism and the Criticism of Culture.* New York: Oxford University Press, 1987.

Harrison, Frank R. III. "The Judeo-Christian Tradition and Crises in Contemporary Technology." *Research in Philosophy and Technology* 10 (1990): 103–18.

Hawkin, David J. *Christ and Modernity: Christian Self-Understanding in a Technological Age.* SR Supplements vol. 17. Waterloo, Ont.: Wilfrid Laurier University Press, for the Canadian Corporation for Studies in Religion, 1985.

Heidegger, Martin. *Discourse on Thinking* (1954). Trans. John M. Anderson and E. Hans Freund. New York: Harper and Row, 1966.

Heschel, Abraham Joshua. *The Sabbath: Its Meaning for Modern Man.* New York: Farrar, Straus, and Young, 1951.

Hodges, Henry. *Technology in the Ancient World.* London: Allen Lane, The Penguin Press, 1970.

Hodgson, Peter C. *New Birth of Freedom: A Theology of Bondage and Liberation.* Philadelphia: Fortress Press, 1976.

Hooke, S. H. "Recording and Writing." In *A History of Technology,* Vol. 1, *From Early Times to the Fall of Ancient Empires,* edited by Charles Singer, E. M. Holmyard, and A. R. Hall. Oxford: Clarendon Press, 1954.

Huning, Alois. "*Homo Mensura:* Human Beings Are Their Technology—Technology Is Human." *Research in Philosophy and Technology* 8 (1985): 9–18.

Ihde, Don. *Existential Technics.* Albany: State University of New York Press, 1983.

———. *Philosophy of Technology: An Introduction* New York: Paragon House, 1993.

———. *Technics and Praxis.* Dordrecht, The Netherlands: D. Reidel, 1979.

Illich, Ivan. "Statement." Trans. Lee Hoinacki. "Statements by Jacques Ellul and
    Ivan Illich." *Technology in Society* 17, no. 2 (1995): 231–38.
———. *Tools for Conviviality*. New York: Harper and Row, 1973.
James, William. *Pragmatism*. New York: Longmans, Green, 1907.
Jonas, Hans. *The Imperative of Responsibility: In Search of an Ethics for the Techno-
    logical Age*. Chicago: University of Chicago Press, 1984.
———. "Seventeenth Century and After: The Meaning of the Scientific and
    Technological Revolution." In *Philosophical Essays: From Ancient Creed
    to Technological Man*. Englewood Cliffs, N.J.: Prentice-Hall, 1974.
———. "Technology and Responsibility: Reflections on the New Tasks of Ethics"
    (1972). In *Philosophical Essays: From Ancient Creed to Technological Man*.
    Englewood Cliffs, N.J.: Prentice-Hall, 1974.
Jones, William B. and A. Warren Matthews. "Toward a Taxonomy of Technology
    and Religion." *Research in Philosophy and Technology* 10 (1990): 3–23.
Juenger [Jünger], Friedrich Georg. *The Failure of Technology*. Trans. not identified.
    Chicago: Henry Regnery, n.d.
Kasson, John F. *Civilizing the Machine: Technology and Republican Values in Amer-
    ica, 1776–1900*. New York: Grossman Publishers, a division of the Vi-
    king Press, 1976.
Kerferd, G. B. *The Sophistic Movement*. Cambridge: Cambridge University Press,
    1981.
Kinsley, David. *Ecology and Religion*. Englewood Cliffs, N.J.: Prentice-Hall, 1995.
Klemm, Friedrich. *A History of Western Technology* (1954). Trans. Dorothea
    Waley Singer. New York: Charles Scribner's Sons, 1959.
Kohanski, Alexander S. *Philosophy and Technology: Toward a New Orientation in
    Modern Thinking*. New York: Philosophical Library, 1977.
Kranzberg, Melvin and Carroll W. Pursell, Jr., eds. *Technology in Western Civiliza-
    tion*, vol. 1, *The Emergence of Modern Industrial Society: Earliest Times to
    1900*. New York: Oxford University Press, 1967.
Kroeber, A. L. and Clyde Kluckhohn (with the assistance of Wayne Untereiner
    and appendices by Alfred G. Meyer). *Culture: A Critical Review of Con-
    cepts and Definitions* (1952). New York: Vintage Books, 1963.
Krois, John Michael. "Ernst Cassirer's Theory of Technology and Its Import for
    Social Philosophy." *Research in Philosophy and Technology* 5 (1982): 209–
    22.
Kuklick, Bruce. *The Rise of American Philosophy*. New Haven, Conn.: Yale Univer-
    sity Press, 1977.
Kundera, Milan. *The Book of Laughter and Forgetting*. Harmondsworth, England:
    Penguin, 1983.
Ladrière, Jean. "Faith and the Technician Mentality." Trans. Margaret House. In
    Christians in a Technological Era, edited by Hugh C. White, Jr. New York:
    Seabury Press, 1964.
Leighton, Albert C. "The Mule as a Cultural Invention." *Technology and Culture*
    8 (1967): 45–52.

Levinson, Paul. "Information Technologies as Vehicles of Evolution." *Technology in Society* 6, no. 3 (1984): 193–206.

Lilley, S. *Men, Machines and History*. Revised and enlarged ed. New York: International Publishers, 1965.

Machiavelli, Niccolò. *The Prince* (1515).

Mander, Jerry. *In the Absence of the Sacred: The Failure of Technology and the Survival of the Indian Nations*. San Francisco: Sierra Club Books, 1991.

Marcel, Gabriel. *Being and Having: An Existentialist Diary* (1935). Trans. Katherine Farrer. Boston: Beacon Press, 1951.

_____. *Man Against Mass Society*. Trans. G. S. Fraser. Chicago: Gateway, Henry Regnery, 1962.

Marcuse, Herbert. *One-Dimensional Man: Studies in the Ideology of Advanced Industrial Society*. Boston: Beacon, 1964.

Margolis, Joseph. "Culture and Technology." *Research in Philosophy and Technology* 1 (1978): 25–37.

Marx, Leo. "Technology and the Study of Man." In *The Sciences, the Humanities, and the Technological Threat*, edited by W. Roy Niblett. London: University of London Press, 1975.

McCorduck, Pamela. *The Universal Machine: Confessions of a Technological Optimist*. New York: McGraw-Hill, 1985.

McGinn, Robert E. "What Is Technology?" *Research in Philosophy and Technology* 1 (1978): 179–97.

McLelland, Joseph C. *Prometheus Rebound: The Irony of Atheism*. Editions SR no. 10. Waterloo, Ont.: Wilfrid Laurier University Press, for the Canadian Corporation for Studies in Religion, 1988.

McLuhan, Marshall, *Understanding Media: The Extensions of Man*. New York: New American Library, 1964.

Mead, Margaret. "Introduction." In *Christians in a Technological Era*, edited by Hugh C. White, Jr. New York: Seabury Press, 1964.

Merton, Robert K. "Foreword" to Jacques Ellul, *The Technological Society* (1954). Trans. John Wilkinson. New York: Knopf, 1964.

Mesthene, Emmanuel G. *Technological Change: Its Impact on Man and Society*. Cambridge, Mass.: Harvard University Press, 1970.

_____. "Technology as Evil: Fear or Lamentation?" *Research in Philosophy and Technology* 7 (1984): 59–74.

Mill, John Stuart. *Utilitarianism* (1863).

Mitcham, Carl. "Computers: From Ethos and Ethics to Mythos and Religion: Notes on the New Frontier Between Computers and Philosophy." *Technology in Society* 8, no. 1 (1986): 171–201.

_____. "Science, Technology, and the Theory of Progress." In *Science, Technology, and Social Progress*, edited by Steven L. Goldman. Research in Technology Studies, vol. 2. Bethlehem, Pa.: Lehigh University Press; London and Toronto: Associated University Presses, 1989.

———. *Thinking Through Technology: The Path between Engineering and Philosophy.* Chicago: University of Chicago Press, 1994.

Mitcham, Carl, and Jim Grote, eds. *Theology and Technology: Essays in Christian Analysis and Exegesis.* Lanham, Md.: University Press of America, 1984.

Mitcham, Carl, and Robert Mackey, eds. *Philosophy of Technology: Readings in the Philosophical Problems of Technology.* New York: The Free Press, 1992.

Mohan, Robert Paul, ed. *Technology and Christian Culture.* Washington, D.C.: Catholic University of America Press, 1960.

Morel, Bernard. "Science and Technology in God's Design." In *Christians in a Technological Era,* edited by Hugh C. White, Jr. New York: Seabury Press, 1964.

Morris, Bertram. "The Context of Technology." *Technology and Culture* 18, no. 3 (1977): 395–418.

Moser, Leo J. *The Technology Trap: Survival in a Man-Made Environment.* Chicago: Nelson-Hall, 1979.

Mounier, Emmanuel. *Be Not Afraid.* Trans. Cynthia Rowland. London: Rockliff, 1951.

Muller, Herbert J. *The Children of Frankenstein: A Primer on Modern Technology and Human Values.* Bloomington: Indiana University Press, 1970.

Mullins, Nicholas C. *Theories and Theory Groups in Contemporary American Sociology.* New York: Harper and Row, 1973.

Mumford, Lewis. *Art and Technics.* New York: Columbia University Press, 1952.

———. *Technics and Civilization.* New York: Harcourt, Brace, 1934.

Nasr, Seyyed Hossein. "Islam and the Environmental Crisis." In *Spirit and Nature: Why the Environment Is a Religious Issue,* edited by Steven C. Rockefeller and John C. Elder. Boston: Beacon Press, 1992.

Newman, Jay. *Competition in Religious Life.* Editions SR, no. 11. Waterloo, Ont.: Wilfrid Laurier University Press, for the Canadian Corporation for Studies in Religion, 1989.

———. "The Faith of Pragmatists." *Sophia* 13, no. 1 (1974): 1–15.

———. *Fanatics and Hypocrites.* Buffalo, N.Y.: Prometheus, 1989.

———. *Foundations of Religious Tolerance.* Toronto: University of Toronto Press, 1982.

———. *The Mental Philosophy of John Henry Newman.* Waterloo, Ont.: Wilfrid Laurier University Press, 1986.

———. "Newman on Christianity and Medical Science." *Paideusis* 3, no. 2 (1990): 28–35.

———. *On Religious Freedom.* Ottawa: University of Ottawa Press, 1991.

———. *Religion vs. Television: Competitors in Cultural Context.* Media and Society Series. Westport, Conn.: Praeger, 1996.

———. "Theology and Some Curricula." *Paideusis* 1, no. 2 (1988): 12–21.

Newman, John Henry. *An Essay in Aid of a Grammar of Assent* (1870). Notre Dame, Ind.: University of Notre Dame Press, 1979.

_____. *The Idea of a University* (1853, 1858). Image Books. Garden City, N.Y.: Doubleday, 1959.

_____. "The Tamworth Reading Room" (1841). In *Discussions and Arguments on Various Subjects*. London: Basil Montagu Pickering, 1872.

Niblett, W. Roy, ed. *The Sciences, the Humanities, and the Technological Threat*. London: University of London Press, 1975.

Nielsen, Kai. *An Introduction to the Philosophy of Religion*. London: Macmillan, 1982.

_____. "Technology as Ideology." *Research in Philosophy and Technology* 1 (1978): 131–47.

Nietzsche, Friedrich. *Beyond Good and Evil* (1886). Trans. Walter Kaufmann. New York: Vintage Books, 1966.

_____. *The Genealogy of Morals* (1887).

Nisbet, Robert. *History of the Idea of Progress*. New York: Basic Books, 1980.

Novak, David. "Technology and Its Ultimate Threat: A Jewish Meditation." *Research in Philosophy and Technology* 10 (1990): 43–70.

Ong, Walter J. *In the Human Grain*. New York: Macmillan, 1967.

Ortega y Gasset, José. "Man the Technician." In *Toward a Philosophy of History*. Trans. not identified. New York: W. W. Norton, 1941.

Pascal, Blaise. *Pensées*. Trans. A. J. Krailsheimer. Harmondsworth, England: Penguin, 1966.

Peters, F. E. *Greek Philosophical Terms: A Historical Lexicon*. New York: New York University Press, 1967.

Peterson, Richard A. "Technology: Master, Servant, or Model for Human Dignity?" *The Philosophy Forum* 9, nos. 3–4 (1971): 201–10.

Pitt, Joseph. " 'Style' and Technology." *Technology in Society* 10, no. 4 (1988): 447–56.

Plato. *Apology*. Trans. G.M.A. Grube. In *The Trial and Death of Socrates*, ed. G.M.A. Grube. Indianapolis, Ind.: Hackett, 1975.

_____. *Euthyphro*.

_____. *Ion*.

_____. *Laws*.

_____. *Protagoras*.

_____. *Republic*.

_____. *Timaeus*.

Plochmann, George Kimball. "The God from the Machine May Soon Be Dead." *The Philosophy Forum* 9, nos. 3–4 (1971): 265–81.

Polanyi, Michael. "The Scientific Revolution." In *Christians in a Technological Era*, edited by Hugh C. White, Jr. New York: Seabury Press, 1964.

Rapp, Friedrich. *Analytical Philosophy of Technology*. Trans. Stanley R. Carpenter and Theodor Langenbruch. Boston Studies in the Philosophy of Science, vol. 63. Dordrecht, The Netherlands: D. Reidel, 1981.

Rasmussen, Larry. "Mindset and Moral Vision." *Research in Philosophy and Technology* 10 (1990): 119–28.

Rescher, Nicholas. "Technological Progress and Human Happiness." In *Unpopular Essays on Technological Progress*. Pittsburgh, Pa.: University of Pittsburgh Press, 1980.

Rockefeller, Steven C. and John C. Elder, eds. *Spirit and Nature: Why the Environment is a Religious Issue*. Boston: Beacon Press, 1992.

Rohatyn, Dennis. "The (Mis)Information Society: An Analysis of the Role of Propaganda in Shaping Consciousness." *Bulletin of Science, Technology and Society* 10, no. 2 (1990): 77–85.

Roszak, Theodore. *The Making of a Counter Culture: Reflections on the Technocratic Society and Its Youthful Opposition*. Garden City, N.Y.: Doubleday, 1968.

Rubinoff, Lionel, ed. *Faith and Reason: Essays in the Philosophy of Religion by R. G. Collingwood*. Chicago: Quadrangle, 1968.

Schadewaldt, Wolfgang. "The Concepts of *Nature* and *Technique* According to the Greeks." Trans. William Carroll. *Research in Philosophy and Technology* 2 (1979): 159–71.

Schiller, F.C.S. "Faith, Reason, and Religion" (1906). In *Humanistic Pragmatism: The Philosophy of F.C.S. Schiller*, edited by Reuben Abel. New York: The Free Press, 1966.

Schillinger, A. George. "Man's Enduring Technological Dilemma: Prometheus, Faust, and Other Macro-Engineers." *Technology in Society* 6, no. 1 (1984): 59–71.

Schrader, David E. "Technology: Our Contemporary Snake." *Research in Philosophy and Technology* 10 (1990): 205–15.

Schumacher, E. F. *Small Is Beautiful*. New York: Harper and Row, 1973.

Schuurman, Egbert. "A Christian Philosophical Perspective on Technology." In *Theology and Technology: Essays in Christian Analysis and Exegesis*, edited by Carl Mitcham and Jim Grote. Lanham, Md.: University Press of America, 1984.

Shairp, J. C. *Culture and Religion in Some of Their Relations*. 3d ed. Boston: Houghton Mifflin; Cambridge, Mass.: The Riverside Press, 1872.

Silver, Abba Hillel. *Where Judaism Differed: An Inquiry Into the Distinctiveness of Judaism*. New York: Macmillan, 1956.

Simmel, Georg. *Sociology of Religion* (1905). Trans. Curt Rosenthal. New York: Philosophical Library, 1959.

Singer, Charles, E. J. Holmyard and A. R. Hall, eds. *A History of Technology*, vol. 1, *From Early Times to the Fall of Ancient Empires*. Oxford: Clarendon Press, 1954.

Singer, Maxine. "Vatican City State: The Pontifical Academy of Sciences." *Technology in Society* 13, no. 4 (1991): 427–32.

Skolimowksi, Henryk. "The Structure of Thinking in Technology." *Technology and Culture* 7, no. 3 (1966): 371–83.

Sommerfelt, A. "Speech and Language." In *A History of Technology*, vol. 1, *From Early Times to the Fall of Ancient Empires*, edited by Charles Singer, E. M. Holmyard, and A. R. Hall. Oxford: Clarendon Press, 1954.

Sontag, Frederick. "Theodicy and Technology: Is God Present in Technological Progress?" In *Theology and Technology: Essays in Christian Analysis and Exegesis*, edited by Carl Mitcham and Jim Grote. Lanham, Md.: University Press of America, 1984.

Sophocles. *Antigone*. Trans. Elizabeth Wyckoff (1954). In *Greek Tragedies*, vol. 1, edited by David Grene and Richmond Lattimore. Chicago: University of Chicago Press, 1960.

Spengler, Oswald. *Man and Technics: A Contribution to a Philosophy of Life* (1931). Trans. Charles Francis Atkinson. London: Allen and Unwin, 1932.

Spinoza, Benedict de. *A Theologico-Political Treatise (Tractatus Theologico-Politicus)* (1670). Trans. R.H.M. Elwes (1883). New York: Dover, 1951.

Stanley, Manfred. *The Technological Conscience*. New York: The Free Press, 1978.

Stevenson, Charles L. *Ethics and Language*. New Haven, Conn.: Yale University Press, 1944.

Sun, P. Hans. "Notes on How to Begin to Think about Technology in a Theological Way." In *Theology and Technology: Essays in Christian Analysis and Exegesis*, edited by Carl Mitcham and Jim Grote. Lanham, Md.: University Press of America, 1984.

Swetlitz, Mark. "A Jewish Commentary on the Religious Origins of Technological Civilization." *Research in Philosophy and Technology* 6 (1983): 197–204.

Taylor, Alva W. *Christianity and Industry in America*. New York: Friendship Press, 1933.

Teilhard de Chardin, Pierre. *The Phenomenon of Man* (1955). Trans. Bernard Wall. London: Collins; New York: Harper and Brothers, 1959.

———. "The Place of Technology in a General Biology of Mankind" (1947). In *Activation of Energy*. Trans. René Hague. London: Collins, 1970.

———. "Reflections on Happiness" (1943). In *Toward the Future*. Trans. René Hague. New York: Harcourt Brace Jovanovich, 1975.

Temple, Katharine. "Doubts Concerning the Religious Origins of Technological Civilization." *Research in Philosophy and Technology* 6 (1983): 189–97.

Thomas, J. Mark. "Are Science and Technology Quasi-Religions?" *Research in Philosophy and Technology* 10 (1990): 93–102.

Tillich, Paul. *Theology of Culture*. Ed. Robert C. Kimball. New York: Oxford University Press, 1959.

Toles-Patkin, Terri. "The Imbecilization of Culture." *Bulletin of Science, Technology and Society* 8, no. 5 (1988): 519–23.

Tomas, Vincent, ed. *Creativity in the Arts*. Englewood Cliffs, N.J.: Prentice-Hall, 1964.

Unamuno, Miguel de. *The Tragic Sense of Life* (1913). Trans. J. E. Crawford Flitch. New York: Dover, 1954.

Vaihinger, Hans. *The Philosophy of "As If"* (1911). Trans. C. K. Ogden (from the 6th German ed.), 2d ed. London: Routledge and Kegan Paul, 1935.

Vanderburg, Willem H. "Technology, Society, and Culture: A Framework for Understanding." *Technology in Society* 7, no. 4 (1985): 411–22.

Veblen, Thorstein. *The Instinct of Workmanship* (1914). New York: W. W. Norton, 1964.

von Hildebrand, Dietrich. "Technology and Its Dangers." In *Technology and Christian Culture*, edited by Robert Paul Mohan. Washington, D.C.: Catholic University of America Press, 1960.

Walker, John. *A Critical Pronouncing Dictionary* (1791).

Wallace, Anthony F. C. *Religion: An Anthropological View*. New York: Random House, 1966.

Waters, Brent. "A Meditation of Fate and Destiny in a Technological Age." *Bulletin of Science, Technology and Society* 12, nos. 4–5 (1992): 204–7.

Watson, Richard A. "Human Dignity and Technology." *The Philosophy Forum* 9, nos. 3–4 (1971): 211–41.

Weber, Max. *The Protestant Ethic and the Spirit of Capitalism* (1904). Trans. Talcott Parsons. New York: Charles Scribner's Sons, 1958.

———. *The Sociology of Religion*. Trans. Ephraim Fischoff from the 4th German ed. (1922). Boston: Beacon Press, 1964.

White, Hugh C., Jr., ed. *Christians in a Technological Era*. New York: Seabury Press, 1964.

White, Lynn, Jr. "The Historical Roots of Our Ecologic Crisis." *Science* 155 (1967): 1203–1207.

———. *Medieval Religion and Technology: Collected Essays*. Berkeley: University of California Press, 1978.

Wiener, Norbert. *God and Golem, Inc.: A Comment on Certain Points where Cybernetics Impinges on Religion*. Cambridge, Mass.: M.I.T. Press, 1964.

Winner, Langdon. *Autonomous Technology*. Cambridge, Mass.: M.I.T. Press, 1980.

———. *The Whale and the Reactor: A Search for Limits in an Age of High Technology*. Chicago: University of Chicago Press, 1986.

Yinger, John Milton. *Religion, Society and the Individual*. New York: Macmillan, 1957.

Zimmerman, Michael. "Technological Culture and the End of Philosophy." *Research in Philosophy and Technology* 2 (1979): 137–45.

Index

About the Author

JAY NEWMAN is Professor of Philosophy at University of Guelph. He is a Fellow of the Royal Society of Canada and a past president of the Canadian Theological Society. He is author of several books including *Religion vs. Television: Competitors in Cultural Context* (Praeger, 1996), *On Religious Freedom* (1991), and *The Journalist in Plato's Cave* (1989). His numerous articles have appeared in such journals as *Philosophy, Ethics,* and *Religious Studies.*

ISBN 0-275-95865-5

90000>

EAN

9 780275 958657

HARDCOVER BAR CODE